Images of Thought

SUNY series in Latin American and Iberian Thought and Culture

Jorge J. E. Gracia and Rosemary Geisdorfer Feal, editors

Images of Thought

*Philosophical Interpretations
of Carlos Estévez's Art*

JORGE J. E. GRACIA

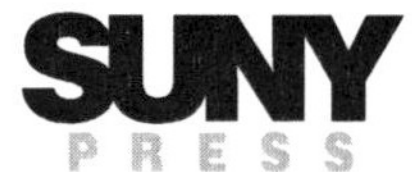

Cover art: Carlos Estévez, *Self-fishing*, 2006, courtesy of Jorge and Norma Gracia

Published by
State University of New York Press, Albany

For information, contact State University of New York Press, Albany, NY
www.sunypress.edu

Production by Eileen Meehan
Marketing by Michael Campochiaro

Library of Congress Cataloging-in-Publication Data

Gracia, Jorge J. E.
    Images of thought : philosophical interpretations of Carlos Estévez's art / Jorge
J. E. Gracia.
        p. cm. — (SUNY series in Latin American and Iberian thought and culture)
    Includes bibliographical references and index.
    ISBN 978-0-7914-9379-3 (hardcover : alk. paper)
    ISBN 978-0-7914-9380-9 (pbk. : alk. paper)
    1. Estévez, Carlos, 1969—Criticism and interpretation. I. Title.

N6605.E88G73 2009
709.2—dc22   2008028300

10 9 8 7 6 5 4 3 2 1

Las Meninas is the visible image of Velásquez's invisible thought.

—René Magritte

Contents

Part 1: Philosophical Interpretations of Estévez's Works

Knowledge

Reality

Society

Destiny

Part 2: Philosophical Interpretations and Art

Appendices

List of Illustrations

Preface

In 2001, I picked up a copy of Holly Block's recently published *Art Cuba: The New Generation*. I browsed through it, looking at the pictures and marveling at the imagination and creativity of recent Cuban artists. I still have the book, with pieces of paper sticking out marking those artists whose work I found more striking. Of the more than three dozen artists included, a dozen were particularly interesting, and one caught my special attention; I could hardly take my eyes away from the images of his art. His name is Carlos Estévez, at that time barely thirty, and represented with three works, all of them extraordinary. *Cité de l'existence* (The City of Existence, 1998) is a watercolor, pencil, and sanguine on paper of a standing, nude man, with legs and arms apart, whose body is covered with an urban landscape with points of emphasis on the heart, the back of the hands, the feet, the center of the face, and the penis. *El mundo del deseo* (The World of Desire, 1999) is also a watercolor, watercolor pencil, and sanguine on Kraft paper, of a moth with open, elaborately beautiful wings and a body suggesting an erect penis surrounded by the lines of a receptacle. *Mecánica natural* (Natural Mechanics, 1997) is a watercolor and pencil on paper of a chicken drawn inside the outlines of a sewing machine and its intricate inner workings.

Where did these images come from? They seemed so different from anything else I had seen. They were imaginative, subtle, and aesthetically pleasing, and they produced in me the feeling I get in the pit of my stomach when I intensely want something that I cannot have. The longing was bad, but Estévez's work was out of my reach. He was in Cuba, which posed enormous difficulties for getting in touch and purchasing and transporting the art. The political situation in Cuba and the United States was not conducive to this kind of process. More important still, I had started thinking about Cuban art in connection to my work on ethnicity. My interest stemmed not so much from a fascination with this particular art, for I am not parochially interested in Cuban art. But as a philosopher I had been working on issues of social identity, specially Hispanic/Latino identity, and this had led me to think that perhaps I could use the case of Cuban Americans to explore the philosophical questions that arise in the context of ethnicity—identity, memory, diaspora, assimilation, discrimination, and acceptance, among many others. This in turn had led me to restrict my recent art collecting to Cuban American artists, so Estévez was completely out of the picture—since he lived in Cuba and was not Cuban American, I had to let him go, with pain. But the memory of his work stayed with me; the uniqueness of his art had made a lasting impression.

Then, in 2005, I was in Art Miami, strolling through the endless corridors filled with artworks, and I saw three pieces that immediately stood out as Estévez's work. One was clever and light, yet intriguing, a juggler of teacups; a second was a female puppet with iridescent wings, superimposed on a black background; and the third was a head full of numbers, moving among the clouds in a flying contraption. Estévez had been in Miami for six months!

I bought the flying head on the spot, and this opened the doors for me to talk to the artist and incorporate him into my web project "Cuban Art Outside Cuba: Identity, Philosophy, and Art" (http://www.philosophy.buffalo. edu/capenchair/CAOC/index.html). This led in turn to several conversations and exchanges and to the interview whose translation is included among the Appendices of this book. Eventually I realized the reasons Estévez's art had such a special attraction for me. His work is profoundly philosophical; almost every piece he produces has philosophical relevance and interest. It raises metaphysical and theological issues in particular, such as the nature of the world, free will and determinism, predestination, and the human condition. And after all, I am a philosopher and have been interested in metaphysics and theology from the beginning. Another aspect of the work intriguing to me is its archaism. Estévez's art is informed by a fascination with Renaissance, medieval, and early modern intellectual history and science. Some of it resembles the drawings of Leonardo da Vinci, as well as the work of explorers, scientists, and inventors. His sources of inspiration are often old drawings, abstruse philosophical doctrines, and articles in centuries-old encyclopedias. In some ways, he is a Jorge Luis Borges of visual art. But this has to be balanced with a futuristic, science fiction strain that mixes humans, machines, and animals. As a philosopher, a medievalist, and an intellectual historian, could I resist such temptation? I surrendered. And in time it became clear that if I were going to explore the question of what philosophy has to do with art, it would be particularly appropriate to use Estévez's work as a point of departure. This book is the result.

The question of the relation between philosophy and art has been investigated from different perspectives, but my strategy here is to challenge the philosophical problem posed by this controversial relation in terms of visual art.[1] The problem affects every form of art, because art generally uses perceptual means to unfluence audiences. Even art forms that use language, as is the case with poetry, conjure up visual images. So the relation of these images to philosophical thoughts and ideas arises. Can art incorporate philosophy? And can philosophy make something philosophical out of art? Or, put in another way, can artists effectively address philosophical issues and ideas in their art, and can philosophers provide legitimate philosophical interpretations of art? Or are art and philosophy diametrically opposed enterprises, in which communication is impossible? These questions are particularly relevant in the case of the work of an artist like Estévez, whose art is intended to be philosophical but takes the form of visual images.

I argue that this problem is founded on a misunderstanding of the natures of interpretation, art, and philosophy. The argument has two parts that correspond to the two parts of the book. The first presents various philosophical interpretations of the work of Carlos Estévez; the second is a theoretical analysis of the concepts at play in the notion of the philosophical interpretations of art. Both parts are essential. The first provides the material for the speculative discussion in the second part, and the second supplies a theoretical articulation necessary to satisfy the requirements of philosophical relevance for the first part. In conclusion, I claim that the relation between philosophy and art, even in the case of visual art, is not necessarily anti-thetical, and that the philosophical interpretation of art is not only possible but enlightening.

Still, the kind of interpretation applied to art cannot be all of the same sort. Art that is not concerned with philosophy can only successfully be interpreted philosophically in relational terms, whereas art that is philo-sophical can be successfully interpreted in nonrelational terms. The key to understanding philosophical interpretations of art is to keep in mind both the kind of philosophical interpretation in question and what the art is about.

The first part of the book consists of seventeen essays that examine various problems of perennial interest, and of particular concern in con-temporary society, in the context of Estévez's work. They are presented as philosophical interpretations of particular pieces by this artist but also are intended to reveal and illustrate significant relations between philosophy and art. They anticipate, but do not reproduce, the points made in the second part of the book, avoiding redundance and leaving room for readers to move in whatever directions they wish. The essays are not of the same size or nature, and they differ depending on the topic explored, the particular artworks they address, and the philosophers used in them. The second part of the book is divided into three chapters that explore the nature of interpretation, art, and the philosophical interpretation of art and suggests solutions to some of the problems posed by the relation between philosophy and art.

The titles I have chosen for the interpretative essays are taken from well-known sayings. I have favored ancient and medieval authors, some traditional sources such as the Bible, and thinkers with whom Estévez or I have some kinship. This artist's work has ties to late medieval and Renaissance traditions, as well as to the thought of some existentialist philosophers. As a member of the Cuban diaspora residing in Miami, Estévez also has been exposed to issues of ethnicity and race. My own preferences, which match his to a good extent, gravitate toward classical philosophy and its medieval interpreters and include contemporary existentialist thought and social philosophy dealing with identity, so I have tried to stay within the parameters relevant to the understanding of Estévez's work and to my own views and philosophical preferences. His work and my interpretations take off from what we know and like, as Ortega would say, from "our circumstances." At the end of each essay I have added a short list of sources used that might be of help to those interested in pursuing further the topics explored in the essays. In cases where there is a short text within a larger discussion that appears to be particularly helpful, I have singled it out, but readers should not think of it as the sole locus in the sources listed where relevant topics are treated or to which readers should restrict their reading. Most of the pertinent ideas are scattered throughout the texts.

Although both the works of art and the philosophical essays contained in the first part of the book address similar topics, they do so differently—the first through images, the second through discourse. The philosophical discussion enters into a dialogue with the particularities of the art in order to illustrate these two different perspectives and to facilitate their comparison. Estévez's work is not presented as an illustration of philosophical ideas but as a source of philosophical understanding and speculation. In addition, the images and essays are intended to prompt readers to formulate views about the relationship between art and philosophy.

The essays are gathered into four general topics: knowledge, reality, society, and destiny. The first raises questions concerning self-knowledge and the origin, means, and object of understanding, including faith and reason. The second turns to the difficulties in grasping change, the nature of the universe, and the place of humans in it. The third explores various relations in society, between social groups, the self and the other, and women and men. And the fourth considers freedom and determinism, providence, and predestination.

The argumentative part of the book closes with a short conclusion. The Appendices that follow include the interview with Estévez mentioned earlier, a short biographical chronology of the artist, and a checklist of the exhibition "Carlos Estévez's Images of Thought," at which many of the works to which this book refers are to be exhibited. A bibliography of pertinent sources for Estévez, Cuban art, and the sources cited is added at the end.

Different parts of this book should appeal to different audiences. The essays on Estévez's art contained in the first part are not intended as technical discussions but rather as accessible interpretations that can give rise to further reflection. The second part of this book is meant as the presentation of the philosophical position that inspires the entire volume and should appeal in particular to those interested in philosophical speculation. The biographical and bibliographical materials are provided for information and research.

Sometimes, the discussion relies on views I have developed elsewhere, although in every case I have added new angles to them and in some cases changed them substantially. Most important among the sources where these perspectives have been previously developed are the following, in chronological order: *A Theory of Textuality: The Logic and Epistemology* (1995), *Texts: Ontological Status, Identity, Author, Audience* (1996), *Metaphysics and its Task: The Search for the Categorial Foundation of Knowledge* (1999), *Hispanic/Latino Identity: A Philosophical Perspective* (2000), *How Can We Know What God Means? The Interpretation of Revelation* (2001), *Old Wine in New Skins: The Role of Tradition in Communication, Knowledge, and Group Identity* (2003), *Surviving Race, Ethnicity, and Nationality* (2005), and *Latinos in America: Philosophy and Social Identity* (2008).

Let me finish by thanking those who have contributed in significant ways to make this project possible. Most of all, I am grateful to Carlos Estévez, without whose inspiring work and efficient cooperation this book would have been impossible. The working relationship between us has been wonderful and one of the most pleasurable aspects of this project. He also was gracious in providing permissions for printing images of the works included here and for helping in the selection process. I am also especially grateful to four friends who read different versions of the manuscript and came up with extraordinarily good suggestions and criticisms. In every case, their comments, arising from very different perspectives, elicited important changes in the book. Carolyn Korsmeyer brought to her reading not only a recognized expertise in aesthetics and feminism but also a fine sensitivity for the interpretation of art. William Irwin's experience with pop culture and hermeneutics introduced a welcome perspective on the text. Eduardo Mendieta provided a strong Continental philosophical point of view and an understanding of Latin American art. And Charles Burroughs added his noted erudition as art historian. I also am grateful to Susan Smith for helping with the bibliography and for compiling the index. The Samuel P. Capen Chair in Philosophy and Comparative Literature at the University at Buffalo sponsored the cost of reproducing the images of the artworks. Lisa Chesnel, acquisition editor at State University of New York Press, took an early interest in this project, which continued with Larin McLaughlin. And

Eileen Meehan at the production end of things, efficiently saw the publication through.

I also need to thank Sandra H. Olsen, Director of the University at
Buffalo Galleries, Sandra Firmin, Curator of the Galleries, and Robert Scalise,
Assistant Director for Exhibitions and Collections for the UB Anderson
Gallery for the time, effort, and enthusiasm they put into the organization
of the exhibition of Estévez's work.

1

Art and Philosophy

On a recent trip to New York City to attend the opening of a Cuban art exhibition organized by Glexis Novoa, an artist and a curator whose work my wife and I admire, we decided to take the opportunity to make a pilgrimage to the Museum of Modern Art (MoMA). When we arrived we saw advertised an exhibition of the work of Martín Ramírez in the Museum of Folk Art, located next to the MoMA. We had seen pictures of Ramírez's work before and had been intrigued by them, so we decided to go in.

Ramírez was a Mexican laborer who came to the United States to work on the railroad. After years of struggles, he ended up in a mental institution, where he was diagnosed as catatonic schizophrenic. He did not talk, but he drew and painted pictures on any pieces of paper he could find. His work is a stream of trains, tunnels, cowboys, *campesinos*, city escapes, and virgins. The human figures usually are trapped in buildings and cells from which escape seems impossible. Visually, the work is appealing to some audiences and disturbing to others, but it is difficult not to be moved by it.

Approximately ninety pieces were displayed in the exhibition, roughly one fourth of the extant work from the artist. After two hours of marveling at the stunning character of the art, we were on our way to the elevators, when my wife, who, unlike me, frequently strikes up casual conversations with strangers, said to one of the guards: "Not bad for a nut, don't you think?" The guard responded with quite a bit of animation: "Nut? No, this guy was not crazy at all! He knew more about life than we do." This was unexpected and serious, so I told Norma, "Let's go back, we better take another look at these pictures."

The guard had struck a chord. He had made us realize that Ramírez's pictures were not just what they looked like; there was something deeper, and perhaps disturbing, in them. Until that point I had been looking at the work in formalist terms, as striking images devoid of a philosophical dimension, but the guard's comment awakened me to a different perspective, which also contrasted with the commentary on the works presented at the exhibition. The curators had done a fine job of assembling opinion about Ramírez. A psychologist spoke about Ramírez's mental condition, and whether he was in fact schizophrenic. A sociologist discussed the social factors that influenced the work. An art historian located the art in a historical context. And the person who discovered Ramírez narrated the story of the discovery and how the art establishment had first turned its back on the work. All of this was interesting and useful, but one thing was missing: the philosophy, which is what the comment from the guard suggested. He had given a brief, but significant, interpretation of the philosophical relevance of the work: it was about life and it showed a kind of knowledge and wisdom sometimes lacking in contemporary society. And indeed, upon reflection it reveals the human condition, its loneliness and *angst*.

If this is not a philosophical interpretation, then what is? But how could it be taken seriously? What did it add to what the psychologist, sociologist, art historian, and biographer had said? And was it significant, or should it be dismissed merely as a reaction of no consequence, by a person without proper credentials? The guard had, in quite simple terms, posed for me a most interesting philosophical question, the relation between philosophy and art, and the consequent issue of the viability and significance of philosophical interpretations of art.

Philosophy has seldom ignored art. Questions about the nature of art go back to the very beginning of the discipline, to Plato in particular, and modern and contemporary philosophers have devoted considerable time and effort to the exploration of philosophical problems that arise in the context of art. Such topics as the essence of the aesthetic, the nature of representation and its role in art, the relation between form and content, the significance of abstraction, and many others are common throughout the history of philosophy. Recently there has been substantial interest in the cognitive and epistemic issues raised by art, especially painting.[1] And the use of artists and their works as sources of philosophical reflection related to the philosophy of art is common. However, it has been comparatively rare in the history of philosophy to find authors who have found in visual art in particular, the source of philosophical inspiration quite apart from issues in aesthetics, such as the problems of free will and determinism, predestination, or the nature of reality.

The twentieth century saw an increase in these latter sorts of discussions. Consider, for example, Jean-Paul Sartre's speculations about distance and emptiness in the context of Giacometti, Jacques Derrida's use of two of Goya's paintings to philosophize about the colossal, Gilles Deleuze's ruminations about sensation based on the work of Francis Bacon, or Michel Foucault's employment of Velásquez's *Las Meninas* to raise questions about the role of representation in Western epistemology.[2] Among the most famous philosophers who have made use of visual art in their philosophy are Walter

Benjamin (Klee), Martin Heidegger (van Gogh), and Michel Foucault (Magritte).[3] Still, this is not as frequent as the use of art as a locus for the discussion of aesthetic issues. Most philosophical analyses of art aim to explain what philosophers think artists are doing and to tell us how to view something as art, in addition to providing answers to other issues that arise from the consideration of art.[4] And many of those who use works of art to address philosophical problems seem to do so as loci for the discussion of these problems largely independently of the philosophical take a work of art might have or the philosophical understanding of the views of the artist who made it or the audience that confronts it. When Deleuze was asked if the aim of his book on Bacon was to make readers better see the artist's paintings, he agreed that it would have that effect if it were successful, but he added that it had a higher aspiration, "to approach something that would be the common ground of words, lines, colors, and even sounds."[5] In short, his primary aim was to achieve a sound philosophical view of art rather than to enlighten us about Bacon's work in particular.

Indeed, many interpretations of art that are presented as philosophical can be disputed because they do not seem to be truly philosophical, or because they do not appear to be interpretations properly speaking, or even because the artistic credentials of their objects are questionable. This is not as frequent with philosophical interpretations of other cultural phenomena or other kinds of interpretations of art. It is easy to find philosophical interpretations of literature, such as the speculations that Jorge Luis Borges's stories have elicited.[6] And psychological interpretations of art, even of the great masters of the Renaissance, abound.[7] The battle between "philosophers" and "poets" goes back to the beginning of philosophy, but it is particularly acrimonious when it concerns philosophy and the visual arts.

The reverse also is true. Much visual art seems to have little to do with philosophy, and many artists, art critics, and even philosophers have argued that it should not have anything to do with it, or, if it does, then this is not a source of value in it but may be detrimental. Still, there can be little question that much visual art involves philosophy. Consider, for example, Raphael's *School of Athens*, Goya's *The Executions of the Third of May 1808*, Picasso's *Guernica*, and Estévez's *Irreversible Processes*. In the *School of Athens*, Raphael presents us with a kind of summary of ancient Greek philosophy, with two central contending philosophical views, the Platonic and the Aristotelian: Plato signals upward, presumably to the world of transcendent ideas, whereas Aristotle points downward, toward the empirical world of experience. In *The Executions of the Third of May 1808*, Goya provides a stark condemnation of the executions carried out by the French and thus voices a cry for national freedom. Picasso's *Guernica* is nothing if not an exposé of the horrors of war and the inhumanity of which humans are capable. And Estévez's *Irreversible*

Processes poses the problem of freedom and determinism: although we seem to be in control of some of our actions, others are clearly beyond it.

Philosophy and art have not had an easy life together. Beginning with Plato, there has been a philosophical tradition that has regarded art with suspicion, often as even dangerous. For Plato, art in general interferes with the grasp of truth and the nature of reality. Artworks are far removed from the real and constitute obstacles in understanding how things truly are because of their engagement with the senses and emotions at the expense of the intellect. A painting is a copy of an idea the artist has, which is itself a copy of objects in the world of experience, which are in turn copies of the real objects of knowledge, Plato's notorious ideas. The Myth of the Cave, presented in *The Republic,* dramatically illustrates this view by showing how the artifacts that humans construct, as well as their shadows projected on a wall, are the objects we see in the obscurity of our existence on earth, where we are surrounded by appearances far removed from the reality represented by the sun and the objects it illumines outside of the cave.[8]

On the opposite side are authors who regard art as something much loftier than philosophy. In the nineteenth century in particular, with the rise of Romanticism and the reaction against the Enlightenment and its emphasis on reason, some authors placed art on a pedestal and devalued philosophy. The true way of grasping reality, of understanding ourselves and the world, they argued, was through emotion, not reason. Viewed as an effective trigger of emotion, art became exalted, and philosophy, as a discipline of knowledge that relies on rational discourse, came to be considered rather a lower means of enlightenment. The analysis proper to philosophical thinking kills what it analyzes—it terminates life in order to examine it—whereas art fully preserves its object. Art is not philosophy, and to try to project philosophy into it and use it in art results in the destruction of art.

Why such resistance to putting together art and philosophy? The answer is not difficult to surmise. For one, both of the approaches mentioned tend to rely heavily on a sharp distinction between emotion, on the one hand, and rational, discursive thought, on the other. Emotion often has been viewed as a matter of sensation and feeling, whereas reason has been regarded as having to do with cognition and propositional thought, although this opposition has not gone unchallenged, and many philosophers argue that emotion includes an important cognitive dimension.[9] Leaving the controversy over the nature of emotion aside, however, at least four other areas are used to contrast art and philosophy and to argue that it is impossible to put them together: medium, means, end, and practitioners.

The argument based on the medium is frequently used in the context of visual art. The favorite medium of philosophy and the favorite medium of visual art differ substantially, indicating a serious rift between them. The main medium of philosophy is language, but it is not for visual art, even though from time to time visual art does use language and there are traditions in which writing is considered high art. Writing as art is common in the East, and it is arguable that it also has been practiced in the West, particularly in the Middle Ages. Still, plastic artists do not generally use words but instead turn to materials and objects that they manipulate in various ways. A sculptor might use marble, a painter paints, and drawing usually requires pencil and paper. Visual art is tied very closely to the material process of production. Painting, for example, seems to be concerned with mixing and diluting materials. There is something alchemic about it, as James Elkins has argued, it is "a kind of immersion in substances."[10] Indeed, in the interview included in the Appendices, Estévez uses the language of alchemy to describe the way he works: "even the feeling of my drawings is . . . material, because I confront the paper as alchemists used their sketch books." On the contrary, philosophers practice their craft with words almost exclusively, used either orally or in writing.[11] And although it is true that philosophers have from time to time expressed their ideas in poetry, and poetry is a kind of art, even then the medium they use seems far removed from the favorite medium of the visual arts.

Philosophers talk to each other, or even to themselves, and they write about what they think, whereas visual artists turn to images, perceptual effects, and material objects and substances. And when artists use words in their art, they have to sort their status, because, as Danto has pointed out, "words are both vehicles of meanings and material objects."[12] Indeed, painters often use words nonlinguistically, because, as Foucault put it, "the relation of language to painting is an infinite relation. . . . Neither can be reduced to the other's terms: it is in vain that we say what we see; what we see never resides in what we say."[13]

The argument against the marriage of philosophy and art based on the medium derives further substance from the fact that visual artists do not, on the whole, produce treatises; they do not write articles; they do not give lectures; and they do not engage in discussion and argument when they function as artists. It is unusual to have an artist respond to the work of another artist, who in turn responds to it, in the way philosophers do. This kind of dialogue, which is essential to philosophy, is missing in visual art. Philosophers regularly produce dialogues—think of the paradigmatic work of Plato—and they engage in disputation and argument with each other. The centerpiece of medieval philosophy, for example, is the oral disputation, which only eventually was put down on parchment. To this day, dialogue and disputation are fundamental in the discipline, as any gathering of philosophers will prove, whereas the identity of a visual work of art depends very much on elements that are not words and of non-linguistic elements in the words the work may use.[14] When plastic artists use words, they do not seem to be concerned with the logic of thinking but with the way words contribute to an overall image. This brings me to the second area that is used to argue against putting art and philosophy together, the means.

The principles that guide philosophers in their craft involve reasoning and logic; they provide structure to their discourse. Philosophers examine claims about the world made by others and themselves, and they subject these claims to scrutiny, frequently finding fault with them. They do this by examining the evidence offered and by subjecting the arguments given in their favor to the test of logic. Philosophical treatises contain such things as the presentation and explanation of theses, the examination of evidence and arguments provided for them, the evaluation of such evidence and arguments, and the development of arguably better alternative views and arguments.

Aristotle, for example, takes issue with Plato's view, that the way to explain knowledge is by reference to a world of ideas independent of experience and located in a realm of their own. The Platonic explanation of how we know triangularity is not through our perception of individual triangles, because none of them fits exactly the definition of a triangle; we know triangularity because we have direct access to the idea of triangularity, independent of our experience. Aristotle then proceeds to show how Plato's theory creates more conceptual problems than it solves, in part because it cannot adequately explain how these ideas are related to the objects of which they are supposed to be models.

In contrast, art seems to have little to do with reasoning, logic, or even affirmation, and if it has to do with reasoning, then the reasoning is very different from that used in philosophy.[15] Artists are not concerned with presenting explicit theses they affirm but rather with the creation of their own worlds.[16] Few of the elements that go into the makeup of a philosophical product are present in art; there is no presentation of evidence or arguments; there is no evaluation of the evidence or the arguments; and there is no reasoning dialectic. Art does not engage in the kind of procedures common in philosophy. This becomes evident when one puts a philosophical treatise, say Aristotle's *Metaphysics*, next to a work of art, such as Estévez's *Self-fishing*. The gap appears enormous. It becomes even more clear when the two works are about the same topic, as happens with Estévez's *Irreversible Processes* and a particular question in Aquinas's *Summa theologiae*. Both deal with the issue of whether humans act freely, but they are worlds apart in their approach.

This gap can be explained in part because the end pursued by philosophers is generally the formulation of hypotheses they aim to demonstrate, even if the hypothesis is that there are no hypotheses. Philosophers defend some view or other or present criticisms of views with which they disagree. And even when a philosopher reaches a puzzling dead end, as happens frequently in the Platonic Dialogues, this is regarded as an achievement, in that it reveals the inadequacy of a certain position assumed by some to be correct.

Artists, however, rarely seek to prove or disprove anything directly, and generally they formulate no explicit hypotheses which they defend or attack. This is why works of art, even those that have a narrative component, can be subjected to a variety of interpretations. Indeed, Adorno has claimed that art disappoints those who seek "conclusions," for these require concepts and judgment, and art in his view lacks both.[17] A work like Estévez's *Forging People* surely tells us something, and what it tells us is supposedly true, but the message, if it can be called that, is not unambiguous or explicit. It is not like most claims found in philosophical treatises; both its character and the way it is presented are different. *Forging People* can be interpreted in diverse ways. The piece does not present us with a doctrine about how groups of people come to be. Rather, it becomes a means whereby an audience can consider various ways to approach this matter: people can be seen as products of divine creation, biology, social forces, or human imagination.

Artists create universes, with their own dialectics and rules, and although some art appears to express views, this is not a necessary condition of art as it seems to be of philosophy. Art may lead observers to formulate hypotheses and draw conclusions, but it is always risky to attribute such moves to the artists. This contrasts with what philosophers usually seek, and may be what Adorno is trying to put into words when he notes that "philosophy bears upon reality and its works," whereas art "is more autarchically organized."[18]

The divide between philosophy and art finds additional support in that the practitioners of art and philosophy generally have different talents, strengths, and weaknesses. Philosophers are trained to detect minor shifts in meaning and logic in sentences, arguments, and claims, but they might not realize the significance of different ways of rendering a leaf, of a brushstroke, of the use of a particular color, or the significance of rhyme, the sorts of things that are essential to art. Philosophers are used to dealing with concepts and their analysis, sometimes exclusively, whereas visual artists work primarily with materials at hand, such as paints, colors, stone, and pencils. Indeed, artists often have difficulty expressing themselves when asked to provide conceptual explanations of what they are trying to do with their art.[19] Philosophers appear to have very different modes of operation, sensitivities, and visions than artists. Philosophy involves propositional understanding, whereas visual art is about perceptual grasp.[20] Even if both enterprises involve truth seeking, as many philosophers and artists have claimed, their approaches appear incompatible to many.[21] And, for others, such as J. M. Bernstein, they are at least irreducible or untranslatable into each other.[22]

The seeming opposition between art and philosophy stands in the way of accomplishing what is suggested in the subtitle of this book. If those who claim that philosophy and art are incompatible are correct, then the philosophical interpretation of art is doomed from the start, in that the task requires establishing a relation between two enterprises that are opposed to each other or at least belong to two different realms. Of course, not every one agrees. If Danto is right and art "has passed over into a kind of consciousness of itself and become . . . its own philosophy," then the philosophical interpretation of art should be possible.[23] But Danto's move has been criticized by those who see it as a misunderstanding of art and the elimination of an important distinction between it and philosophy.[24] And, for our purposes, it would not work in any case. Obviously, if one of the opposites of an opposition is eliminated by turning it into the other, then the opposition vanishes. But to do this is not to explain how the opposites are related. It does not help to argue that the philosophical interpretation of art is possible because art is philosophy or philosophy is art. What we need is an account that maintains their integrity, seeing how they are different and in conflict, and yet explains how they can be related in the philosophical interpretation of art.[25]

But are those who find an irreconcilable opposition between art and philosophy correct? The interpretations of Estévez's works included in the first part of this book are presented as evidence that they are not. Still, the essays do not explain why. For that, as Plato would say, we need more than examples; we need an understanding of what a philosophical interpretation of art is and how it works.

Our task begins with two initial questions: What is art? What is a philosophical interpretation? Without answers to these questions, we would be hard-pressed to claim that we have understood all that is involved in the philosophical interpretation of art, or that we understand in what sense the essays on Estévez's art given here can qualify as philosophical interpretations. But the answers to both questions are highly contested. The degree of disagreement concerning the first is evident in ordinary life from the fact that the same objects are regarded by some as important artworks and by others as mere rubbish. This is matched by the number of conflicting definitions of art among philosophers of art. And the views concerning philosophical interpretation are not less contested, in particular because both philosophy and interpretation are highly controversial notions. The hermeneutical literature is full of conflicting views about interpretation, whereas philosophers themselves disagree strongly about what is and what is not philosophy.

Here I cannot examine even a small number of the views that have been proposed about the notions of interpretation, art, or philosophy. Rather, I shall have to make do by proposing views of them that I have more extensively defended elsewhere and that hopefully will help readers think about this relationship and the essays in this volume. I begin with interpretation and then move to art and its philosophical interpretation. The reason is that certain conceptions of art and its relation to interpretation and philosophy can muddle the discussion if we begin with art without first making clear some things about interpretation. The overall moral of the story is that the philosophical interpretation of art is not only possible, but indeed enlightening, apart from being fun, for both the philosopher and the artist. I plan to offer support for this first by presenting philosophical interpretations of the work of Carlos Estévez and second through conceptual analysis. Before I turn to this double task, however, let me say something about Estévez and his art.

2

Carlos Estévez and His Art

Carlos Estévez is a Cuban-born artist now residing in Miami. He was educated and trained in Cuba but has also lived in France, Norway, Mexico, and England, and he has visited many other countries. Although still under forty years of age, he has been very prolific, having produced hundreds of works. His art has attracted substantial attention in Europe, the United States, and Latin America. The range of the work extends from sculptures and installations to oil and acrylic paintings on canvas and paper, drawings on paper, assemblages, collages, and combinations of these. Particularly prominent are the works on and with paper, for Estévez seems to have a fascination with this medium and has explored it in multiple ways.

Estévez's technique, like that of most Cuban-trained artists, is superb and broad. He can work with any traditional materials but also has incorporated nontraditional elements in the art. For example, he regularly collects objects of various kinds, particularly artifacts such as bottles and gadgets he finds in rummage sales and flea markets, which he later integrates into his works.

Unlike many Cuban artists, Estévez does not seem to be explicitly concerned with Cuba or the events precipitated in 1959 by the triumph of Fidel Castro's revolution. Nothing in his art suggests anything about Cuba. It contains no iconic images related to the island, no forts or palm trees, no papayas or bags of *chicharrones,* and no portraits of Cubans, whether ordinary citizens or political leaders. Nor is there anything in the work that deals with the particular social and political issues that have so concerned many Cubans for the past fifty years. The images used are universal, and so are the themes explored.

This contrasts with the work of many other Cuban artists who find inspiration in Cuban themes. Cuban art in the twentieth century tried to integrate recent artistic developments in Europe.[1] In doing so, it also attempted to explore Cuban culture, *lo cubano,* and embed the developments of European art in a local context. The use of African themes by some of the masters of twentieth-century art in Europe, such as Picasso and Modigliani, became for Cuban artists the use of Afro-Cuban themes, or of themes that have to do with the Cuban landscape and the Cuban reality. The great master of the *Vanguardia* of Cuban art, Wilfredo Lam, produced a Cubism inspired in Afro-Cuban topics. His most famous painting, *La jungla* (The Jungle, 1943), is an example of this approach.

The trend to explore the Cuban situation in art has continued in the work of more recent artists.[2] Most of José Bedia's paintings until recently explored the Cuban religious traditions that can be traced to an African heritage, and even his recent work that does not deal with this topic goes back to events in the history of Cuba.[3] Gustavo Acosta has painted many Cuban buildings; much of the work of Leandro Soto refers back to the island; and Arturo Rodríguez frequently incorporates themes related to the Cuban situation in his paintings. Even Alberto Rey, who left Cuba when he was three years old, has a series of paintings of Cuban icons, ordinary Cuban cultural objects, and even portraits of Cubans. And much conceptual art from Cuban artists involves political and social criticism, as is the case with some of the pieces by Ana Mendieta and Glexis Novoa. Indeed, the work of some artists seems to be completely absorbed by the exploration of Cuban themes.[4] Even an artist like Baruj Salinas, whose style has a very strong abstract component, has occasionally introduced Cuban elements into his work.

Other artists, however, have stayed away from Cuban topics, such as Rafael Soriano, Mario Bencomo, and María Brito. Estévez follows this line and has avoided anything typically Cuban, or even distantly related to Cuba. None of the recurring images in his work has anything to do with Cuba. As he notes in the interview included in the Appendices, even when his work arises from a particular Cuban situation, eventually it transcends it.

> Human beings are like plants. We are born in one place and grow roots. We assimilate the nutrients from the earth and that marks a fundamental guideline in life. I am Cuban. I was born in Cuba. My way of seeing life I believe is Cuban. I am aware that, compared to Europeans and Americans, I have a very definite culture, and that is like a sieve through which I filter all the information that comes to me from reality. However, the interaction with other realities continues to enrich that vision, and from the beginning I aimed as an idea for my work to discover the depths of humanity beyond the confines of a specific place, be it Cuba or Africa. There is a universal human concern, deeper than particular spaces and contexts, common to human beings: feelings, passions, and thought. In this sense, I am interested in how a human being from a particular latitude can make an experience an important event for another human being in another latitude. It is in that sense that my work goes beyond particular

social, political, and cultural contexts. I cannot deny that many
of my works had a local source at the outset, but with practice,
when one starts to polish the work and outline the idea, I think
it transcends to what I really want.

Estévez does not explore the ethnic elements of Cuban traditional art, nor
does he take up Cuban motifs or engage in commentary on the social and
political situation of Cubans on the island or outside it, all common themes
in recent Cuban art. But this does not mean that Estévez's art is completely
estranged from Cuban artistic traditions. His work shows some important
continuities with the history of Cuban art in the extensive use of drawing
and in the display of a certain cleverness, irony, and play. The widespread
depiction of puppets, for example, harkens back to this line of development
in the history of Cuban art.

Cuban artists have had a long tradition of caricature, humor, and irony
generally rendered in drawings. Some of the best-known Cuban artists today,
such as Tonel (Antonio Eligio Fernández), exploit this genre. Consider his
ironic response to Edvard Munch's *The Scream*. Munch's work is a frightening figure that conveys all of the existential *angst* associated with the human
condition and the horrible catastrophes of the twentieth century. Tonel's work,
with the same title, but in Spanish (*El grito*), depicts a toilet mimicking a
large mouth screaming "Help!" Among other current Cuban artists who use
caricature, humor, and irony are Pedro Vizcaíno and Carlos Luna.

Three undercurrents tie Estévez's work to Cuban culture in general. One
is the interest in theological and religious issues. Cuba was the last colony of
Spain in the Americas and has always had strong ties to the Peninsula. The
tradition of Spanish mysticism and interest in the medieval scholastic tradition
have maintained an influence in Cuba, even after the Cuban Revolution. Many
of the formative figures in Cuban intellectual history were clerics trained in
that tradition. And painters such as Emilio Falero and Juan Carlos Llera
have been inspired by it. In a stunning work entitled *Across* (2006), Falero
takes a Christ from José de Ribera's painting of the Trinity and puts him
on a raft in the middle of the ocean, representing the plight of Cubans who
use this means of transportation to cross into the United States. To this one
needs to add the interest in African religions, mentioned earlier. Estévez does
not have the explicit references to the Spanish or African traditions present
in some other artists, but he shows a marked concern with theological and
spiritual issues, such as the relation between humans and God, free will and
determinism, and predestination.

Another aspect of Estévez's work that ties it to Cuban culture is its
subtle eroticism. Cuban society is infused with the erotic. This is evident
in the work of writers such as Gustavo Pérez Firmat and artists such as

Carlos Luna. Estévez's art is not as explicit as the work of other Cuban American artists in this respect, but it does contain depictions of genitalia and erotic suggestions. A recurrent motif is the relation between males and females at various levels, which inexorably leads to the exploration of their sexual connections.

Finally, particular Cuban experiences have in some cases been the origin of Estévez's art, although the work has eventually been translated into a universal language that appears disconnected to anything Cuban. A good example is *The True Universal History* (1995), a piece he discusses in the interview in the Appendices. The topic of this installation is the way past history is viewed; how the past is rewritten by new generations, governments, institutions, historians, and even individuals, under new circumstances. This is a common phenomenon in human society, but in this case it was prompted by the perception of how the Cuban Revolution modified the way Cuban history is conceived.

In spite of these ties to Cuban cultural phenomena and traditions, Estévez's art is unique and its style easily recognizable. Its originality is a most prominent characteristic. One author that comes to mind as a background influence is Leonardo da Vinci. We find the same interest in machines, wheels, and contraptions. Estévez also has a fascination with anatomy, although for him this tends to concentrate on bugs, birds, fish, butterflies, lizards, and other animals. His humans are frequently puppets, mechanical devices with minds and emotions. Other common images found in the work are buildings and balloons. The fascination with some of these objects can be traced back to his childhood. His father was an engineer, and Carlos grew up among drafting tables and other engineering paraphernalia; he was slated to follow in his father's footsteps.

A performance dimension also is present in Estévez's art. In the project *Botellas al mar* (Bottles to Sea, 2001 and continuing), described in greater detail in the interview presented in the Appendices, Estévez periodically throws sealed bottles into the sea in various places. Each bottle contains a drawing in the style of medieval illuminations as well as historical details about the production of the work and how to get in touch with the artist. The event is filmed and recorded, and the act of throwing the bottle is part of the art, which can be considered mixed media, including performance. In his boxes, Estévez integrates diverse objects and techniques to create unique worlds—"a new reality," in his own words—bringing together the naturalist and the collector.

The mind behind the work seems to be as fascinated with new discoveries and the mechanics of the world as that of Renaissance and Enlightenment scientists and explorers. In the interview included in the Appendices, he tells us: "Among my gods is . . . Leonardo da Vinci. But apart from that I am interested in the work of Jesuits from the seventeenth century like Kircher. It's a time when man begins to discover the world, starts to investigate, [to develop] the pseudoscience." This quality is quite evident in his use of balloons and early models of machines. Balloons figure prominently in several of the paintings whose images are reproduced here, including the flying brain of *Horror vacui*. And *Difficult Loves* includes an image of a model of a flying machine by Otto Lilinthal.

Much of this art alludes to the age of exploration, when Europeans were engaged in the expansion of their world. Estévez does not catalogue newly discovered species—he is not a Humboldt or an Audubon—nor does he draw machines as models with the aim of building them—he is not a Leonardo. Most of his contraptions are impossible, as is the case with the work of such other artists as Escher and Magritte, and he is not a compiler of data. He aims, rather, at pushing the boundaries of the imagination, while using wheels, pulleys, and levers to explore the nature of the world that surrounds us, especially the world of the mind and our emotions. He mixes humans with animals, and both with machines, which ties his archaism to the future, the world of cyborgs and science fiction. His art is a laboratory of sorts, an observation platform. Indeed, one of the works reproduced here is entitled *Observatorium*.

This quality accounts in part for the philosophical character of Estévez's creations. Every piece seems to pose a conceptual puzzle, to present a controversial view, to reveal an existential predicament, or to uncover an intuition about humans and their surroundings. As he puts it in the interview, "My work is a kind of personal existential philosophy translated into the world of images. Each piece is a reflection, a meditation focused on the topic of being human." This is revealed sometimes in the titles of the works but also in the way the images elicit questions and pose conundrums that call for philosophical reflection and solutions. They dare the audience to develop views of the sort philosophers seek.

Estévez may be one of the most philosophical of all contemporary artists, and certainly of living Cuban artists, but he also explores the psychological makeup of humans and their relationships and idiosyncrasies. In many ways, the art is childlike, in that it has a playful, ingenious character associated with our early lives. And, indeed, he describes some of his pieces as toys. But the work also is scientific in its clever engineering feats; it always displays a deep curiosity and insight into the world and humanity. We are asked to look at it and ponder, as children do in a puppet show, fascinated by the possibilities opening before our eyes.

With all of this conceptual apparatus behind it, one would think the art would be, like much contemporary art, shocking, ugly, and even repugnant. And Estévez does not shy away from graphic portrayals. Some paint-

ings depict headless figures, as well as other provoking images, as we see in
the flying brain of *Horror vacui* and the decapitated puppet of *Waverings of
Faith*. But the art always has an aesthetic dimension that is engaging and
often appealing, and is frequently captivatingly beautiful. I cannot imagine
anyone failing to appreciate the extraordinary beauty of *Difficult Loves* or
of *Self-fishing*.

The modern and archaic, the avant-garde and traditional, the conceptual and formal, and the strong and delightful combine in Estévez's art to
draw the observer into a world of wonder. And although the art seems to
be driven by ideas, it is never didactic or preachy; it makes no statements.
Its inherent ambiguity leads to questions rather than answers, a reason, as
the essays in part 1 of this book indicate, it eminently serves as an instrument of philosophical reflection.

Estévez's statement about himself and his art appropriately begins with
questions, for this seems to be one of the primary functions of his enterprise:
to question, to ask, to probe into the depths of human existence and the
nature of the world. As he puts it:

> What is man? What is life? What do we represent in the
> universe? What is happiness? There is my obsession. . . . My
> work is, in essence, the representation of a vision that nurtures
> itself from lively and reflexive processes, assimilating the world in
> order to reintegrate it once more into itself by means of images
> that symbolize my marks on the universe. I think of my work
> as fragments, essays or phrases that come to me intermingled
> with the dynamic of human thinking. The pieces are not ends,
> or expressions of style or formal harmony. They are by and large
> directed toward diversity but originating in a unique source, "The
> Creator," and having the same goal, cognitive experience. Each
> piece pretends to be a query or an answer that depletes itself,
> attentive to the ideas' exigencies, developed from the communion
> between the symbolic-suggestive connotations of the image and
> the material that contains it. My main resources have been ency-
> clopedias—which I use as metaphors of confinement within an
> object (book) that originates from "human knowledge"—universal
> history—from which I acquire symbols and images to represent
> my ideas—and life as a cognitive experience—through which I
> pretend to rework the treatise of human existence.[5]

These words provide a clear justification to interpret Estévez's art in philosophical terms. They also add support to the project undertaken in this book.

Part 1

Philosophical Interpretations of Estévez's Works

Knowledge

3

Know Thyself

Socrates, as reported by Plato

In *Self-fishing* (Plate I), Estévez has composed a collage that integrates drawing, painting, and pasted images. The central figure is a puppet whose limbs, head, and genitals are painted but look like pieces of paper that have been cut out and pasted on the surface. Their color is mottled, mimicking in some ways the variety displayed in the color of human flesh. They are attached to a transparent torso, which is merely indicated through lines that establish its contours. The limbs, head, and genitals are connected to it by what look like dowels. At the joints, black points signal movement: where the head, the arms, legs, and penis join the body, and where the different parts of the legs and the arms come together. Red dots are placed on the forehead, the hands, the feet, and the glans of the penis.

The puppet is sitting on an invisible surface, its legs turned inward as if it were resting on the ground, with the feet also turned, reflecting a traditional position of meditation. Inside the partly transparent body, whose torso resembles an odd-shaped fishbowl—a kind of vase—swim fish of all kinds: twenty-one in the torso and four in a circle in the head. The fish have different shapes and colors. Those in the torso generally display a greater variety of colors, and the colors are more intense. The fish in the head are darker and less striking, perhaps faded. The head is turned upward, to allow for a straight path into the body. In his hands, the puppet holds upright a fishing rod, which goes through his mouth and into the body. The rod ends with lines going to different parts of the body where the fish are swimming; a hook signals its purpose, to catch fish. The fish in the head are not reachable with the rod.

This work suggests, in a vivid and graphic way, a view concerning the acquisition of knowledge that has been a major player in philosophy since its beginning. Socrates made it central and did more than anyone else to pass it on to posterity through his disciple, Plato, who developed it in his Dialogues.

The notion that the source of knowledge and wisdom is the self responds to a serious problem: Where do our ideas come from? What is the source of wisdom? The possibilities worked out by philosophers over time tend to break down into three large groups: the external world, the internal world, or a combination of the two. Radical empiricists or externalists, like David Hume, think that the source of our ideas is experience. We know by looking out, going outside of ourselves, leaving the inner workings of our being behind, and considering what is in the world. Even when we think about ourselves, we do it by turning ourselves into objects of reflection and examining these objectified selves as we do things that populate the universe. We become, in a sense, passive observers, *tabulae rasae*, in John Locke's expression, on which images of what is outside imprint themselves. These images become manipulated in various ways by us, through mechanisms that are already in place, and in time become ideas, vague renditions of the original imprints. These ideas do not belong to us, they are not part of who we are, and they do not originate in us; we are the subjects on which they find a home, even if in the process they change.

Externalist views of knowledge encounter difficulties of various kinds. For one, according to them human subjects play a largely passive role in the process of establishing our ideas, which seems contrary to our intuitions. And for another, our ideas appear to be very different from what external-ists claim they are. The idea of triangle is not the same as the image of a triangle I get from perception; and cat is not what I see when I look at Hunter, one of my cats.

This leads internalists, such as Socrates, Plato, and René Descartes, to argue that the source of knowledge is not outside of us but inside of us. These authors usually are called "rationalists," because they generally hold that ideas come from reason, not experience. For someone like Plato, we acquire ideas through a process of reasoning based on a dialectic that leads us to remember what we once knew and remains in us. For Descartes and others of the same ilk, ideas are innate and form part of our mental makeup. We just need to get inside of ourselves, into our minds, and find them there. They do not come from outside at all.

But internalism also has problems, some of which are more obvious than others. For example, from this view it would seem to follow that we have within ourselves all of the ideas of all things, and that the same ideas are shared by everyone. In fact, however, we seem to have ideas only of things we have sensed, and the ideas we have about them differ. Not only do people from different cultures have different ideas, they have different ideas about the same things. How can this be explained without reference to the history of particular cultures and the experiences of their members? Without experience, as John Locke pointed out, our minds appear to be blank tablets.

Difficulties have led to intermediate views. Aristotle and Thomas Aquinas, for instance, propose a reconciliation between externalism and internalism, empiricism and rationalism: all knowledge begins in perception, but it is not equivalent to perception. What we sense goes through a complicated process in which what we get from the outside is modified in important ways to become our ideas. This process is not the mechanical manipulation suggested by David Hume. There is a real alteration of the product, because ideas and the images we acquire through experience are quite different. The image I have of my cat Hunter is significantly different from the idea of cat. Hunter is individual and has features that do not apply to every cat. He is black, but to be a cat does not require being black; cats come in many colors.

So who is right? The issue for us is not about which position ultimately makes sense but about how Estévez's painting helps us understand the problem at hand and whether it prompts reflections that deepen our grasp of both the issue and its possible solutions.

At first the painting seems to support an internalist approach. The source of knowledge and wisdom, the place where we find our ideas, is inside of us, both in the mind—where the fish swim in a small circle—and in our bodies, in the bigger fish bowl of the torso. Socrates, Plato, and Descartes are right. But is this all that one can get out of the painting? Consider a couple of other facts. The fish cutouts of paper are incorporated into the painting from the outside. The fish are not painted inside the puppet, suggesting that what is in us might not have been there originally.

Another intriguing point is that the fish are pictures of actual individual fish. This leads us to surmise that what is inside of us is exactly like what is outside, at least in appearance: our ideas are replicas of the external world. And this seems to argue in favor of the externalist view—Locke and Hume are right after all!

Three other points merit attention in the painting. One is that the fish that presumably represent our ideas are located in two places, some in the torso and others in the head, but the ones in the head have less intense colors than the ones in the torso. One way of reading this is that the painting emphasizes the abstract character of ideas in the head; they are more isolated from other parts of our humanity, such as our emotions and appetites, our allegiances and relations. Knowledge can be abstract and detached, but most of our knowledge, and perhaps the one that is more relevant—could we say vital?—is close to our hearts, guts, and sex. As Estévez puts it in the interview presented in the Appendices:

What is inside me does not seem very clear because it is inside.
Until I undergo this process of externalizing it, of taking it out,
I cannot analyze it, as happens when you take things from reality

and into a laboratory to study them. This happens a bit with the human spirit. Inside of us there is a vast darkness, because all our feelings and emotions are mixed there. And when you succeed in bringing them out, they become part of the world, and that is when you can reflect on them.

The character of the fish in the head may also suggest that they are derived from the ones in the body. The second might represent, as empiricists would say, vivid perceptions or impressions, in which the colors are strong. And the first might represent reflections on the first, where the colors have faded, becoming less vibrant.

Another significant aspect of the painting that merits attention is that the fish are alive, which means that ideas are not static replicas of the external world but more like functioning organisms in a process of change, growth, and decay. They are moving, swimming, and touching each other, occupying different spaces, making connections to other ideas. They might even be competing for food, for whatever sustains them. They prey on our feelings and appetites in our bodies and on our thoughts in the mind.

But what happens when the fish are fished out? They die. Still, we need to fish them out in order to see them, for the puppet's torso is not meant to be transparent for the puppet. It is not a bowl; it is a body, and the ideas are within it. To look at the ideas, to consider them, to objectify and manipulate them, the puppet needs to take them out. But by doing so, these ideas find a new life, albeit a different one. Fished fish die, but ipso facto become sources for something else; something is lost, but something is gained.

This kind of existential predicament is very much part of what Estévez's *Self-fishing* is about. It brings back the famous words by William Wordsworth in *The Tables Turned*: "We murder to dissect." The objectification of our ideas kills them, leading to the unwelcome suggestion that, after all, we do not have access to them as they are in themselves.

Where does the painting fall in the controversy between externalists and internalists? The work is not a treatise, or a statement of a philosophy; it is a visual metaphor for knowledge and some aspects of how it occurs. It leaves us with questions rather than answers, which is, after all appropriate insofar as philosophy begins in wonder.

SOURCES

Aristotle. *Posterior Analytics*, Bk. II, ch. 19. In *The Complete Works of Aristotle*, vol. 1, ed. Jonathan Barnes. Princeton, NJ: Princeton University Press, 1984.

Descartes, René. *Discourse on Method*, Part II. In *A Discourse on Method and Selected Writings*. Translation by John Veitch. New York: Dutton and Co., 1951.

Hume, David. *An Inquiry Concerning Human Understanding*, Bk. I, part I, S. I. La Salle, IL: Open Court Press, 1963.

Locke, John. *An Essay Concerning Human Understanding*, Bk. II, ch. 1. 2 vols. New York: Dover, 1959.

Plato. *Meno*. 80e–86c. In *The Collected Dialogues of Plato*, ed. Edith Hamilton and Huntington Cairns. New York: Pantheon Books, 1961.

Thomas Aquinas. *Summa theologiae*, I, qq. 74–76. Edited by Thomas Gilby. Garden City, NY: Image Books, 1969–.

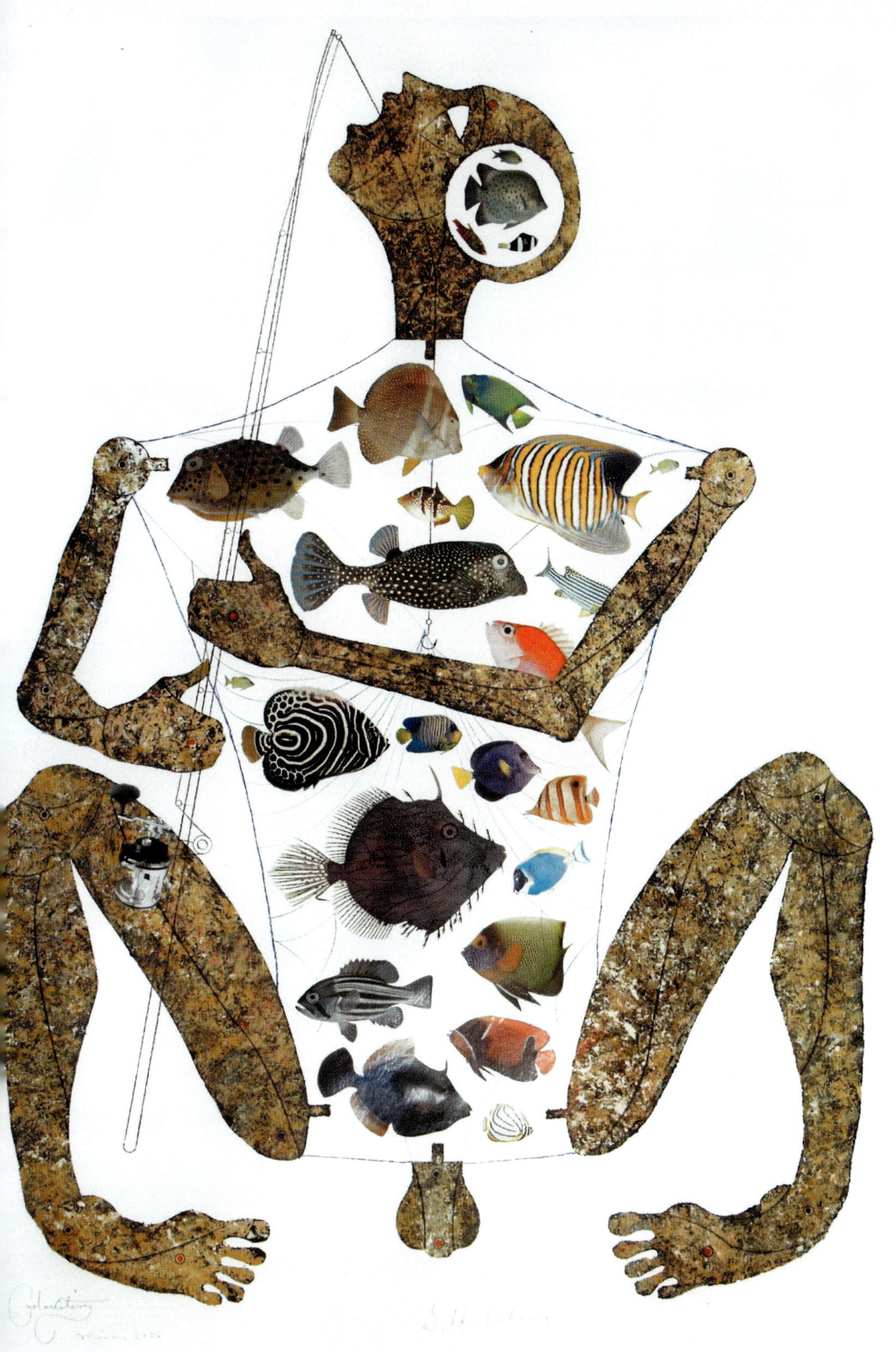

Plate I. *Self-fishing*, 2006, 39" × 27.5", collage on paper

4

I Am Myself and My Circumstances

José Ortega y Gasset

In *No One Can See through My Eyes* (Plate II), the figure of a man stands erect, on a circle of dark earth within a larger circle of red earth, whose center is another circle stained black, and from which radiate twelve lines that go toward the periphery but do not reach it. Hands on his side and feet aligned, the man is made of wood, and his body is anatomically correct. He stands alone and nude. Branches arch from the head until they reach the end of the lines drawn within the circle. Between the ends of any two lines spring two thinner branches in opposite directions that are in turn tied to lines arising from similar points and to the main branches coming out from the man's head.

Although a good number of contemporary philosophers have been concerned with the perspectival nature of our knowledge, few have made it as pivotal a point of their thought as Spanish philosopher José Ortega y Gasset. Moreover, his influence in the Spanish-speaking world to which Estévez belongs has been enormous.

Ortega formulated his view in the claim "I am myself and my circumstances." He thought of human beings as located in unique contexts that affect not just who they are but also what they know. I am not separated from what surrounds me: an island detached from the mainland, to use John Donne's metaphor. My surroundings are part of who I am, of my world. My situation belongs to me and no one else, giving me an irreproducible perspective on myself and the world. I am the center of my universe and intrinsically related to it, both in reality and thought.

This view is intended to make sense of the human situation and how it affects us individually and collectively. Are my life, my experiences, and my surroundings not intrinsically tied to who I am? Do the place where I live, the things around me, and the people with whom I associate not influence me in significant ways? Who could dispute this? My place of birth and where I grew up have given me my native tongue, and what can be more influential in the way I think than my language? But Ortega went beyond this, claiming that our unique individual situation creates an epistemic environment that is also unique. No one else knows what I know, and no one else sees what I see. This view has been dubbed perspectivism and has taken many shapes in the philosophies of such authors as Friedrich Nietzsche and Martin Heidegger.

Perspectivism makes considerable sense. Take my own situation as I write this essay. I am sitting here in my study, looking at the computer screen in front of me, but also occasionally looking at an image of Estévez's installation on the screen of another computer. What I see and think is prompted by this unique situation, which is different from that of the readers of this essay. Are the readers subjected to similar epistemic pressures? Surely not. They are not writing the essay and what they see is an image of Estévez's work printed on a page of this book. More important still, readers are influenced by what I say, by my text. We cannot see through each other's eyes. The readers also are influenced by who they are, by their histories and experiences, and by their goals. They are not writing for an audience, and they may not be philosophers, and if philosophers, they may have never read Ortega, but I have. And I have a different history and experiences, and a different goal.

One of the major strengths of perspectivism is that it explains the source of disagreements among human beings. If you and I disagree about the color of the apple we see hanging from a tree in the yard, then this could be explained because we see different things. The apple looks different from my perspective than it looks from yours, affecting its shape, color, and the reflection of light on it. Our particular circumstances determine what we see, and the differences in our vision explain why I claim the apple is red and you claim it is pink.

But there is another side to this issue: if everything we know is known from particular perspectives that are unique and unshareable, then how do we explain universal knowledge? How do we account for the knowledge that applies across perspectives and is the foundation of science? Can we ever agree that the world is round, that water boils at 100 degrees Celsius, or that humans are capable of reason? This is one of the great challenges to Ortega's point of view. Perspectivism accounts for particular knowledge, but it has difficulty accounting for universal knowledge.

Estévez's installation is an effective representation of the perspectival view of knowledge. The title of the work, *No One Can See through My Eyes*, is a reminder that we see only from a unique vantage point and that the instruments through which we see belong to each of us in a way that cannot be avoided. This applies to all knowledge. We are alone in our epistemic conditions because no one can take our places. Indeed, the claim suggested by the installation might be more radical than that made in some versions of perspectivism. Although some perspectivists hold that knowledge is always perspectival, they allow that in principle it is possible for persons to change places and vantage points and therefore to see what others see. I can look at a valley from the top of a mountain, but you can take my place and see it also.

Still, not every perspectivist shares this less radical view. Some believe, as Ortega does, that each perspective is unique because of the historical context surrounding it. Every event in history, including our perceptions and our thoughts, are single happenings that cannot be replicated. This view may be dubbed epistemic historicism, because it holds that the conditions of our knowledge (epistemic) are historically unique (historicism).

The title of Estévez's work suggests this more radical position: my eyes are mine, and no one can ever have them or the sight they give me. This is not just a matter of my present location and the perspective it gives me, it is a matter of I being who I am and having the eyes, the mind, and the body I have, and of experiencing the world through them. Because my body, my eyes, and my mind are mine—otherwise I would not be who I am, and what I would perceive would not be what I perceive—no one can use them. Each of us lives in a unique world, all our own. The circle on which the figure of Estévez's installation is placed suggests this unique world. And the branches that form the cage from which the figure cannot escape suggest that epistemic liberation is impossible insofar as the branches are connected to the head of the figure. The head can be identified with ourselves, and the fact that the branches come out of it indicates that release from the cage is impossible because the cage is not just a product of our circumstances but also in part of our own making. The unique situation of the figure makes it see something no one else sees, so there is an advantage to the epistemic circumstances of the figure: it has some privileged knowledge. But by the same token, the unique situation shuts the figure up in a dimension not accessible to others; the figure's horizon is always its horizon, and the world is always its world.

How can we reconcile the radical perspectivism of our knowledge, based on the unique historical condition in which we find ourselves, with the universalist claims of science? Is science a mere invention? Is scientific knowledge no more than a myth created by one or more persons for purposes of their own? Perhaps with the aim of power and domination? Can I impose my view on others by force? Or perhaps by the use of rhetoric and propaganda?

The world is full of examples that support affirmative answers to these questions. Although individual knowledge seems to be authentic, as

Michel Foucault argues, universal knowledge appears to be no more than the imposition of one individual's perspective on others. No perspective takes into account all perspectives, because perspectives are not shareable. There is no God's eye view, because there can be no God outside of history; only historical entities exist, and these are bound by the contingencies of space and time. No history applies to everyone and everything. History is always my history or yours; it cannot be my history and yours. The history that is both mine and yours amounts to the history of someone else that incorporates, in a unique way, what may appear to be mine and yours and as a result belongs to neither of us. A perspective cannot be shared; common knowledge is impossible.

And yet science works! Scientific knowledge involves predictions, and the predictions are fulfilled. Males who take an aspirin every day have fewer heart attacks than males who do not, other things being equal. The sun rises every morning in the East, and when I get up and turn on my computer, the screen lights up and I see the text of this book on which I have been working. I do not live in a world of random and unexpected events. On the contrary, things seem to be regular for the most part, and the perception of regularity is shared by other humans. My expectations and those of others around me are often matched. How can we make sense of this, if all knowledge is radically perspectival, if no one can see through my eyes?

Estévez's installation may suggest a way out: the perspective of the figure is unique, but the figure could be interpreted to represent not just one person, but all humans; nor do we need to consider the circle on which it stands to be a particular world, we could think of it as standing for each and every one of our worlds. This suggestion opens up because the figure is not a portrait of a particular person in unique circumstances. It is any person in his or her circumstances. There is no recognizable clothing, no particularities in the installation. Even the features of the figure are indistinct, specific, or generic, not individual. The only particularity in the work is its masculinity, but this could be taken to be no more than a reflection of the artist's sex and his use of it to reveal a perspective, or the common use of a male to symbolize humanity as a whole. Besides, in order for the piece to be credible as a historical figure, and history is of the essence for perspectivism, it has to have a particular sex, even though the claim it makes may be applicable to all human beings.

The universalizability of this claim makes it possible to avoid the most extreme consequences of perspectivism. Yes, no one can see through my eyes, and no one can take my place, but because we are all humans, there is something common to our situation that can be the basis for universal, nonperspectival knowledge. The very sentence, "No one can see through my eyes" is true, and universally so, because the "my" applies to everyone, not just to Estévez. The figure in the installation is a symbol of all humans and our condition, and one characteristic of that condition is that some of our knowledge is perspectival, even if not all of it is. The question that we need to answer, then, is which and how each of them is developed and can be tested. The cage that traps the figure in the installation is partly of his own making, the knowledge built by each and every one of us is ours, but precisely because of this we have a basis of common understanding, of communication, and of escape. We can always change what we make.

SOURCES

Foucault, Michel. "Truth and Power." In *Power*, ed. James D. Faubion and translated by Robert Hurley, et al. New York: New Press, 2000.

Heidegger, Martin. *Being and Time*, I, 44a–c. Translated by John MacQuarrie and Edward Robinson. London: SCM Press, 1962.

Nietzsche, Friedrich. *The Will to Power*. Translated by Walter Kaufmann and R. J. Hollingdale. London: Weidenfeld and Nicolson, 1968, 493–507, 567–69.

Ortega y Gasset, José. *Man and People*, ch. 3. New York: Norton, 1957.

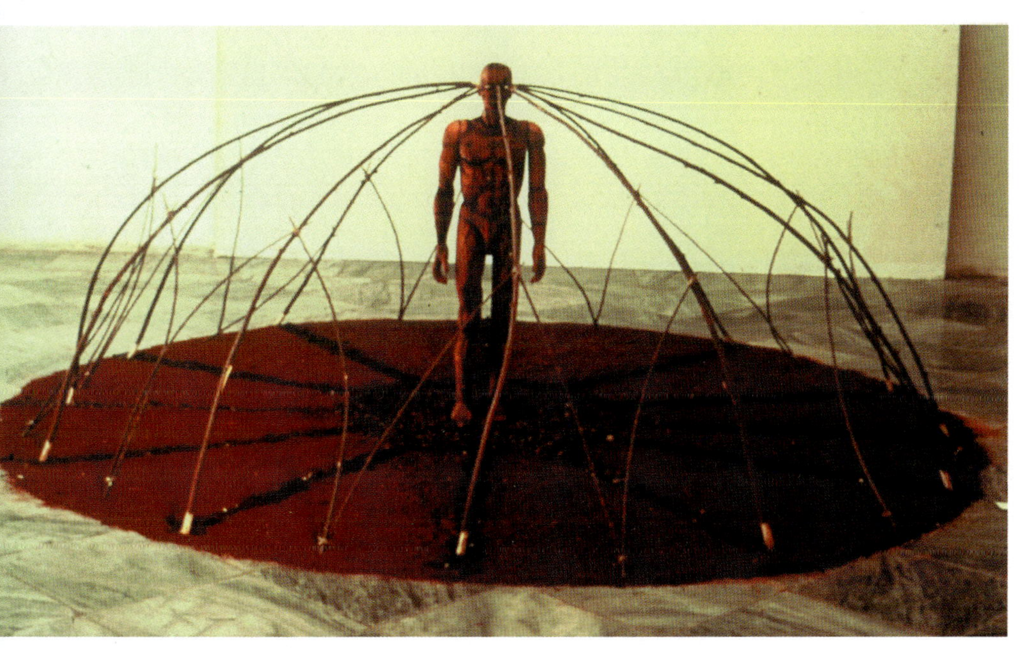

Plate II. *Nadie puede ver por mis ojos* (No One Can See through My Eyes), 1994, 43" × 118" × 118", wood, earth, and branches

5

Everything We Know Is Numbers

Pythagoras

On a textured sky on which green clouds float, a black head in profile rests on a bicycle-like flying machine, in *Numerical Thoughts* (Plate III). The wheels of the machine are tied to other wheels on the head, which in turn go around a large wheel placed in the cranial area. From this wheel issues a triangular structure, the skeleton of a fuselage, with one more wheel and several triangular supports. This contraption ends in a propeller that is both tied to a smaller wheel by the protruding structure and to the large wheel on the head. The wheel in the head contains concentric circles, going all the way to its center, with numbers along their perimeters. Some numbers seem to follow a certain order, but others do not.

Pythagoras seems to have been the first Western thinker to put numbers at the center of human knowledge and reality. His view was that everything consists of numbers. What could he have meant by this cryptic claim? Speculation has been rampant ever since, but two things are certain. One is that he was thinking of numerical relations, such as the relation between the sides and the hypotenuse of a right triangle. After all, Pythagoras is best known for the Pythagorean theorem, according to which the square of the hypotenuse of a right triangle is equal to the sum of the squares of its two sides. The other certain point is that these numerical relations explain the way the world is and works. Why are things the way they are? Because of these relationships.

Other pre-Socratic philosophers also were concerned with this question. Thales, known as the father of philosophy, said that the answer is water: everything is made up of water. And if you think about it, his view, which at first appears perplexing, turns out not to be so strange. Water can become airborne, it is often liquid, and it can be solid ice. So here is something that can have a variety of properties to explain why things are what they are.

Several of these pre-Socratics turned to what they thought were the basic elements that compose the world (earth, water, air, and fire) and their combinations to explain the nature of things and how they change. But Pythagoras was the first to come up with the idea that numerical proportions are of the essence. This is so and so because it has certain proportions, and that is so and so because it has different proportions. His theory even attempts to explain sounds, for particular numerical relations result in determinate sounds. A string of a certain thickness and tightness produces a certain sound when struck, which is not produced by strings with another thickness or tightness.

From the moment Pythagoras introduced numbers into the explanation of the nature of things and how they change, numbers became a subject of intense speculation. Two questions about them have fascinated philosophers ever since. One is their nature: What kind of entities are numbers? The second concerns their origin: Where do numbers come from?

It is not surprising that Plato, who was greatly influenced by Pythagoras, developed sophisticated answers to both questions. Although he presented them in several of his Dialogues, they are most captivatingly elaborated in the *Meno*. Meno has a slave boy who has no formal education and Socrates, who generally appears in the Platonic Dialogues as the philosopher in search of wisdom and leader of discussion, engages him. With his usual savvy, he asks the slave boy questions about numbers, geometrical relations, and the like. The boy readily responds. Most surprising, he can answer very sophisticated questions about mathematics and geometry, even though he has no training in these disciplines. Indeed, Socrates is able to elicit from the boy an understanding of the Pythagorean theorem itself by drawing pictures on the dirt at their feet. Where does the boy's knowledge come from?

Plato's view is that it could not possibly have come from teaching, for the slave has had no appropriate instruction. Nor could it come from experience, for numbers and numerical relations are universal, and the things one experiences in this world are individual. The sum of two plus two, which is four, is nothing individual. It is not the sum of only these two white balls and two black balls I have in front of me; it applies to any two things that are added to any two other things. Here is another example that may be more perspicuous: "triangle" is universal, but "this triangle" is not. The notion of a triangle applies to every triangle: this triangle, that triangle, and the triangle I am currently imagining. To be a triangle is to be a geometrical figure with straight sides and three angles, and this is true of any figure that satisfies these conditions. But the case of particular triangles is different, such as the one I am looking at on the screen of my computer at this moment. This triangle is idiosyncratic; it is unique.

But what does Plato mean exactly? That things like number two, or the sum of two and two, are not perceivable in the way these two balls I use to play are. Two is something we use to think about the two balls, but it is not like the balls. And this applies not just to the balls but also to any two things we encounter in the world. What is the nature of two, then, and where do we get this idea?

For Plato, numbers and numerical relations are nonsensible entities in a world outside perception; they have an existence in a realm not affected by the contingencies of the world. They are eternal, universal, and abstract, and they exist in an immaterial universe of their own that is more real than the world surrounding us. The things we experience are mere copies of them. But if this is so, how did we get to know them? How does Meno's slave know about two, and about the sum of two and two, when he cannot perceive them? A very difficult question that Plato sidestepped by narrating instead a myth.

Humans are composed of an immaterial soul and a material body, but the soul preexisted the body, and in its preexistence was exposed to the ideas of everything: numbers, animals, cats, humans, trees, and even beds. The soul was in direct contact with these ideas, but unfortunately, it became trapped in a body, and this caused it to forget its prior existence and all it previously knew. The process of remembering that knowledge is difficult and involves a dialogical procedure of probing and questioning. This is what Socrates does with Meno's slave, asking him questions that lead eventually to his remembrance of the ideas of numbers he formerly knew. Ideas are not physical or sensible, and they can be accessed only in the mind, through reason.

Estévez's *Numerical Thoughts* can be interpreted as a particularly suggestive representation of some aspects of the Platonic view. Several elements of it seem pertinent. One is the activity depicted in the work. A traveler is going somewhere and coming from somewhere, but it is not clear that there is any particular place from where the traveler is coming or toward which he is going. The location is a sky with indefinite clouds. This is no location as we find in our world of experience—only a suspended existence, a kind of Avicennian man. There is motion, but without any identifiable end or provenance. The field of action is rather diffuse, suggesting no place at all, or if anything, "the clouds," which is especially appropriate, since that is the title of Aristophanes' famous play in which he ridicules Socrates for losing touch with the world.

The traveler himself is merely a head. There is no body. And it is colored black and rather indistinct. There are no particular marks on it. This is an individual, clearly, because it is *a* head. But it is a mind rather than a part of the body, properly speaking, and not my mind or yours but *any* mind. Individual heads have individual features, and this one does not. The open eye is empty, because vision and sensation are immaterial in this trip; the interest is in the inside, not in the outside. We are dealing with thinking and meditation, not with sensation and experience, which follows

Plato's stipulation about the remembrance of numerical ideas. We need to delve within, not without, which brings us back to *Self-fishing.*

There is also a mechanism, a kind of flying machine that carries the traveler. It has wheels and pulleys and various mechanical parts, indicating the movement of reason. Plato held that reasoning involves a process he called "dialectic," in which logic is paramount. In this process we go from premises (All humans are mortal, and Socrates is human) to conclusions (Socrates is mortal). We engage in a procedure that Plato's famous disciple, Aristotle, sought to establish for all times in *The Organon.* The motion of the traveler is not intuitive, because intuition is like a flash of insight. It is, rather, a process similar to that of a well-oiled machine, such as a bicycle, that when used properly carries us from one place to another. That the machine in the painting is composed of wheels—circles have generally been regarded as the most perfect shape—and of lines—which are directional—cannot but enlighten us as to the nature of the process.

And what is the end product of this trip through the clouds? Numbers. They appear in concentric circles in the part of the head identified as the locus of the brain and the mind. We find numbers and proportions of numbers, or, as Plato would put it, we remember. Nothing else and nothing more: proportions, relations. Which takes us back to Pythagoras. The traveler has reached the end, the contemplation of the essence of the universe, numerical ideas that explain why things are the way they are.

But in Estévez's painting not all of the numbers follow the discernible order sought by Plato and Pythagoras. The order of some numbers defies understanding, bringing to the fore the possibility that either the world is not completely rational, or that our understanding of it is not. By doing this, Estévez has gone beyond Plato and Pythagoras and has opened the doors to the existential predicament he explores in much of his other work. Plato and Pythagoras may have been turned upside down. Unlike the Pythagoreans, who kept secret their discovery of irrational numbers, Estévez makes that irrationality perspicuous in *Numerical Thoughts.*

SOURCES

Aristophanes. *The Clouds.* In *Two Classical Comedies,* comp. Peter D. Arnott. New York: Appleton-Century-Crofts, 1967.

Aristotle. *Posterior Analytics,* Bk. II, ch. 19. In *The Complete Works of Aristotle,* vol. I, ed. Jonathan Barnes. Princeton, NJ: Princeton University Press, 1984.

Plato. *Meno,* 80e–86c. In *The Collected Dialogues of Plato,* ed. Edith Hamilton and Huntington Cairns. New York: Pantheon Books, 1961.

Pythagoras. *Fragments.* In *An Introduction to Early Greek Philosophy; The Chief Fragments and Ancient Testimony, with Connecting Commentary*, ed. John Mansley Robinson, ch. 4. New York: Houghton Mifflin, 1968.

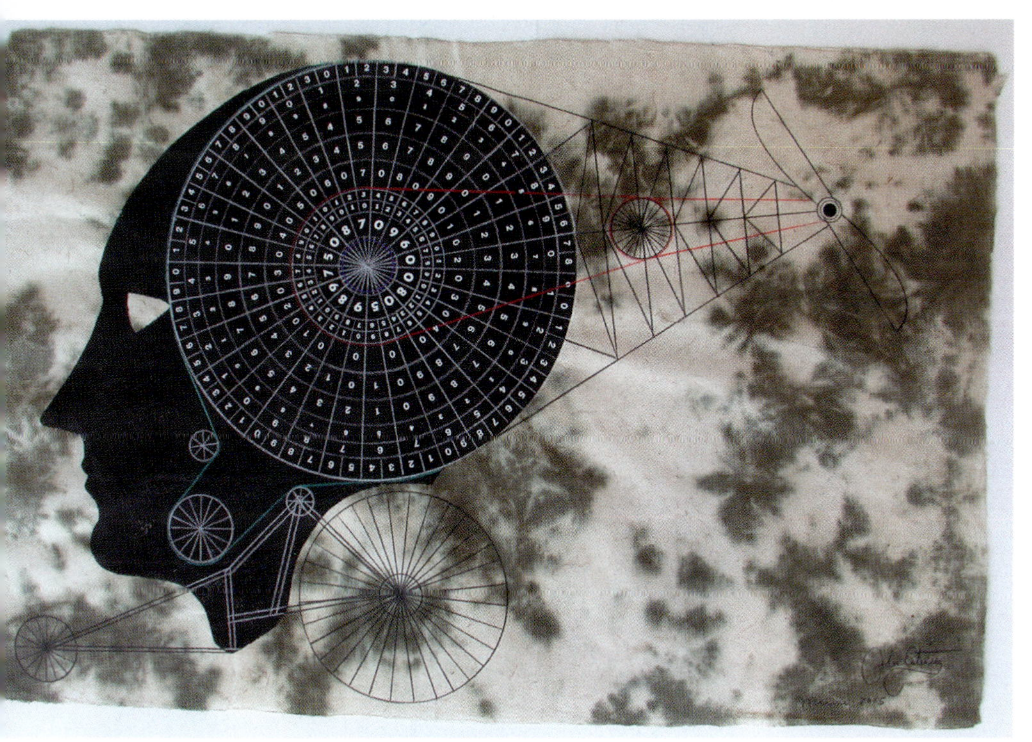

Plate III. *Pensamientos numerales* (Numerical Thoughts), 2005, 20" × 30", mixed media on paper

6

No Man Knows the Whole Truth

Xenophanes

What do we know, and how do we know it? This seems to be the topic of Estévez's *Observatorium* (Plate IV). The painting is a collage in which the artist presents us with three heads and a brain. On the left, two heads in black and in profile, with faint lines suggesting facial features, look in opposite directions. The top head is filled with architectural structures, large buildings, churches, palaces, monuments, and tombs, originating in various places, times, and cultures. In the vicinities of each of these structures are located white circles with red dots at the center. Inside the lower head we find solar systems, including our own, with planets and stars. Around it, on the surface, we see ground instruments of observation, telescopes, magnifying glasses, and other contraptions. The third head is on the right, at the bottom of the work. It is of a color that simulates human skin with all of its variety, richness, and imperfections, mounted on a kind of vehicle with a pair of wheels and three propellers at the top, resembling a flying machine with wave receptors. It displays various instruments of observation in the place of eyes, nose, mouth, ears, and forehead. The fourth figure is not a head but a brain seen from above. It has been made to look quite realistic, but its two halves are held together by door handles, and many doorknobs of various sorts are stuck into it.

An observatory is a place where one observes, where one collects information. It is a place for the acquisition of knowledge. Normally one would think of this as a room in which instruments of observation are located. And the observations one makes in an observatory usually have to do with the heavens; they are matters of astronomy. But Estévez's painting consists of four figures, and only one suggests anything about astronomy. What is involved here?

One way to look at it is to see the painting as a metaphor for both the means of knowing and the object of knowledge. What are the objects at play? Four primarily. One is expected, from the title: the heavenly bodies,

45

what we find and study in astronomy, such as solar systems, the stars, and their interrelations. The head filled with buildings suggests another sort of object, human-made objects, cultural artifacts. Buildings are perhaps the most perspicuous of human creations and include everything developed by cultures: laws, religions, art, social organization, and so on. It is intriguing that the buildings that Estévez has chosen were produced by different societies at different times and have different purposes, all suggesting great variety in this source of human understanding.

And how is it that these heads represent different ways of knowing? In the case of the head with solar systems, one might conjecture that it has to do with the instruments proper to the science of astronomy, what astronomers use to observe the heavenly bodies. But there are no instruments available in the head full of buildings. Perhaps the structures themselves point to the means of observation, for if they stand for different cultures, then the principles developed by those cultures to understand the world would be represented by the buildings.

The head at the bottom on the right, unlike the others, is fully looking at the spectator. It is communicating with us, and observing. And it has a means of transportation and flight, which entails that it can move and observe from different perspectives. What is the object of observation, then? You and me. This figure represents our observation of ourselves, of what we are, of who we are, and of our individual and collective histories. Consider that the central instrument of observation is a view master for looking at photographic representations, an instrument used to see images from the past. The picture it presents is a landscape on one side, but on the other some structures lurk. And the central part is omitted from view, perhaps telling us that it is the viewer himself or herself who is the center of attention. The means of observation varies a great deal, going from instruments of sight to instruments of sound. Humans are complex entities, with physical, social, cultural, and mental dimensions. There is no one single way to observe ourselves. Unlike the solar systems, at which we look in one fundamental way through science, humans approach themselves in a multiplicity of ways and through a multiplicity of mediums.

The last figure is a brain. Its place, at the top and the right-hand side of the painting, suggests its importance. The fact that it is a human brain and realistically portrayed indicates that the object of observation is the brain itself. This would in turn lead us to the idea that we are dealing not with us as a whole package, as we have in the previous figures, but only with a part of ourselves, the locus of thinking and knowing. But do we have any indication that we are dealing with something more than a brain? Doorknobs and handles stick out of it, giving us a way to move in this direction, for the brain is not self-contained and restricted to itself; it is a door to something else. They suggest thoughts and their transmission. The fourth object of observation is the mind and its communication with others; and the means of communication is not sensible. The brain has no eyes, no organs of sensation; it has no physical movement. Its motion is imperceptible, suggested only by the equipment sticking out from it.

Philosophers have disagreed strongly about the object of knowledge and its means. Some tell us that we only know ourselves, our minds, as it were. We know the world only as it is present in us, and only through us. This is the famous position of Socrates discussed in the context of Estévez's *Self-fishing*. For others, the reverse is true. We do not know ourselves except through others. We cannot find anything through introspection. We need to perceive, to go out of ourselves in order to acquire knowledge. This is the view of Hume and other empiricists, again discussed in this book. And philosophers also disagree about the object of knowledge. For some it is the self, as Socrates seems to have believed; for others it is nature, which seems to have been the case with some of the pre-Socratics; and still for others it is the world of culture, for they believe there is no nature apart from culture, which is a favorite position of the nineteenth century and more recently of postmodernists.

Estévez's painting suggests a more encompassing approach. The object of knowledge is multifaceted: the heavenly bodies, the world of culture, ourselves, and our minds. And each of these objects requires specialized instruments through which the knowledge is accomplished: instruments of science, the principles embedded in culture, the observation of ourselves and our past, and the reflection within the mind. I think he is right!

SOURCES

Aristotle. *Posterior Analytics*, Bk. II, ch. 19. In *The Complete Works of Aristotle*, vol. I, ed. Jonathan Barnes. Princeton, NJ: Princeton University Press, 1984.

Descartes, René. *Discourse on Method*, Part II. In *A Discourse on Method and Selected Writings* translated by John Veitch. New York: Dutton and Co., 1951.

Hume, David. *An Inquiry Concerning Human Understanding*, Bk. I, part I. S. I. La Salle, IL: Open Court Press, 1963.

Locke, John. *An Essay Concerning Human Understanding*, Bk. II, ch. 1. 2 vols. New York: Dover, 1959.

Plato. *The Republic*, Bks. VI and VII. In *The Collected Dialogues of Plato*, ed. Edith Hamilton and Huntington Cairns. New York: Pantheon Books, 1961.

Thomas Aquinas. *Summa theologiae*, I, qq. 74–76. Edited by Thomas Gilby. Garden City, NY: Image Books, 1969–.

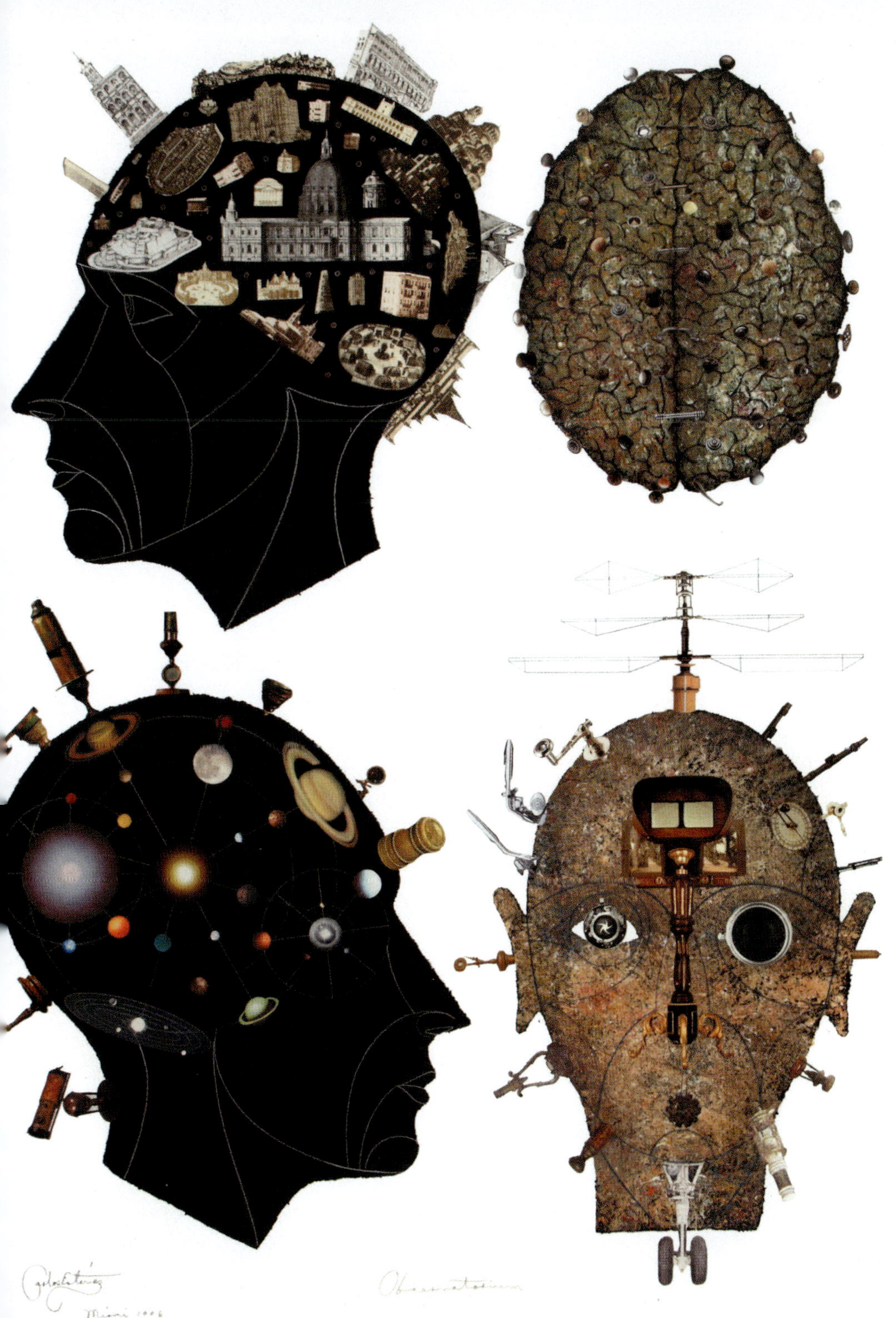

Plate IV. *Observatorium* (Observatory), 2006, 39.5" $\times$ 27.5", collage
on paper

7

Faith Seeks Understanding

Anselm

A background of shades of red. On the sides, two pillars support two heads facing each other holding a line on their mouths that runs across *Waverings of Faith* (Plate V), but is weighted down by a puppet ballerina balancing herself on it. Between the pillars, and in decreasing height all the way to the center, are drawings of building structures, church towers, domes, spires, and minarets. The puppet is balanced precariously, but graciously, on one leg, the other leg and the arms helping to keep her in place. She holds a line between her hands, weighted down by a wheel to which the puppet's head is tied through another line, disconnected to the body. Other lines are tied to the feet and hands, running to the edge of the picture.

Tertullian made the controversial statement, "I believe because it is absurd" (*Credo quia ineptum*), which centuries later became the guiding principle of Søren Kierkegaard's philosophy. Faith is irrational, contradicting our most cherished rational principles and requiring a leap. For Kierkegaard, the paradigm of faith is Abraham, in that he was willing to obey God's order to sacrifice his son and heir. This made no sense to him. It would mean not only excruciating pain but also committing murder and eliminating his line. Yet Abraham raised his hand and was ready to strike, on God's command, trusting his faith rather than his reason.

This view receives support from St. Paul, for whom Christian wisdom appears to be foolishness in the eyes of the world. But is this a sound position? Can we give up the certainties of science for the certainties of faith when they contradict each other? Can I hold something that science tells me makes no sense? Can I believe that the world was created in six days when geology and evolutionary theory tell me it took millions of years? Or, alternatively, should we give up faith for science? Most religions grapple with this problem, for at stake is the very nature of faith and reason and the kind of certainty each provides.

The main battlefield for these issues in the West was the Middle Ages, an eminently religious period in which faith ruled every aspect of human life. On one side were those who, like Tertullian, held that faith provides the only kind of certain knowledge. Every source of knowledge other than faith, which they identified with the truths revealed in the Judeo-Christian Scriptures, is suspect and must be confirmed by faith. If it is not, then its certainty is in doubt, and if it should contradict faith, then it must be abandoned altogether.

Bonaventure went so far as to establish a hierarchy of authority and certainty in knowledge to guide us. At the top are the Christian Scriptures, God's revelation to humanity, and therefore unquestionable. Next come the writings of the Fathers of the Church, authors such as Tertullian and Augustine, who were the first to comment on the Scriptures and attempt to develop a theological framework to understand them. The authority of these is not as high as that of the word of God, but they have to be taken seriously and can be trusted only as long as they do not contradict revelation. Next comes the work of the masters, the writings of Bonaventure's contemporaries who taught at medieval universities. These sources of knowledge have even less authority than the work of the Fathers of the Church, therefore their claims need to be closely watched and controlled by the authority of Scriptures and of the Fathers of the Church, for error may have crept into them. Finally, there are the writings of the philosophers, authors from ancient Greece, Rome, and from the Islamic world, such as Aristotle, Seneca, and Averroes. These works are filled with mistakes, and it is difficult to separate truth from falsehood in them. They should not be trusted at all. As Bonaventure put it, "The water of philosophical science is not to be mingled with the wine of Holy Scripture."

On the other side were those authors who gave priority to secular knowledge over faith, arguing that the certainty of faith was subsumed under that of scientific knowledge. Faith has to make sense in order to be acceptable, therefore it must be harmonized with science. Peter Abelard, among others, tried to show the need that faith has of reason. He argued for the dependence of faith on reason by quoting side-by-side Scriptural texts that seem to contradict each other, in a controversial work entitled *Sic et non* (Yes and No).

Finally, there were authors who sought a middle ground between those who downgraded reason and those who downgraded faith, stressing one to the detriment of the other. Anselm of Canterbury attempted to harmonize the claims of faith and those of reason, arguing both that faith seeks understanding and understanding begins with faith. We cannot do without either. There is perhaps no better illustration of Anselm's approach than his notorious argument for the existence of God. In the *Proslogion,* he begins by stating that he believes both that God exists and that he is "that being of which a greater cannot be thought." Then he proceeds to show that once this formula is understood, it follows that such a being exists. Otherwise that being than which a greater cannot be thought would not be that being than which a greater cannot be thought, but rather that being than which a greater can be thought, for one could think of one that also exists, and that would be greater.

Anselm's argument is presented as a demonstration that God exists, which provides a certainty different from that of faith. The argument supplies a proper understanding of faith. Faith seeks arguments such as this when it seeks understanding. Anselm spoke of them as "necessary reasons."

The spirit revealed in Anselm's procedure led to the most famous medieval attempt at resolving the issue concerning the relation between faith and reason. In the *Summa theologiae*, Thomas Aquinas goes deeper into the understanding of this issue than anyone before him in order to resolve the controversy, and his view remains one of the most clear and satisfactory solutions to this day. According to him, faith and reason are ways in which we acquire knowledge. All knowledge has an object, but not all knowledge is acquired in the same way. Each way of knowing approaches its object differently, and this in turn requires a different method of drawing conclusions about it. Aquinas used some jargon to express this point. He said that an object has to be considered according to a certain "formality," which we might take to mean a certain aspect, and that this formality is in line with faculties knowers have, such as the powers of sensing, thinking, and reasoning.

If we want to know the color of a particular physical object, say an apple, we must look at it. The sense of sight will tell us the color—whether the apple is red or green. But if we want to find out how an object tastes, then the sense of sight is not helpful in giving us the knowledge we want to have. No matter how much we look at an apple, it will look red or green, but we will not find whether it is sweet or sour. In order to know how the apple tastes, we need to use other means of knowing, namely, the sense of taste; we must bite into the fruit and savor it. The reverse is also true; by biting into the apple we will find out its taste, but we will not learn its color. Obviously the same object can be known in different ways, and the knowledge that we have of it can, as a result, be quite different. An apple can be known as red and also as sweet.

Just as the sense of sight and the sense of taste are two different powers that yield two different ways of approaching an object and help us reach different conclusions about it, so are faith and reason. Reason looks at the world in natural terms, as opposed to supernatural ones. It investigates the world as it is presented to us through our experience by using the natural powers that we have. These powers include both the powers of perception and of reason. The job of scientists is to observe the world and to come up with conclusions about it that are justified by reliable perceptual and rational processes. In this way they can formulate truths such as the world is round, water boils at 100 degrees Celsius at sea level, or the square of the hypotenuse of a right triangle is equal to the sum of the squares of its sides. Of course, the scientific knowledge we derive from the exercise of reason breaks down into different disciplines. Some of these have different objects that serve to distinguish them, as happens with astronomy, which studies the heavenly bodies, and psychology, which studies the mind. But other sciences may have the same objects and use different methods to investigate them, as happens with chemistry and physics, both of which study the same things but in different ways.

Both faith and reason have as their object of study the entire universe, including God. But there is a very important difference between them in that faith studies the world under the guidance of what God has revealed to humans about it and reason does not. Revelation, according to Aquinas, is found in the Scriptures. But the source of secular knowledge is the world, the Book of Nature, as the medievals called it, to contrast it with the Book of Revelation, that is, the Bible. We have two perspectives, two ways of investigating the world, and two sets of conclusions about it. The certainty of conclusions is traceable to the certainty of the foundations of those conclusions. In the case of science, the certainty is based on the reliability of the method we use to draw them and the assumptions we make. This is the evidence provided by our natural faculties. In the case of faith, the certainty also depends on the reliability of the method used to draw them and the assumptions we make. For faith this reliability is provided by the Scriptures and the validity of the belief that they constitute a revelation from God.

Aquinas realizes that both faith and reason use each other to some extent. Reason assumes certain things without question for the purposes of investigation. And faith uses reason (including perception) in its study of the world guided by revelation. In each case the ultimate determining factors are different: for science they are our natural powers, whereas faith rests on a belief in the supernatural.

This poses an apparently unresolvable dilemma, for it is always possible that what makes sense from a rational point of view does not from a faith point of view, and vice versa. What do we do when these procedures lead us to what appear to be incompatible conclusions? The situation is tough only for believers. Those who have no faith do not encounter this problem insofar as they only have to deal with reason. But believers are in a different situation, which brings us back to Estévez's painting.

We can consider the ballerina in two ways. In one, we might think of her as representing a believer, that is, a person with faith. In another way, we might think of her as representing faith itself. If we go with the first interpretation, then the precarious balancing act belongs to the believer. The rope on which the ballerina is trying to balance herself comes out of the mouths of two heads and could be taken to signify words coming out of two sources. One is the word revealed by God in the Scriptures; the other is the word of reason. The tension in the rope represents in turn the tension between these two different sources of authority. Depending on who gives more or less, the rope will have a different tension and will cause the believer to move and seek a new balance, whence the waverings.

The varying tension of the rope also is reproduced at a different level, complicating the balancing act of the believer, because the head of the ballerina is severed from the body and balanced through a wheel by her hands and arms, while the body is seeking equilibrium also through the legs. Perhaps the body can be taken to represent faith, which is commonly associated with the heart; and the head, with the wheels in it, can be taken as representative of reason. All of this is further complicated because the figure is a puppet, some of whose moves seem to be controlled from above, from outside the picture altogether. Could this mean that a supernatural agent has a hand in determining what is happening, although we are not shown to what extent?

The believer finds herself pulled by different epistemic forces. She has two external sources of knowledge—one is revelation and the other is science. And she has two internal faculties—faith and reason. What happens when this fine balance is lost? The puppet falls, which can indicate either the end of a believer's faith or the end of her use of reason. The ballerina enters the world of reason and science, or she moves into a dogmatic world of religious sectarianism. Both are symbolized by the buildings outlined in the painting, which in one case represent human products and in the other places of worship.

We also can go with a second interpretation, thinking of the ballerina as representing faith itself: it is not the believer who is engaged in a balancing act, but faith. The fact that the figure in the painting is female suggests that perhaps this is the better interpretation, for two reasons. First, both the Latin *fides* and the Spanish *fe* are feminine nouns, and Estévez's native tongue is Spanish, which is a Romance language. Second, in the history of the West, females often have been associated with what is nonrational or even irrational, and faith also has been regarded by many to have these characteristics. So let us assume that faith, considered as a body of beliefs and doctrines, is represented by the ballerina.

There are, again, two sources of doctrine and beliefs: one is properly speaking the set of views revealed in, say, the Bible, and the other is the set of conclusions demonstrated by science. Clearly the set of religious doctrines cries out for understanding and integration, as Abelard noted. Besides, they have implications that have to be drawn from them. Indeed, this is the nature of theology, to which Aquinas often refers as Sacred Doctrine to indicate that it is revelation articulated into a coherent system of teachings. The two heads that hold the rope on which faith is balanced can be taken as the sources of knowledge, revelation and science, and they need to be integrated and their implications spelled out; the rope has to be held and tightened sufficiently for the puppet, faith, to stand on it.

But the rational source carries much baggage and relies on methods that are very different from those used in faith. This makes equilibrium precarious. If reliance on sources other than Scriptures goes beyond a certain point, then faith might lose its balance and fall. This could mean that faith has ceased to be what it is in order to become something else. Or perhaps its falling into one or the other of the buildings below the rope signals how the articulation of revelation gives rise to different denominations and interpretations of the same revelation. Does each building suggest a different organized church, or religion—Christian, Muslim, Jewish?

Likewise, if science is abandoned in favor of revelation, then equilibrium also is destroyed, and the ballerina falls. The falling again would be into a particular building, which could indicate a dogmatic acceptance of revelation without science that becomes intransigent and closed: a building separate from others and closed to them.

Of course, the ballerina is tied by ropes to a source above, which suggests that ultimately a transcendental deity guides at least part of the process. So the situation of faith might not be as precarious as it appears after all, but that remains an open question in the painting and gives comfort only to those who believe.

SOURCES

Anselm. *Proslogion*, chs. 1–4. In *Monologion and Proslogion*, trans. Jasper Hopkins. Minneapolis, MN: A. J. Banning Press, 1986.

Bonaventure. *Sermons on the Six Days*, Vision III, Discussion VII. In *Philosophy in the Middle Ages* ed. Arthur Hyman and James J. Walsh. Indianapolis, IN: Hackett, 1973.

Kierkegaard, Søren. "The Knight of Faith and the Knight of Infinite Resignation." *In Fear and Trembling.* Translated by Walter Lowrie. Princeton, NJ: Princeton University Press, 1941.

Peter Abelard. *The Story of Abelard's Adversities.* Translated by J. T. Muckle. Toronto: Pontifical Institute of Mediaeval Studies, 1954.

Tertullian. *On the Prescription of Heretics*. In *On the Testimony of the Soul and On the "Prescription" of Heretics*, trans. T. Herbert Bindley. London: Society for the Promotion of Christian Knowledge, 1914.

Thomas Aquinas. *Summa theologiae*, I, q. 1. Edited by Thomas Gilby. Garden City, NY: Image Books, 1969–.

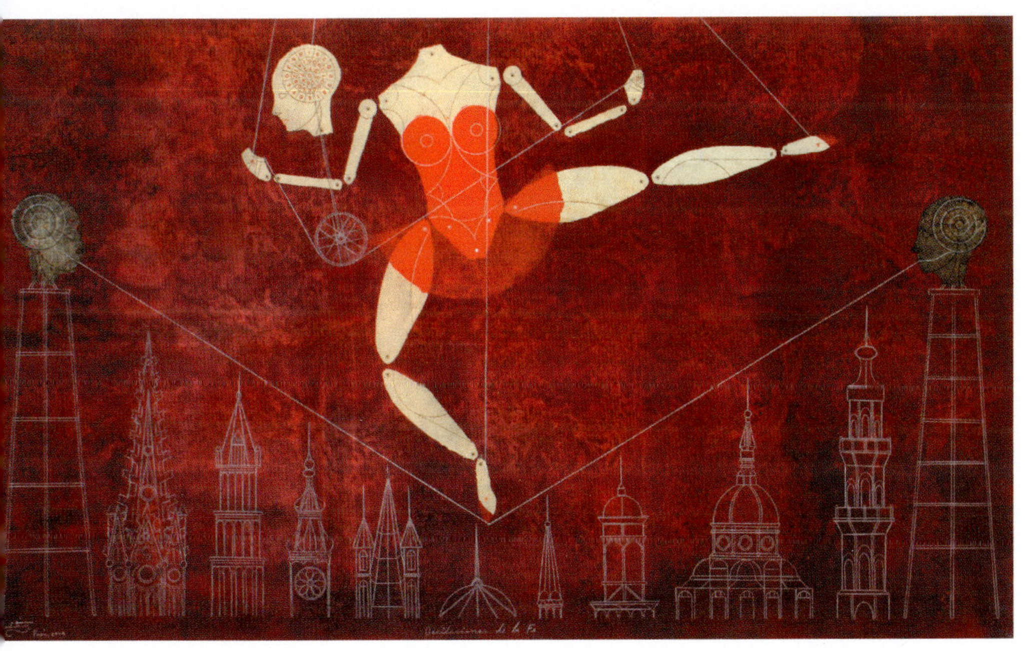

Plate V. *Oscilaciones de la fe* (Waverings of Faith), 2003, 37" × 64", oil and pencil on canvas

Reality

8

You Cannot Step into the Same River Twice

Heraclitus, as cited by Plato

On a background of undefined greys, blues, greens, and occasional ochers and reds, four figures are located in Estévez's *Undetermined Being* (Plate VI). All four have human parts, but none of them is completely human as we know it. The first on the left is standing and frontally presented, but the head is turned and looking toward its right. The figure is vertically divided into two halves. The left side looks solid and is composed of a face and torso, with an arm and a leg attached. The face has lips and eyes. Body joints and muscles are indicated by lines and points. Red dots stand at the center of the chest, the penis, and the head, on both halves of the figure. The foot and the hand also have red dots with attached lines that disappear on the upper part of the painting, confirming that the figure is a puppet. The right half of the figure is not solid and is drawn with lines that suggest a machine; instead of a hand and a foot, it has wheels. Wheels also take the place of genitals, the navel, the heart, and the brain.

Next in line, going from left to right, stands a column with a black head resting on its top. The stylized face, with eyes, nose, and mouth, is looking at the observer. On the forehead rests a red dot at the center of an off-white small circle. Tied to it is a tube connected to a veritable maze of other tubes extending throughout a good part of the canvas, in a Medusa-like maze; they end with openings. The pedestal on which the head rests is white and divided into several parts. Immediately below the head, a transitional part goes from the head rest to the capital of a column. There we find a black dot encircled by some space divided by a red line. The shaft of the column has four parts; the first three are separated by spaces on which are drawn red circles with dots at the centers. Each of the first three parts is further divided into small squares, some of which contain numbers. The fourth part of the shaft contains more designs. Below it is the base, with a transition to a larger square with the inscription *El sentido de la vida es su falta de sentido.*

63

La esencia del ser está en su incompletez (The meaning of life is its lack of meaning. The essence of being consists in its incompleteness).

The third figure is black, partly frontally presented and partly in profile. Its top is a human puppet looking sideways to its left, holding in its left hand a lighthouse in which a climbing staircase is visible. The light is represented by a small blue dot encircled by a black line. On the right hand the puppet holds a lamppost with a large blue dot at the top. The lights in the lighthouse and the lamppost are tied by lines to three concentric wheels with red dots located in the cranial area of the puppet's head. The black figure ends at the bottom of the abdomen, where another part begins; it looks like the body of a horse, with four legs composed of multiple wheels, circles, and lines and populated by numbers.

The fourth figure is placed in the right-hand corner of the work. It is composed of a head in profile looking to the left. Like the other figures, it is colored black and has circles with red dots on its skull. It is connected to a large set of concentric circles, with lines that form cubicles with numbers. It suggests the opening of a transparent shell revealing the snakelike body of a mollusk, extending all the way to the end of its portable dwelling.

Conceptions of being have tended to fall into two groups. Some are finished and static, others unfinished and dynamic. The first emphasizes permanence, the second change. Among early Greek philosophers, these two positions acquired classical formulations in the thought of Parmenides and Heraclitus. For Parmenides, being was one, unchanging, and, as a result, eternal. As Zeno put it, change is a matter of appearance; an arrow never leaves its source or reaches its target, even though it looks as if it travels from one to the other through space. Heraclitus held just the opposite view. Being is characterized by change, so that, as cited by Plato, "one cannot step in the same river twice." Nothing stays the same, nothing is fixed, and nothing is eternal, except perhaps for change itself.

Parmenides' view was extreme, but it nonetheless had enormous influence in the thought of Plato and Aristotle in the ancient world, and through them, in the philosophy of medieval, Renaissance, and early modern philosophers. It is not until the nineteenth century, with the development of empirical science, that the influence of this view wanes. In Plato we find this Parmenidean idea in his claim that the real world consists of eternal and unchanging abstract ideas, separate from the material world of sensation and change. The real world is composed of such things as goodness, justice, oneness, and catness. This is a rather difficult position to maintain, but it was nonetheless borrowed by some Christian philosophers, beginning with Augustine, who placed these ideas in the divine mind. Through these archetypes, which they referred to as *exemplars*, God created the world. The Platonic ideas became the models God used in creation.

In spite of Aristotle's empirical bent and his interest in biology, he also was influenced by the Parmenidean conception of being, although his view is more dynamic. For him, the organic world is composed of individual entities he called substances, such as a cat or a woman. These substances fall into different groups of genera and species. Mary and Peter belong to the genus animal and the species human, which are characterized by properties common to all of their members and without which the beings in question would not be what they are. The necessary properties of things constitute their essences, which are nothing but sets of properties in virtue of which things are kinds of beings and are able to exist. A human being is both an animal and has the capacity to reason, and it is in virtue of these that it can exist.

Essences are sets of properties that make things what they are, and specific essences make things members of particular species. The part of this idea that goes back to Parmenides is the view that species are here to stay; they are fixed and cannot change. It was this conception of species that authors such as Aquinas, through the influence of Augustine, adopted to explain God's relationship to the world. The human species, just as the species dog, has its foundation in the divine mind, and like that mind, it is eternal and unchanging.

The nineteenth and twentieth centuries in particular did much to change this Parmenidean insight in favor of a more Heraclitean position. Not everyone agreed with Heraclitus, that everything is in flux, but many philosophers rejected the view that things have eternal and unchanging essences.

Two developments were important in this process. The first is the Darwinian theory of evolution, which claims that current species are the result of contingent processes that could have been otherwise. These species are in a process of change and could very well have evolved into species very different from the ones that gave them origin. Indeed, they may still evolve into entities different from what they currently are. This view influenced later philosophers, such as Friedrich Nietzsche and Henri Bergson, and particularly process philosophers, such as Alfred North Whitehead, because they think the world is not static but dynamic; it is not composed of things but of processes.

The second development was the realization that any kind of rigid conception of human essence puts constraints on human action, going contrary to our intuitions—humans seem to be free to act as they wish, as least in certain occasions. Suicide is the proof of the pudding, as Jean-Paul Sartre pointed out. The decision to end one's existence proves that we are free. Besides, any rigid conception of humans undermines human moral responsibility, and this is intolerable. Insulating the catastrophes of the two World Wars and their horrors from responsibility and blame is untenable.

The alternative to the Parmenidean view is to conceive being as dynamic and changing rather than static and fixed. There are no definite boundaries to the way being manifests itself, except for contingent ones. Things could have been otherwise and often are. The future is open, and beings are undetermined and, if human, free. This preserves human responsibility and makes us masters of our future.

This principle can be used to approach Estévez's painting. The painting is focused on humans rather than being in general, because there is no such thing as being in general, and there is no way to represent it. There are only individual beings of particular kinds. Still, the title of the painting suggests the more general topic. Besides, there is also a need to communicate with a human audience, and human illustrations make the point of the work easier to grasp.

The canvas displays four figures, each of which has two parts. The first has human and mechanical halves. The second figure is partly human and partly stone. The third is a man with the body of a horse. And the fourth is a human head with a body of a mollusk. In all cases, one part appears to be real and human, similar to the way we are; the other part is suggestive of what we could have, or could, become. We could have been, or could become, machines, robots of some kind, figures of stone, horses, or even mollusks. And we could have become, or could become in the future, the very mixtures depicted: androids, centaurs, mollusks with human heads, or even beings made partly of stone.

And how is it that we became what we are? The painting suggests several factors. One is the mysterious influence of whatever is outside of the picture. Perhaps a god, or a superior race of entities from outer space, or the very circumstances that govern our existence on Earth, such as physical or cultural processes. The puppetlike figures make room for speculation about the ultimate causes of the changes that bring about what we are. In all of the figures, certain points of importance are emphasized, such as the brain as the seat of thinking, the heart as the seat of feeling, the genitals as the seat of sexual attraction, and the hands and feet as the seats of manipulation and movement.

We are not locked into an essential frame that constraints and limits us. Life, as the caption on the column suggests, lacks a definite meaning. But this does not entail that it is rudderless, that there is no direction, or that there is no significance to it. It means that being is incomplete and open, and that we can make of it what we want in the appropriate circumstances. Being and essence, contrary to what Parmenides, Plato, and even Aristotle, to some extent, thought, are not closed but indeterminate and open to change and transformation. Sartre and Nietzsche are right: existence precedes essence, and not the other way around. This thought is both liberating and frightening. It is liberating in that it frees us from the shackles of the past, and it is frightening because it makes us understand the uncertainty of the future.

SOURCES

Aristotle. *Metaphysics*, Bk. VII, chs. 1–6. In *The Complete Works of Aristotle*, vol. I, ed. Jonathan Barnes. Princeton, NJ: Princeton University Press, 1984.

Bergson, Henri. *Creative Evolution*, ch. 3. Translated by Arthur Mitchel. New York: The Modern Library, 1944.

Darwin, Charles. *On the Origin of Species*, ch. xv. New York: New York University Press, 1988.

Heraclitus. *Fragments.* In *An Introduction to Early Greek Philosophy: The Chief Fragments and Ancient Testimony, with Connecting Commentary*, ed. John Mansley Robinson, ch. 5. New York: Houghton Mifflin, 1968.

Parmenides. *On Nature.* In *An Introduction to Early Greek Philosophy: The Chief Fragments and Ancient Testimony, with Connecting Commentary*, ed. John Mansley Robinson, ch. 6. New York: Houghton Mifflin, 1968.

Plato. *Timeus*, 50. In *The Collected Dialogues of Plato*, ed. Edith Hamilton and Huntington Cairns. New York: Pantheon Books, 1961.

Sartre, Jean-Paul. *No Exit.* In *No Exit and Three Other Plays.* New York: Vintage International, 1989.

Thomas Aquinas. *Summa theologiae*, I, q. 15. Edited by Thomas Gilby. Garden City, NY: Image Books, 1969–.

Whitehead, Alfred North. *Process and Reality: An Essay in Cosmology*, ch. II. New York: Free Press, 1978.

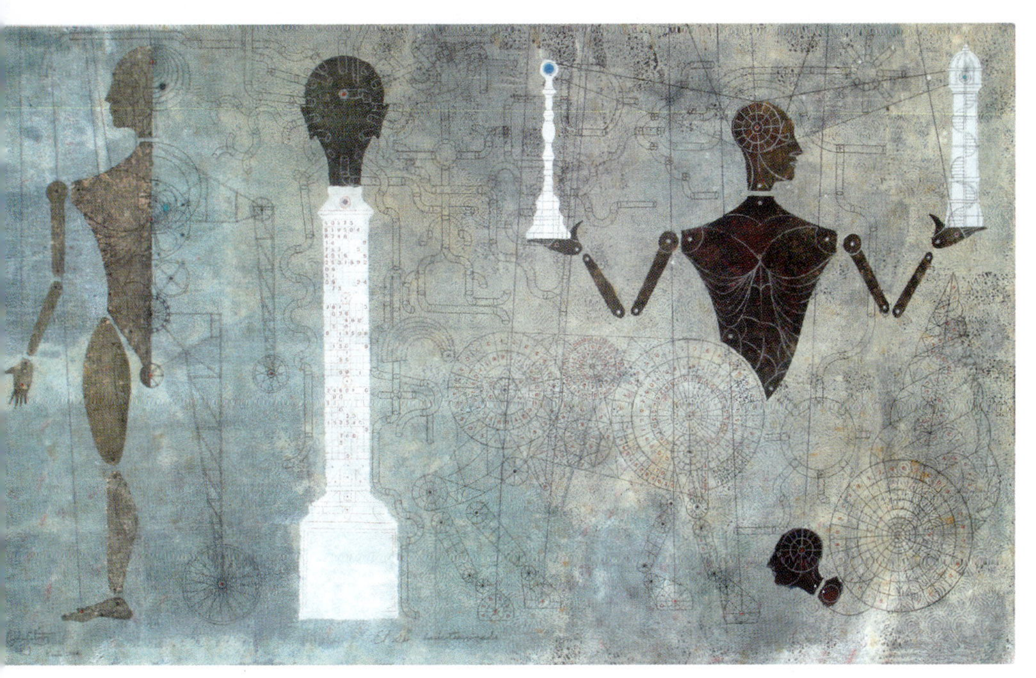

Plate VI. *El ser indeterminado* (Undetermined Being) 2004, 38" × 64", oil and pencils on canvas

9

No Part of the Whole Is Empty

Empedocles

In *Horror vacui* (Plate VII), the background appears to be an aerial view of the Earth through the clouds. On it we see a balloon with a gondola hanging from it. The gondola is a head in profile whose sawed-off crown reveals an empty cavity where the brain is supposed to be. It is attached to the balloon with multiple strings that end up on a band that encircles it. The balloon is tied to strings that meet in three points at its top to prevent it from escaping; two sets of strings end in points, and the third ends in a circle, forming a mesh that partly encases it. The balloon is a human brain of enormous size if compared to the head to which it presumably belongs, and it is appropriately depicted in tones of yellow and grey, with occasional hints of red. The color of the head is a peculiar yellow.

The most common way of thinking about the fear of empty spaces, the title of Estévez's painting, is as a phobia, an uncontrollable panic that grips some people when they find themselves in vast and open terrains. In art, the *horror vacui* refers to an attitude in artists that leads them to fill up entirely the space available to them. But here we are not concerned with psychology, and ironically, neither with art as such but rather with philosophy. Can this painting have a philosophical dimension?

Two things come to mind. First, the painting has to do with knowing and explanation. After all, the head in it is superimposed on a view of the earth, suggesting an observer. If so, the fear of empty spaces can be used to understand an attitude contrary to one of the most widely cherished principles of science, the so-called Principle of Parsimony, or Ockham's Razor. According to this principle, a simpler explanation of why something happens is preferred to a more complicated one. In William of Ockham's terminology, entities should not be multiplied beyond necessity. Conceptually, a good explanation is lean, with as few elements as possible, uncrowded by unnecessary paraphernalia. A bad one, on the contrary, is often suffocated by details, full of irrelevancies included from a false sense of completeness.

Consider, for example, the observable fact that if I let go of the glass I am holding on my hand, it falls to the ground. One explanation of why it does is that two powerful gods are engaged in a struggle for power, and one wants things to fall down, whereas the other does not. The first gets help from another god, whom he has bribed, and thus he is able to get his way in this particular instance, which leads us farther into speculations about the two gods and their histories. Another explanation is that material objects attract each other in proportion to their mass. The glass falls to the ground because the earth is a very large material body and attracts the glass to itself, which is a small one.

According to the Principle of Parsimony, the second explanation is preferred to the first, because it is much simpler. But those who oppose the Principle of Parsimony argue that its application often results in inadequate understandings, yielding simplistic and incomplete conceptions of the world. Their view can take two forms: one is metaphysical and concerned with reality, while another is epistemic and concerned with knowledge. The metaphysical view has given rise to a concept that has surfaced from time to time: the Principle of Plenitude. In epistemology, it has been responsible for the elaboration of extraordinarily complex explanations.

The Principle of Plenitude holds that there can be no holes in being, that being can have no gaps. The universe is completely full, although this fullness often is understood differently by different authors. In some cases it is understood spatially: the universe is a box in which every part has something in it. In other cases it is combined with another idea, that of the great chain of being: it is not just that there is no vacuum, no empty spaces, but that every possibility must be realized in the universe. From this we get the name of the principle, for plenitude means fullness.

The Principle of Plenitude has been used in philosophy for many purposes. One of the most interesting ones is as an explanation of why God created the world as he did. The issue can be divided into three questions. First, why did God create a world of multiplicity? Second, why did God create species that seem to conflict with one another? And third, why did God create this world rather than any other?

In all of these cases, the answer can be that God did it because of the Principle of Plenitude. Being seeks to multiply itself, to give itself richly; it seeks fullness. Because of this, God created multiplicity, for a world of uniformity would not reflect fullness insofar as fullness requires variety. God created the species that he created, even though they conflict with each other, because every possibility has to be realized, and this requires that different, and conflicting, things be produced. God created this world rather than any other, because this world is full of things both in terms of not having any empty spaces and in terms of having every possible kind of thing in it. This is why this is the best of all possible worlds, as Pangloss so eloquently states in Voltaire's satirical novel *Candide*.

Estévez's painting illustrates dramatically the consequences of the *horror vacui*. The brain of someone with this attitude seeks to fill every detail and posit every entity in its explanation of the universe. The cavity that is naturally its place can no longer accommodate it because it has grown disproportionately to include this explosion of being, conceptually and metaphysically. Ironically, because the brain has become enormous, it can no longer fit the head, leaving it empty, as it travels in search of ever increasing expansion.

Is the fear of empty spaces warranted? Is the painting a criticism or an endorsement of such fear? At first it looks as if it is indeed a criticism of it. But one also can note that the contrary attitude, where we conceive the world in limited terms and our explanations are lean, confines us to the cranial cavity. We miss the soaring flights and insights that occur when we liberate ourselves from the boundaries within which we generally function. Perhaps it is better to let our thoughts and imagination, symbolized by Estévez's brain balloon, fly into the sky of possibilities, carrying with them the rest of us, beyond our unperceived limitations. Estévez's work does not answer this philosophical question; it merely poses it, suggesting what appear to be the consequences of some answers to it.

SOURCES

Augustine. *On Free Will,* Bk. III, v. 13. In *Augustine: Earlier Writings,* vol. 6, trans. J. H. S. Burleigh. London: SCM Press, 1953.

Empedocles. *On the Nature of Things.* In *An Introduction to Early Greek Philosophy: The Chief Fragments and Ancient Testimony, with Connecting Commentary,* ed. John Mansley Robinson, ch. 8. New York: Houghton Mifflin, 1968.

Lovejoy, Arthur. *The Great Chain of Being: A Study of the History of an Idea,* ch. 4. Cambridge, MA: Harvard University Press, 1936.

Voltaire. *Candide.* New York: Bantam Classics, 1984.

William of Ockham. *Ordinatio,* d. 30, q. IE. In *Philosophical Writings: A Selection,* trans. Philotheus Boehner, pp. xx–xxi. Indianapolis, IN: Bobbs-Merrill, 1964.

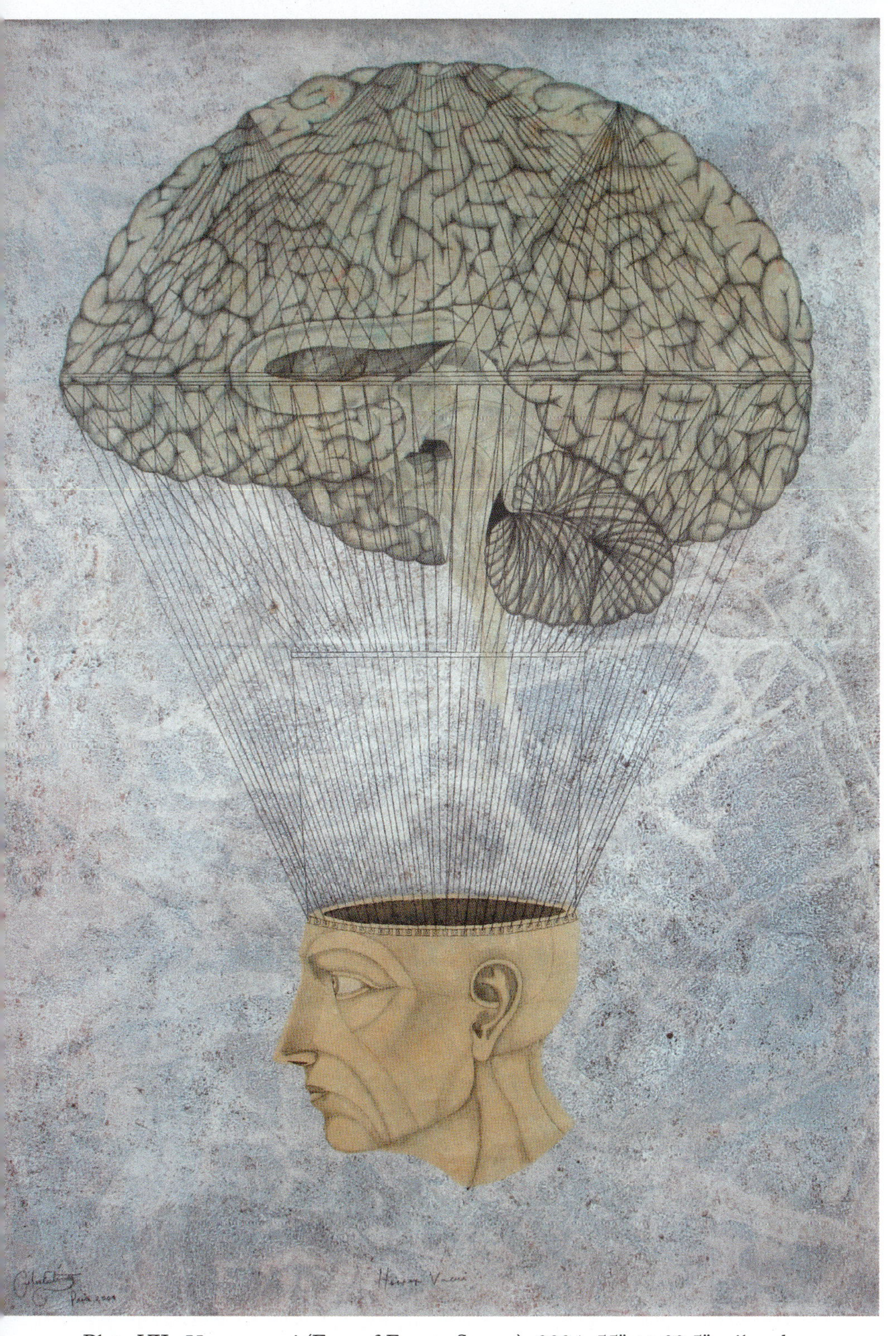

Plate VII. *Horror vacui* (Fear of Empty Spaces), 2004, 55" × 39.5", oil and pencil on canvas

10

There Is No New Thing under the Sun

Ecclesiastes

A headless figure with puppetlike arms, legs, hands, and feet rides a bicycle whose wheels fill the cranial capacity of two heads in profile, looking in opposite directions, in *Stationary Journey* (Plate VIII). The heads themselves are ensconced in riding machines. From a point on the neck, where the head of the puppet is supposed to go, comes a string tied to a balloon from which hangs a gondola. The background is in a faux finish of orange, ocher, yellow, and greys. The figures are black, as are the lines that make up the riding vehicles. The skeleton of the puppet is visible and consists of wheels and mechanisms of various sorts. Dots of red and shades of green pinpoint centers of power. The line that ties the puppet to the balloon continues inside the puppet's body, circling around and connecting inner springs.

Two philosophically interesting ways to interpret Estévez's work suggest themselves. On the one hand, the work can be taken as a depiction of the universe and of human history within it. On the other hand, it can be taken as a depiction of individual human lives. These interpretations are not incompatible, for the second may be an application of the first. The message is the same: we are stuck where we are in spite of our efforts to the contrary.

This idea is very old and has taken many forms. It first surfaced in a philosophical context with the Greeks, who also held the contrary view, according to which both the world as a whole and individual human beings are going somewhere, and there is direction and advance toward a goal. Some ancient Greek philosophers believed that history is cyclical, that it all occurred before and will occur again. What is happening today will happen tomorrow and has happened yesterday, and so on with every event in the history of the world and the history of individual lives. There is no beginning or end, the world has always existed and will always exist. It moves in a circle, not a line; there is no goal that can be achieved to give meaning and sense to the process, only an endless recurrence.

In spite of its popularity, ancient Greeks were not uncritical of this view. Aristotle undermined it by arguing that every activity in the universe happens for a purpose, that it has an end toward which it moves. The stone moves toward the ground to find rest there, and the sculptor toward the production of a statue, where he reaches satisfaction and fulfillment. Everything has an end and moves toward an end, otherwise movement could not happen and would be unintelligible. The sculpture is necessary to explain why the sculptor engages to produce it. It would make no sense to say that the work of the artist has no goal, that there is, in Aristotle's term, no *telos* toward which it strives.

Whatever exists requires an explanation in four terms. If we want to account for the existence of a statue of Aphrodite, first we need to think about the material out of which it is made, such as marble. Then we have to think about the shape that the marble has and which makes it to be a statue of Aphrodite and not one of Apollo. In addition, we have to think about the process of sculpting through which the artist produced the statue. These are material, formal, and efficient causes according to Aristotle, but not enough to account for the end product or to explain why it exists. We need to think also about the statue as realized, for this is the object of desire, the goal that the artist wants to achieve all along, and without which she or he would not have started the process of creation. This is called final cause.

Aristotle believed not only that each change in the world has an end, he also held that the world as a whole has an end, an object of desire toward which it moves through the accomplishment of many intermediate ends. This ultimate object of desire, perfection itself, is found in the unmoved source of all movement, the Unmoved Mover. This being is fully perfect and as such has nothing to desire and admire but itself; its movement is merely self-contemplation. In principle, Aristotle's view is not incompatible with the old Greek cyclical view of history, for the very end of the universe has no end other than itself, is not in motion, and the movement it generates makes no ultimate progress; no one can become the Unmoved Mover.

The view Augustine presented later was very different from the cyclical view favored in ancient Greece. Inspired by Christian eschatology, he conceived the world and human history as progressive. The world is moving toward a goal, and each of its parts, each of its events, is unique and a contributing factor to the achievement of that goal. This will be the crowning moment of all history and the achievement of a plan God has for the universe. The City of Man has for its end the City of God. There is a supernatural denouement to human existence, which is assured by God's benevolent Providence. Humans are destined to share in God's happiness, in a state of unending beatitude, marked by the contemplation of their maker in a glorious vision.

The idea of progress is deeply ingrained in Western thinking. Augustine is regarded by many as perhaps the most influential thinker in Western thought, and his eschatological view of human history and world movement became integrated into our way of looking at things. In early modern philosophy this notion was stripped of its divine dimension and became the idea of progress in nonreligious or even antireligious philosophies such as positivism, idealism, and Marxism. In the positivism of Auguste Comte, it turned into a historical process marked by stages through which humanity passed, until it reached a stage of science. The idealism of Hegel ends in the self-knowledge of the Absolute, again developed through a process of progressive self-consciousness. And in Marx it becomes the communist state in which capital is eliminated and human beings reach the condition of true humanism: human beings are no longer used as means for the increment of capital but as ends.

Neither of the extremes represented by the early Greek cyclical view of human history and the Augustinian view of linear progress seem to be what Estévez's painting is about, philosophically. The work is, rather, attuned to the Aristotelian notion of a telos that is beyond attainment but maintains motion. The cyclist is working hard at moving forward, motivated by the view of a larger horizon visible from, or represented by, the balloon—a goal, an idea, floating in the air in front of the figure. But he is kept in place by the very motion in which he is engaged, because he is tied both to the head that is looking and trying to move forward and the head that is looking and trying to move backward.

The central figure of the painting represents us individually or human history as a whole. We have ties to the past and are pedaling hard to move to the future, inspired by a mental goal, an idea, or an object of desire but never moving effectively toward the end. We are in many ways like the movers of the Aristotelian heavens, bound to circle endlessly around the Unmoved Mover, drawn by the desire for it and hampered by their inability to achieve it. We move in circles, and so does human history, but not because there is nothing new under the sun, or because everything is bound to be repeated, but because the end is unattainable, even though we are bound to strive for it. And it is perhaps in that striving that our nature and happiness consist.

SOURCES

Aristotle. *Physics*, Bk. II, ch.3. In *The Complete Works of Aristotle*, vol. I, ed. Jonathan Barnes. Princeton, NJ: Princeton University Press, 1984.

Augustine. *The City of God*, Bk. XIX. 2 vols. Indianapolis, IN: St Maur Theological Center, 1979.

Comte, August. *The Positive Philosophy*, ch. I. New York: AMS Press, 1974.

Hegel, G. W. F. *Phenomenology of Spirit*, VIII. Translated by Howard P. Kainz. University Park: Pennsylvania State University Press, 1994.

Marx, Karl. "Private Property and Communism." In *Economic and Philosophical Manuscripts of 1844*, ed. Dirk Struitk, trans. Martin Milligan. New York: International Publishers, 1964.

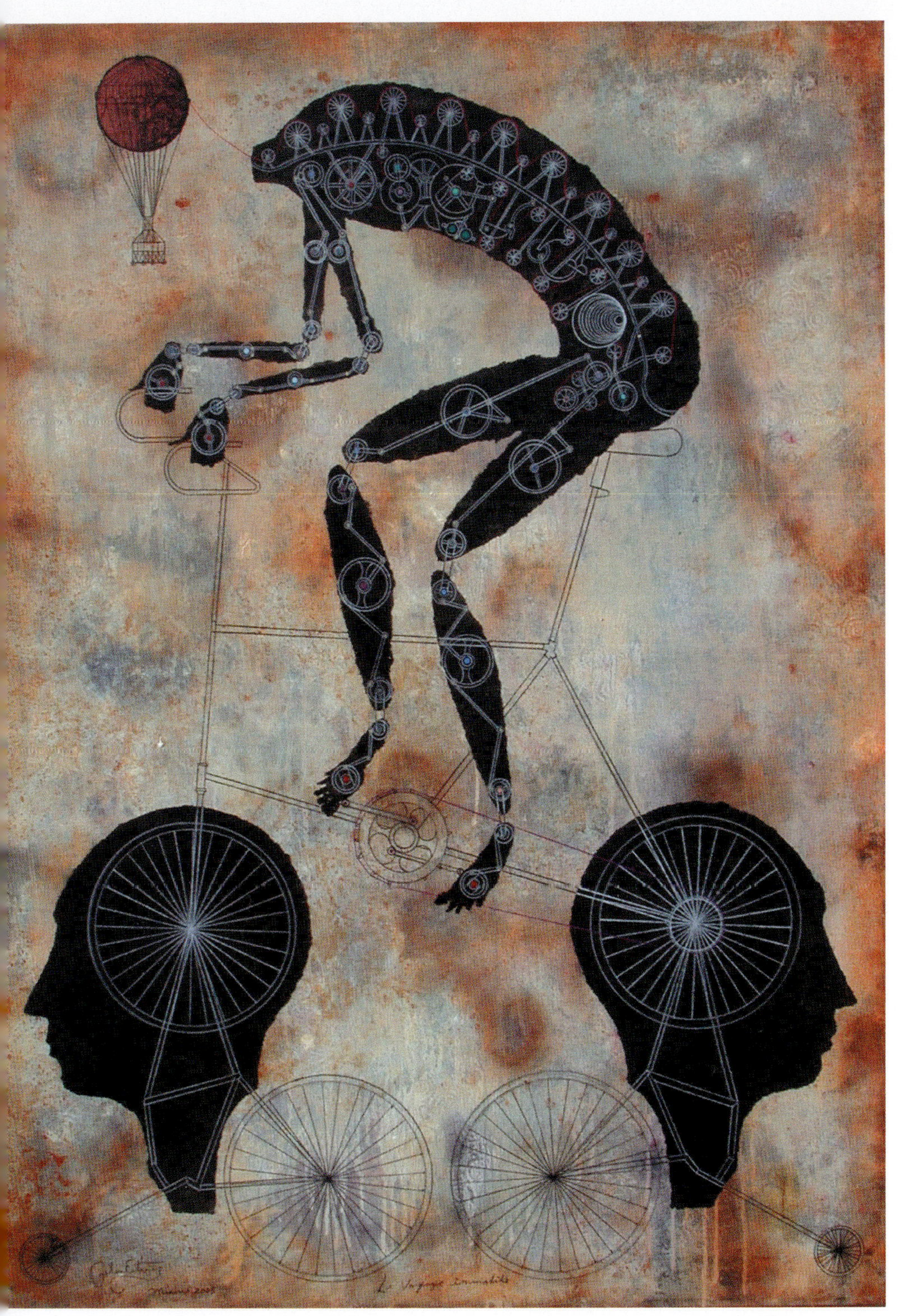

Plate VIII. *Le voyage inmobile* (Stationary Journey), 2005, 55" × 39", oil
and pencil on canvas

11

The Living Creature Is a World Order in Miniature

Anaximenes

The notion of a microcosm goes back to ancient Greece in the West. This idea has fascinated many for thousands of years, so it is not surprising that Estévez, who is frequently inspired by history and philosophy, has tried to produce a work that presents it in a visual way. He does it in *Walking Universe* (Plate IX) by presenting us with an image of a woman whose transparent body and dress reveal her true composition and nature. The woman is in fact the cosmos in miniature.

The theme of the microcosm has at least two important philosophical dimensions. One is metaphysical and concerned with the way the world and human beings are. The other is epistemic and involves the way humans know.

The idea that human beings are metaphysically a universe in miniature may seem strange at first but receives support from various sources. Some scientists have occasionally held that understanding humans in this way also is a way to account for the evolutionary process. This takes the form of a claim that the history of the human individual replicates the history of the evolutionary process that gave rise to the species. This view is frequently known under the motto "Ontogeny recapitulates phylogeny." Ontogeny is the process whereby an individual entity develops from its origin, through various stages, into the complete individual entity it is. Phylogeny is the process whereby a type of entity develops from its origin, through various stages, into the complete type of entity it is. To say that ontogeny recapitulates phylogeny is to claim that the process whereby an individual entity develops into a complete individual repeats in some sense the process whereby a type of entity develops into the complete type of entity it is. For example, it has been argued that because, biologically speaking, the human species is the product of a process consisting of various stages of development, the production of an individual human being mirrors in some way that process. Indeed, so the argument goes, if we observe the stages of development through which a human embryo passes, we can pair them with stages in the development of the human race.

As an individual, I am supposed to have gone through stages that mirror the stages through which the whole human species has come to be what it is. The process of individual genesis mirrors the process of evolutionary genesis. If human beings evolved from water creatures, then there is a point in gestation where we are water creatures, and so on with other stages of development. We are our history. Moreover, since species evolve from some common foundation, one could argue that the process, and the ultimate product that we have become, replicates the whole process of universal development and the nature of the universe. We are small versions of the macrocosm.

This view is not common among scientists, and few philosophers take it seriously today; few would argue that we are, metaphysically, microcosms. But there is another sense in which one can speak about a human being as a universe in miniature that makes more sense. This is because humans seem to have the capacity to know the universe and every dimension of it, and not only through one means but through various means. Knowledge is a kind of mirroring, a representation and recreation of the object of knowledge in the knower. The fact that we can understand the universe, that we can see it and touch things in it, that we can think about it and understand its complexities, is a kind of appropriation of it. To know something is to become it in some way. When I look at a tree, I make it my own by recreating its image in me and by thinking about what it is. The image and the thought may be imperfect, and different in some ways from what I see and think about, but they are there, within me. Indeed, a traditional theory of knowledge has maintained that knowledge consists precisely in the appropriation and recreation of the object of knowledge within ourselves.

Aristotle held a version of this view. According to him, the world is composed of two principles, matter and form. Matter is the stuff out of which things are made, the marble of a statue of Aphrodite, the bronze in the statue of Poseidon. Form is the shape, the structure that makes the marble a likeness of Aphrodite and the bronze a likeness of Poseidon. The properties of things come from form rather than matter. The statue of Aphrodite is what it is because its shape is like that of Aphrodite. The same applies to Poseidon, or even, say, to a dog. A dog is what it is because it has a certain form, because its matter is organized in a way that is different from the way the matter of a cat is organized. A dog is made to bark, but a cat's vocal cords do not allow it to bark, only to meow, because the structure is different. Something similar applies to human beings and their capacity to think. We can think because we have a brain, a chunk of matter organized as an organ composed of neurons and other cells that make thinking possible. Ultimately, if we take a human being and separate the material elements of which it is composed, we get a kind of mush. The mush itself has properties, of course, because nothing exists as just matter. Everything is matter of a certain sort, but the mush is no longer a human being and would be similar to the mush resulting from a monkey, a lion, or a shark.

Aristotle's view of knowledge is that it occurs when our minds function as the matter of the forms of the things we know. When I know a dog for what it is, my intellect abstracts the form of "dogness" from the matter it informs out there in the world and imprints it on my mind, which functions as a kind of immaterial matter. To know is to become informed by what we know, to become it in a way different from the way things we know are, but still it is to become them in the important respect that we are informed as those things are; the forms are the same. To think about a dog is like becoming a dog in the mind. This is not very different from what happens with a mirror, a reason most knowledge theory is infused with mirror metaphors. Imagining is a form of knowing in which the image of a physical thing is reproduced in the mind without the physical aspects of weight and volume.

Knowing is appropriating the world; we become what we know. But there is more to it than this, according to some philosophers. Because of this very fact, that we can know and in knowing we become what we know can be explained only if there is an affinity for being it. This brings us back to the metaphysical side of the theory of the microcosm: we have the capacity to become the universe in our minds, precisely because we are, in a sense, a world in miniature.

It is significant that Estévez's painting is of a woman rather than a man. Often Estévez represents humanity through a male, partly because he himself is a male and is searching within himself for answers, and partly because it is a commonplace in Western history to use the male to represent humanity. But in this case we have a woman. Why? Perhaps because the woman has been traditionally a symbol of nature. She is the mother of our race, in that we come to be through her womb. Conception takes place within a woman, and it is her organism that yields a human being. So if we can find out what a woman is like, we will find out something important about all of us.

The figure in the painting has two other significant aspects. The first and most graphic is that the body is transparent, allowing the spectator to look inside it. And what we see in it is a universe composed of what appear to be heavenly systems, or perhaps even atomic systems, in various stages of movement and rotation. Is Estévez thinking of the heavens, of the inner, atomic makeup of the universe, or of both? The theme of the microcosm also has been tied to the notion that the very elements of our molecular structure mirror the macro structures of the universe, so both make sense.

In the painting, these systems are arranged on a line that goes from the heart all the way to the lower abdomen of the figure and have four different centers: the heart, the stomach, the navel, and the uterus. The systems are connected through lines that suggest relations of various sorts. Nothing is isolated; everything is tied to something else. In addition, the figure displays three circles, two on the breasts and one on the brain, which could themselves be systems of some sort. The breasts are a symbol of what gives sustenance to the system; they are the source of nourishment. The brain stands for our understanding and intellect. Again, they are not isolated but connected to the other elements that make up the painting.

There is also the matter of the dress. The figure is not nude, but has two garments. One is solid and covers the torso, much like the way a one-piece swim suit does, although one can see the heavenly systems through it. The other is an outline of a rather elaborate dress, so that the body and its contents are visible through it. What could this mean? I take it to be a symbol of culture. There is nature, the microcosm that a human being is, and there is culture, what humans create and through which they often discover the understanding of themselves as small universes, as replicas of the universe at large and as capable of knowing and grasping it.

Does Estévez's painting make a metaphysical or an epistemic claim? It can be taken to make both. Human beings are in fact mirrors of reality, but in the small. And they also are capable of understanding it, in that their minds include a circle that mirrors the whole.

SOURCES

Anaximenes. *Fragments*. In *An Introduction to Early Greek Philosophy; The Chief Fragments and Ancient Testimony, with Connecting Commentary*, ed. John Mansley Robinson, ch. 3. New York: Houghton Mifflin, 1968.

Aristotle. *Metaphysics*, Bk. I, chs. 4–7. In *The Complete Works of Aristotle*, 2 vols., ed. Jonathan Barnes. Princeton, NJ: Princeton University Press, 1984.

———. *On the Soul*, Bk. III, ch. 9. In *The Complete Works of Aristotle*, 2 vols., ed. Jonathan Barnes. Princeton, NJ: Princeton University Press, 1984.

Plato. *The Republic*. Bk. VI, 509–11. In *The Collected Dialogues of Plato*, ed. Edith Hamilton and Huntington Cairns. New York: Pantheon Books, 1961.

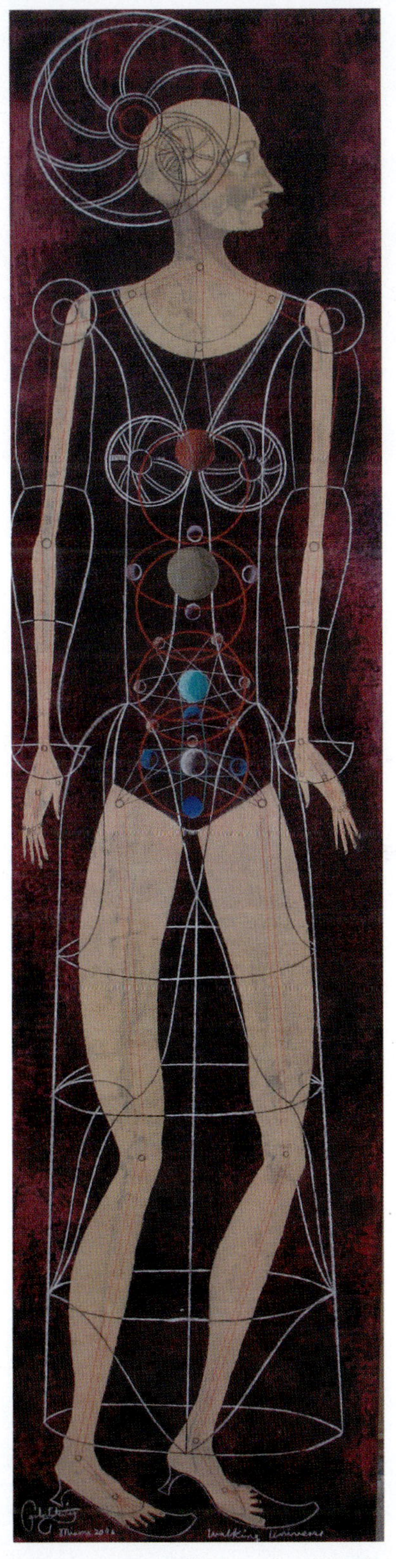

Plate IX. *Walking Universe*, 2006, 48" × 12", oil and pencil on canvas

Society

12

____

Negotiating Identities

NEH Summer Seminar, 2006

Let me introduce myself: I am Jorge Jesús Emilano Gracia. This is the way I think of myself; it is the way I sometimes introduce myself to others, although most often I leave out the two middle names; and it is the way many others think of me. I have a proper name that identifies me as the individual person I am, and not as any of you readers or some other person who is currently walking on the street, outside the house where I am writing. Or in fact any other person in the whole world, past, present, and future. I am the only Jorge Jesús Emilano Gracia there is, has been, and will be. Of course, my name could change. I could use an alias in times of war or when I am persecuted. But that would not alter who I am. And it is possible that someone else is also named Jorge Jesús Emilano Gracia. Indeed, I am sure this is so, although the Internet tells me otherwise. But that does not interfere with the point I am making, for my point is that I am who I am, and no one else is the same individual person I am. That several persons share their names is just a result of the poor imagination we have creating unique names.

But who am I, really? This is not an easy question to answer in the absence of a context. In the classroom where I teach between such and such hours, I am the professor. At home, I am the husband of my wife and the father of my daughters. To the United States and Canadian governments, I am a naturalized citizen. To the Cuban government, I am a natural-born citizen who left Cuba in 1961 and therefore am under permanent suspicion. In Buffalo, I am a resident. To the concierge of The Matrix, the building in Toronto where I spend some of my time, I am the owner of unit 808. To the United States Census bureaucracy I am Hispanic, and many of my friends think of me as Latino. And on and on. The list could be very long. So we may ask: Am I all of these things? Surely I am. The sentences that describe me as so are true.

But does this mean that all of these things I have mentioned are part of my identity? Another difficult question, perhaps even more difficult than the one I asked earlier. In some ways they are, and in some ways they are not. I do not think that anyone would believe that owning unit 808 in The Matrix is part of my identity in such a way that if I did not own it I would not be Jorge Jesús Emilano Gracia. There are so many other things that could have interfered with the purchase of this particular condo! It is all very contingent. I could have moved to "the City" instead, which I almost did in 1996. Would I have had a different identity if I had moved to New York City and did not own a condo in Toronto? I do not think most people would say yes. And most of them would invoke some sort of Aristotelian distinction between essence and accident and say something like this: There are some things that make Jorge Jesús Emilano Gracia the person he is, and there are some things that do not, and owning a condo in Toronto is not one of those that do. So we could say, using the language of identity, that having a head is part of my identity, but owning a condo in Toronto is not, even if the concierge in Toronto knows me exclusively, or primarily, as the owner of unit 808. And this is probably all he knows and wants to know about me—although most likely he also is interested in the size of the tip I give him at Christmastime.

But what is an identity? To talk about the identity of something in particular is to talk about what makes the thing to be the particular thing that it is. We can talk about the identity of anything whatever, and philosophers often do so. There is no reason we cannot talk about the identity of cats and dogs, or even of tables and chairs. But usually, in ordinary language, we reserve the term *identity* for what we think are important entities, such as individual persons.

Philosophers have raised all sorts of questions about personal and other kinds of identity. Some challenge the idea that one can account for the identity of any person at all. And some relish talk about such things as Theseus's famous ship—Does it preserve its identity after all the pieces of wood of which it was originally composed have been replaced during a long voyage?—and about brain transplants—Would a human being change identity if her or his brain were transplanted into another body? But these matters are not our concern here. The issue I want to consider in the context of Estévez's painting has to do with how I negotiate my identities, how I juggle them, because his work is about a juggler.

On a black background, Estévez's *The Juggler* (Plate X) presents us with a central male figure, in white and grey lines, who is juggling eight other human figures similar to himself, who in turn are juggling eight figures each. The main juggler is actively engaged in the act of juggling: his arms in position, his legs well anchored for equilibrium, and his head tilted slightly back, following the course of the figures he is juggling. The figures he juggles are not found in the same position, their arms and legs making different moves; and the same is true of the figures they in turn are juggling. And there are points of connection, the most important of which is the center of the chest, where all the figures have a red dot. The areas of the brain, the hand, the feet, and the penis, display green dots. Four lines cross the drawing, going up from the hands and feet, and disappearing at the edge of the work.

Unlike some of the other works by Estévez included in this book, this one does not have a title that suggests a philosophical theme. *The Juggler* could represent a number of things that apply to human existence in general, not just to philosophy. After all, how many things do we juggle in our everyday lives? Ideas, commitments, interests, schedules, jobs, and relationships, to name just a few. One thing stands out about the work, however, that leads me to use it to illustrate a particular juggling act in which all of us are involved: the fact that the things being juggled by the juggler are replicas of himself, except for their size. This indicates that in some sense we juggle ourselves. But how is this possible? Am I more than one person? And what does all of this have to do with philosophy?

I began by introducing myself as Jorge Jesús Emilano Gracia but went on to talk about many other things that also I am. I have other identities, including the fact that I am Hispanic, Latino, Latin American, Cuban American, Cuban, Canadian, American, a professor, a husband, a philosopher, a father, and a grandfather. All of these are important to me. Some of these identities are ethnic, such as Latino, Hispanic, and Cuban American. Others are national identities. I am a Cuban national because I was born in Cuba, and I am both Canadian and American because I became nationalized in both countries. And still others tie me to other people, such as being a member of the Gracia family, a philosopher by profession, the father of my children, or grandfather of my grandchildren. These identities involve roles that I play, ways in which I present myself and act, and sources of feelings. These identities function in different ways and move my life in different directions, sometimes in opposition, sometimes in harmony, and sometimes by complementing each other.

The central figure in Estévez's painting suggests my central identity, my individual self. But the others, although less prominent and somewhat peripheral, also play important roles regarding who I am. They all make me act in certain ways and influence each other and contribute to my overall balance. Every identity also is a juggler, trying to accommodate and deal with all of the others that apply to me. The jugglers I have in the air would fall if I did not respond. My identities respond to each other in that they call for attention and give rise to actions that are interrelated and required for balance.

But how is this juggling act possible at all in real life? One feature of the painting is particularly helpful in this regard. It is standard to think of my various identities in essentialistic terms. The standard view is that either identities consist of essences, or I do not have them at all. The choice is between what philosophers call essentialist or eliminativist conceptions.

Essentialism is the view according to which things have essences, and essences consist of sets of properties that characterize the things that have those essences. Thomas Aquinas was an essentialist with respect to human nature, because according to him human beings share a set of properties specified in a definition that expresses their essence: humans are rational animals. If one is an essentialist with respect to Hispanic identity or Mexican identity, then one holds that there is a set of properties that characterizes anyone who is Hispanic or Mexican. For me to be Hispanic means that I must share something with all other Hispanics, and this is different from anything shared by members of other groups.

At the opposite end of the spectrum is *eliminativism*, the view that there are no essences. Jean-Paul Sartre was an eliminativist with respect to human essence. His position is known as existentialism rather than eliminativism, because he argued that humans exist (whence the term *existentialism*), but what they are (their essence) is the result of their free choice. I prefer to call it eliminativism in this context rather than existentialism because of its negative claim about essence and the common use of this term in contemporary philosophy. According to Sartre, we are free to be whatever we want to be, and there is no set of properties that we necessarily share. When this view is applied to our question, the answer is that there is no such a thing as a Hispanic or even a Mexican identity, for there is no essence to Hispanics or Mexicans. There are only individual identities forged by individual humans. I am Jorge Jesús Emilano Gracia, and nothing more.

Neither of these positions makes sense—eliminativism, because our identities are very real to us and function as sources of actions and feelings, and in essentialism, because our identities do not involve sets of unchanging properties that rigidly distinguish us from each other. I am certainly Hispanic, Latino, Cuban, and American, but I share no nontrivial set of properties with all other Hispanics, Latinos, Cubans, or Americans.

In Estévez's painting, the figures are not different except in dimensions and gestures, which suggests that the person is the same and whatever identity is being juggled is not something different from himself, whence the juggling, the adaptation and negotiation, and the moving to accommodate a variety of realities to seek balance. My Cuban self has to negotiate my Canadian self, and the father in me has to juggle the husband and grandfather.

Identities need to be conceived in flexible terms, as groups of properties that tie people in different ways as families are tied. The members of families do not all have the same properties, or even some properties throughout the history of the families. Indeed, not all members of a family are related by descent. The very basis of the family, marriage, is a union between two people who are not tied through descent. But all members of a family share a family resemblance in the sense Wittgenstein used, that is, in the sense that every member shares at least some property with some other member of the family. A family resemblance cannot be cashed out in terms of the same properties. Particular members of families resemble other members in various ways, including nonphysical characteristics and customs. But not all members of families resemble all other members in the same ways. And this resemblance, in an appropriate context, is sufficient to establish and identify membership.

Likewise with our identities. To be Latino does not mean that I have a set of properties that I share with all Latinos. It only means that I am tied to the group as a member of a family is to the family. These ties are historical and contextual and change with time. Identities are flexible and changing. This makes it possible for the same person to have multiple identities and to relate them in various ways—the juggling act will depend on the juggler, the identities juggled, and the context. I can be Latino, Hispanic, Cuban, American, Canadian, a philosopher, a husband, a father, and a Gracia, but I need to be able to juggle these various dimensions of who I am, as Estévez's *malabarista* seems to do so effectively.

SOURCES

Gracia, Jorge J. F. *Latinos in America: Philosophy and Social Identity*, ch 1. Oxford: Blackwell, 2008.

———. *Hispanic/Latino Identity: A Philosophical Perspective*, chs. 3 and 5. Oxford: Blackwell, 2000.

———, et al., eds. *Identity, Memory, and Diaspora: Voices of Cuban-American Artists, Writers, and Philosophers*. Albany: State University of New York Press, 2007.

Sartre, Jean-Paul. *Being and Nothingness*, IV, ch. 1. New York: Routledge, 2003.

Thomas Aquinas. *On Being and Essence*, ch. 1. Edited by Thomas Gilby. Garden City, NY: Image Books, 1969-.

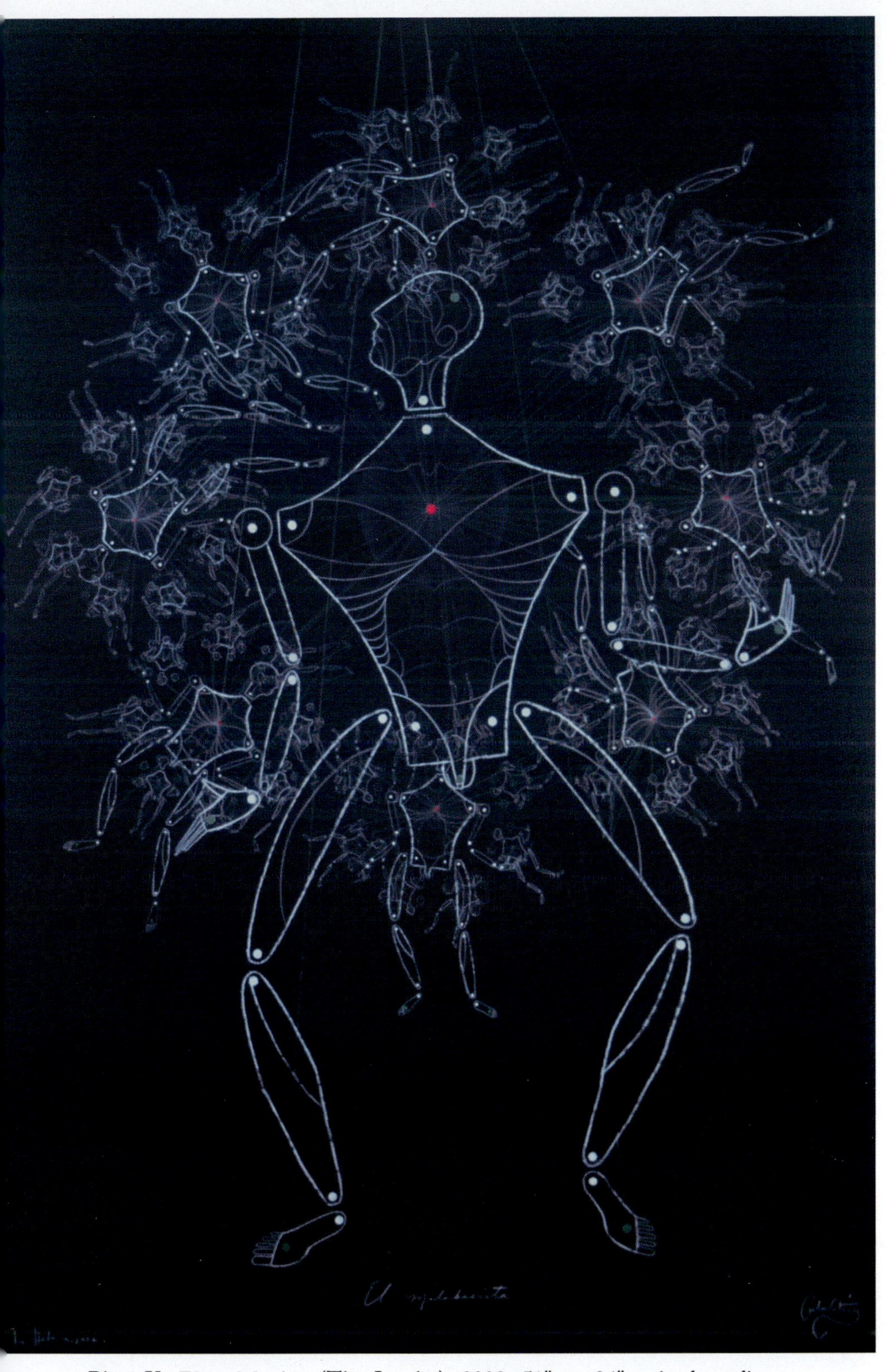

Plate X. *El malabarista* (The Juggler), 2002, 51" × 36", mixed media on watercolor paper

13

____

What Then Is a Race?

W. E. B. Du Bois

On a washed background, greenish-brown in tone, are located what appear to be two moths facing each other, on a vertical arrangement. The top figure in *Difficult Loves* (Plate XI) is elaborately decorated. The wings are symmetrical, with circles, waves, bands, and suggested and explicit patterns in colors that blend, while contrasting with a richly defused context. The body also is decorated, with a head that displays strong, round eyes and a body where faded red-and-blue lines suggest the interior structure of the animal. Three pairs of legs and a pair of antennae issue from the body.

Facing this moth, and different from it in many ways, stands the other. Its color appears at first to be white, with some shades of darker colors, but upon closer inspection these traces seem to be the result of translucent wings. Unlike the top moth, this figure is not anatomically credible. It is composed of four white parts that appear quite substantial and include the wings, something like a head, and a tail. The complicated body, which is a mere outline, looks more like a skeleton, or perhaps the structure of a kite or the fuselage of a plane. There are no eyes, and the wings are in a full, open position. It does not have legs, but it does display antennae. In fact, this entity was inspired by a model of an airplane created by Otto Lilinthal.

One of the most disputed issues in contemporary philosophy is the reality of race, and *Difficult Loves* can be used to think about it. The discussion of race goes back to the eighteenth century, when philosophers such as Immanuel Kant and David Hume first talked about the nature of race. From these first discussions and subsequent scientific investigations came what is generally called the biological view of race. According to it, racial groups are the result of physical features that are genetically determined and transmitted through heredity. Different groups of human beings not only appear different through features such as skin color and bodily shapes but also have different mental capacities, all arising from genetic biological factors.

The biological view of race was first challenged by sociologists and philosophers who pointed out the difficulties in demonstrating that there is a biological basis to the features regarded as racially determining. W. E. B. Du Bois was among the pioneers in formulating this challenge, which continued throughout the twentieth century and to this day. Recent scientific discoveries have revealed serious obstacles in any biological theory of race. The challenges to race in general have come from many sides, but two in particular have had the greatest impact. One is factual, the other epistemic.

The factual argument points out that the notion of race does not correspond to anything real outside the mind and therefore needs to be abandoned. Among the facts frequently cited in its support are the following: first, the genetic differences between races, say "blacks" and "whites," are minuscule if compared to what they have in common. Indeed, the bases for racial distinctions are negligible and flimsy, for there can be greater genetic differences between two individual human beings, presumably belonging to the same race, than between what are usually considered two races. Second, science has shown that either single genes or the various forms they can take (known as alleles) are present in all populations. This means that no single gene or allele is sufficient for dividing humans into systematic categories, let alone racial ones. Third, there is no strict correlation between the directly observable traits of a person, known as *phenotypes*, such as skin color and hair texture, and genetic specifications inherited from parents, known as *genotypes*. The reason is that some phenotypes are the result of very complex genetic relationships and also involve environmental factors. And fourth, particular phenotypes can be the result of different gene combinations and do not adhere to stable racial boundaries. Again, this is in part due to environmental factors, for phenotypes are produced by the interaction between a genetic program and the environment.

The epistemic argument against race points out that we have no effective means of determining membership in racial groups. It is usually thought that racial membership can be easily ascertained, but the facts seem to reveal otherwise, for the criteria used to determine it vary from individual to individual, group to group, context to context, place to place, country to country, and time to time. Consider, for example, that in Cuba, being "black" (i.e., *negro*) entails that one appear as if one has no mixture with the "white" (i.e., *blanco*) race, and a person who looks to be mixed is not *negro* but *mulato*, that is, a mixture of *negro* and *blanco*. But in the United States, the situation is quite different. To be "black" requires only that one have some "black" blood, that is, that one have a "black" ancestor going back a certain number of generations. This is known as the One-Drop Rule: one drop of "black" blood is sufficient to make a person "black." In Cuba, persons of mixed "black" and "white" ancestry are supposed to be mulattoes, as long as they appear to be mixed, and therefore neither "black" nor "white." If they do not appear to be mixed, then they are considered "white" or "black," depending on where the appearance lies. So the question is, who is right? Epistemically, we have a serious conflict, for what is known as a "black" in Cuba is also a "black" in the United States, but what is known as a "black" in the United States is sometimes considered a mulatto, and even in some cases a "white," in Cuba. Differing epistemic racial criteria preclude agreement as to who qualifies as a member of a race.

The epistemic difficulties posed by the instability of racial criteria are not restricted to the variability of the criteria. There is also the problem of the accessibility of the evidence used to satisfy the criteria. In Cuba, a mulatto is supposed to be a mixture of "black" and "white," but we may ask, how is one supposed to tell that someone is mixed? Through a blood test, DNA analysis, or some such procedure? Of course not! The category *mulato* was developed before any of these tests were available and still today is used without reference to them. The judgment that someone is *mulato* is made in terms of visual inspection, as is also done with "blacks" or "whites." Because of this, a *negro* in Cuba can never be considered "white," insofar as he or she cannot change the color of his or her skin, his or her features, and the texture of his or her hair. To be considered "white" would require drastic changes that are, at least currently, impossible. On the other hand, "black" and "white" racially mixed persons can be considered "white" if they do not have the physically perceptual features associated with "blacks." "White" nose, lips, hair, and skin color may be sufficient to have someone qualify as "white," even if he or she has a "black" grandmother. This is why a popular saying in Cuba asks: Where is your grandmother? It is assumed that many, and perhaps even most, "whites" have in fact a racially mixed ancestry.

The epistemic situation with "blacks" in the United States is similar to that of *mulatos* in Cuba, for one drop of "black" blood surely does very little to make a person qualify as "black." Just as in Cuba many racially mixed persons eventually join the "white" population, in the United States many "blacks" do so as well. For how can we possibly tell if a person had a "black" ancestor twenty generations removed unless we provide a DNA analysis or reconstruct the genealogy? But the DNA analysis is never done, and the establishment of a genealogy is seldom attempted, so the knowledge we have of someone's race in the United States is not determined by DNA analysis but rather by simple inspection, and this is deceptive and imprecise when it comes to the application of the One-Drop Rule. Indeed, even if these tests were carried out, their significance has been undermined in science.

Here again we have serious epistemic questions that remain unresolved. We act as if we could be certain who is, and who is not, "black" in the United States, but we cannot be sure of this knowledge on the bases that are regularly used to do so. Clearly—so this argument goes—the criteria of races we use are ineffective, even when they are not in conflict. In some cases, we use color; in others, it is lineage; and still in others, it is culture. "Indian" is a racial term associated with physical appearance in the United States, but in many places in Bolivia and Peru, it refers to culture. To be an Indian in those places is not to have adopted the ways of the European.

Is race real, then? Estévez's work suggests several points that can be useful in the understanding of the issues involved in this question. The most obvious difference between the two moths depicted in the painting is their color, although there also are important differences in shape and composition. All of these are easily observable features. If we take the two moths as examples of two individuals belonging to two races, then it is clear that the differences are phenotypical, and that color, more than anything else, followed by shape, is a determining factor. One of the moths appears to be white, and the other has color. One of the moths appears to be anatomically correct, but the other is not. Yet when we look more carefully at the painting, we see that the colors that appeared originally as solid and "pure" are anything but that, and that one of the moths is an artifact rather than a natural organism.

In the colored moth it is obvious from the beginning that there is a mixture of colors, but this is so even in the supposedly white moth, although the mixture is not obvious at first. Upon inspection, we can see that its whiteness is not pure, that it contains shades of other colors, though these are subtle. This is applicable to race. The whiteness of the white race, just as the whiteness of the white moth, is not really white, nor is it pure. Phenotypical colors, whether they appear pure or not, turn out in fact to be mixtures and impure. What appears to be one color initially upon closer inspection turns out to be more than one. Are white people truly white? Are black people truly black? Are we not all colored, even if the ranges and intensity of colors vary? How can we, then, draw hard-and-fast lines between color phenotypes and people who are supposed to have them?

And what if the supposedly white moth is actually translucent? Does this mean, as many believe, that to be white is not to have color or to be colored? Clearly, whether we take the apparently white moth to be white or to be colorless, it can represent certain widespread attitudes about the so-called white race.

But this is not all. Something else comes to the fore, namely, the implication that pure races are creations. Estévez's painting illustrates this for us with the white moth, for this bug is more like a kite than an organism. It is an artifact, created by us, perhaps even by the other moth, which leads to the question, is the colored moth imagining it? Races, just like the white moth, are artifacts of human making. At bottom, a moth is a moth. Whether white or colored, we are fundamentally the same. We are colored human beings, and the differences between races are artificial creations of society.

An additional suggestion of the painting is the attraction between the moths—the title is *Difficult Loves*. Although the white moth seems to be barring the colored one from approaching it, it is facing it, which could suggest an attraction to which perhaps it does not want to give in, whereas the colored moth, with fully open eyes, seems to want the white moth. Is this a love for the other, for what is believed to be different? Is it a love for a state that is different from the one in which we find ourselves, or is it a love for another because we are at bottom the same, or a yearning for what we consider a perfection and purity that we know we do not have? Opposition and attraction are evident in the moths, just as they are among members of different races. These are certainly difficult loves.

SOURCES

Cavalli-Sforza, Luka L., et al. *The History and Geography of Human Genes*, ix. Princeton, NJ: Princeton University Press, 1994.

Du Bois, W. E. B. *The Conservation of Races. American Negro Academy Occasional Papers, no. 2*. Washington, DC: American Negro Academy, 1897.

Gracia, Jorge J. E. *Surviving Race, Ethnicity, and Nationality: A Challenge for the Twenty-First Century*, ch. 4. Lanham, MD: Rowman & Littlefield, 2005.

van den Berghe, Pierre L. "Does Race Matter?" In *Race and Racism*, ed. Bernard Boxill. Oxford: Oxford University Press, 2001.

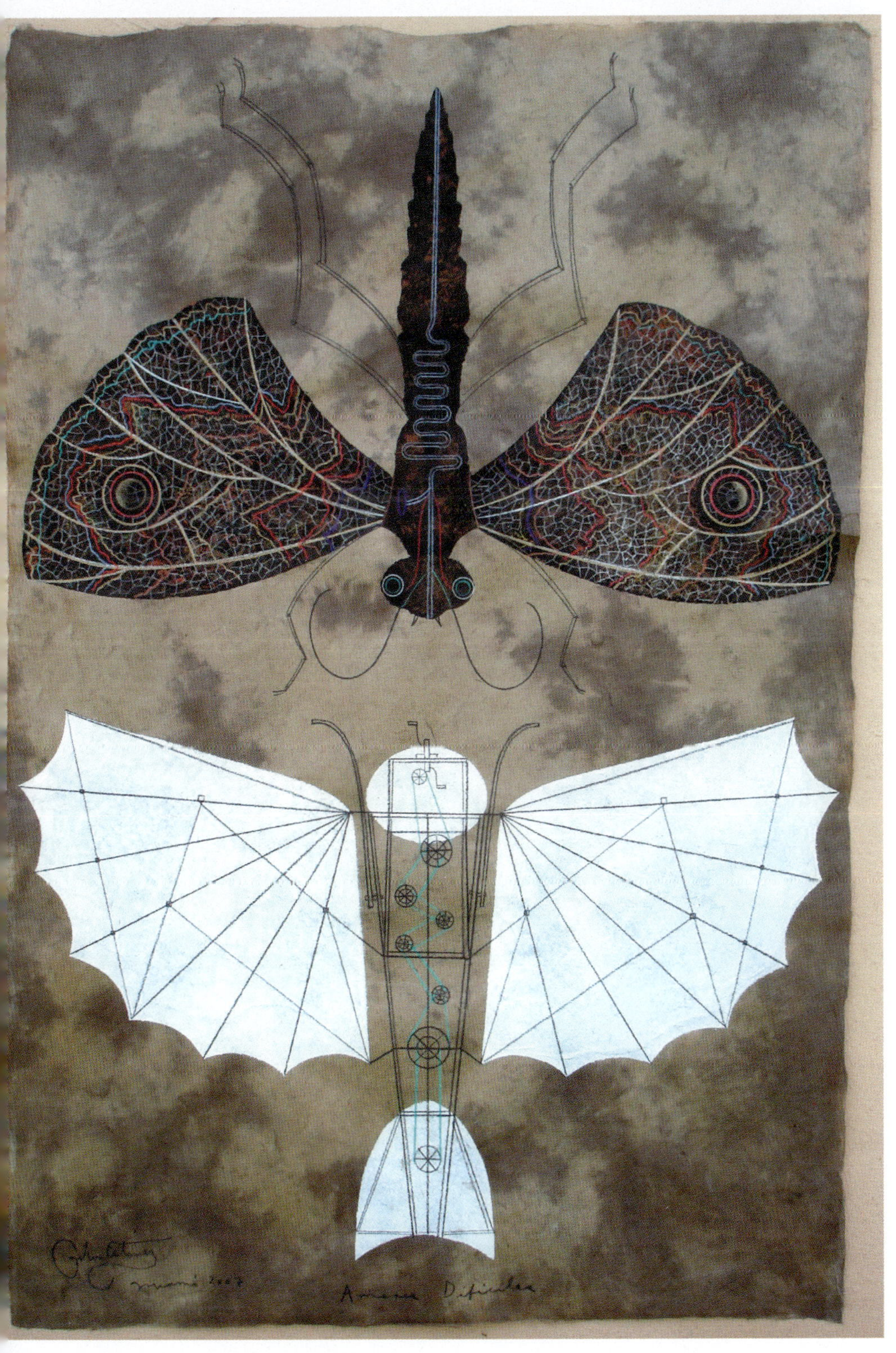

Plate XI. *Amores difíciles* (Difficult Loves), 2007, 30" × 20", pencil and gouache on Nepal paper

14

Imagined Communities

Benedict Anderson

Social groups are ubiquitous in our experience. We begin with the family but quickly move to others such as the extended family, friends, religious communities, members of a club, and colleagues in the workplace, among others. All of these have been the subject of philosophical speculation, sometimes intense. The discussion of nations and nationality began in earnest with the rise of modern nations in the sixteenth century. Most early modern philosophers of note had much to say about this, and the discussion has not abated. Race became a subject of intense interest in the nineteenth century as a result of developments in natural science, the classification of species, and the exposure of Europeans to different groups of people through their explorations of the world.

One of the most often discussed issues concerning social groups of whatever kind has to do with their origin. Members of some religious groups hold that their particular groups are the result of divine intervention. Most ancient myths, from Mesopotamia to the Americas, contain stories about how gods originated various peoples. Ancient Hebrews believed that they had been chosen as a people by God himself, and many Christian denominations have inherited this view, which is in some cases supported by doctrines such as predestination and providence, both of which are discussed in this book. The first doctrine holds that God himself, in the second person of the Trinity, namely, Christ, founded the Christian Church, and that the members of the Church have been elected by God from all eternity for salvation, which is the second doctrine mentioned. In contrast, most sociologists hold that churches and other religious communities are not the result of divine intervention but rather of diverse social factors, including particular needs that bring people together, as well as conquests and the desire for security, commerce, and hegemony.

Many social groups, not just religious ones, have been thought to be the product of divine intervention. Race, for example, according to some

Christian groups, is believed to be also part of divine creation. This is a reason some of these groups have argued for the segregation of different races. In the case of race, most of the discussion among philosophers and scientists has not been related to a divinity but to whether race is a natural phenomenon, that is, the product of biology, or of social engineering, and the debate still rages, although most scientists today reject the idea of race as a biological fact. The issue was taken up in the previous chapter.

For Estévez, the matter of social belonging is particularly critical. As a Cuban he has been closely acquainted with social racial classifications from birth, for Cuba is a racially diverse society. And as an immigrant to the United States, residing in Miami, he has been exposed to a medium where ethnic divisions thrive. It is not farfetched, then, to think of *Forging People* (Plate XII) as being concerned with the topic of how people come about, the matter of their origin. The question, however, does not concern how individual persons originate but how groups of people do, for there does not seem to be any reference to individuals in the work. So we may ask, does the painting fit into the contemporary philosophical controversy concerning the development of social reality?

The piece consists of a very stylized black head painted on an indefinite background that suggests the sky, or perhaps a medium indicating a separation of the head from anything resembling the world. This points to a meditative state, but the head has its eyes wide open, fixed on some indefinite point, while showing great concentration. The multicoloring is perhaps intended to signal this effort. Two circles are displayed on the forehead: a smaller one is right above the nose, and the other higher up. Both include balloons, the lower one with what appears to be a kind of square gondola, the upper one with a sort of machine hanging from it. They are tied to two springs in two parts of the area of the head associated with the brain. The balloons float in the middle of the circles, but the circles are connected to lines that are themselves connected to other parts of the head, in some cases to what look like wound-up motion movements, but also to the eyes. These lines also connect to what seem to be transmitters leading to the head's surface, from which sprout red tree trunks with branches. From the end of the branches hang the heads of people in various positions, with different shapes, and some in apparent interaction. The numbers of heads and branches in the trees differ. Some trees come from transmitters in the ears, and others are connected to transmitters connected to the mouth, but all transmitters are connected to each other.

Now let us go back to philosophy. Three different philosophical views have been devised to account for the origin of social groups, although not all of them are always applied to the same kinds of groups. One claims that groups are the result of divine creation. Whether we are talking about races, nations, churches, or even families, a divinity is ultimately responsible for the social groups into which humanity is divided. This does not mean that these groups are created by fiat and independently of humans and what they think. Divinities work through the world. So, for example, a religious group might hold that in the case of races, God devised a certain genetic difference between certain peoples, and some others might think that God's choice of people and the revelation he gave to them is responsible for creating nations. This is a commonplace in creation myths and is found, for example, in the Jewish, Christian, and Native American traditions, to mention just three of particular interest to Americans.

A second view of the origin of social groups is that they are based on biological factors. There used to be a time in which human races were generally thought to be the result of biological makeup. Negroids were taken to differ from Caucasians in their physical nature, which included such things as dimensions, blood characteristics, and head structure. Sometimes these characteristics were extended to the brain. Ethnic groups also have sometimes been conceived biologically. Some anthropologists argue that humans are hardwired to develop into groups, because humans are genetically structured to recognize people similar to themselves and to feel safer with them.

Finally, there are those who think that social groups are merely the result of our own imaginative making. There is no biology that determines that we are black or white, or that we are Latinos or Anglos, or that we are members of this or that nation. We are so because we have developed an idea of who we are, we have created an image of it, which is no more than a projection of our own wishes and lucubrations. This idea is then used to bring about changes in society. This view makes considerable sense when one thinks about, say, the American people. How did this nation come about? Surely as a result of the imagination of the Founding Fathers, who created an idea that ever since has been used to understand and think about the people we know as Americans.

Which of these views does *Forging People* illustrate for us? At first it would seem that it is the last one. The head seems divorced from the world, unaffected by the happenings in it, suggesting that whatever the head is thinking is a matter of its own speculations, something that is happening within, a mere imagining. Could the balloons located in the places for the brain signify the flights of the imagination, their taking off on their own? If so, the trees sprouting out of the head—family or group trees—would be the result of those flights of the imagination, and the people gathered into groups would be tied to those branches by the mind. We could think of this head as our mental world, the world of consciousness, which is free and open to connections and interconnections, to devising new paths, independent of anything that might have to do with the way the world really is.

But there is also another factor that needs to be considered. The head is individual, it is one and this head, although it is not particularized. It could be the head of a woman or a man, of an old person or a young one, and it has no features of the sort that distinguish individuals. There is no hair, no realistic proportions. It is an idea of a head. So perhaps it is not intended to stand for an individual, but for humankind, all humans, each and every one of us. This means that it is not a particular person, you or I, that creates human groups, although a particular person may contribute much to it, and in some cases she might have the upper hand in doing so. No, it is groups of people and the intersections of their views that do it. Humanity divides itself not according to what you or I think but according to what groups of us think. This is suggested in the painting by the interaction between members of the family trees—some heads interact with each other, giving rise to further changes and ties.

But let us probe further and ask whether the head could not symbolize the divinity. Well, why not? It is presented in the heavens, in an indefinite medium, and it is stylized, something that could be intended not to represent humanity but a model of humanity. And there is no body. Perhaps the head could be taken to be the divine mind, which, because it is immaterial, cannot be shown, and needs the cloak of a generic human form to reveal itself to us. And of course, if what we have in the painting is the divine mind, then this brings back the religious view of the origin of social groups. But I do not think so.

The color of the head provides for us a point that is helpful here: the head is black. Why? I surmise that because the origin of our species is Africa, we are black in our origins. It is only later that we break into a rainbow. So it is not the divinity that has divided us but ourselves, through our actions within our circumstances.

Is there something else? Yes, indeed, at least two things. Perhaps the head should not be taken to indicate that social groups are merely imagined after all. Consider that the eyes are open. One would think that if the head is supposed to be completely insulated from perception and the world outside it, it would have its eyes closed. But no, the eyes are open and intent on observing, piercing what is in front of them. And what is that but the audience of the painting? Now for the balloons: they could suggest that the head is compiling knowledge of the world based on observation, not just on a flight of the imagination, while bringing back the possibility that the third theory might still be at play—social groups could be the result of natural factors as well.

And there is another thing: the trees of people come out of different parts of the head, some seeming to be primarily connected to a certain sense, whereas others are primarily connected to the area of the head associated with thinking. Is the suggestion here that the forging of some groups of people is more influenced by thinking, whereas others are more influenced by sight? Does it not make sense that in some cases our perceptual apparatus is more important than in others? For example, vision appears to play a decisive role in racial classifications, but nationality may have less to do with that and more to do with a certain conceptual agenda.

This leads me to the philosophical significance of this painting. It is not that it presents us with a definite and an exclusivist view of the origin of social groups, it is that it presents us with several possibilities that can be used to match some current theories about this matter, without picking one to the exclusion of the others. The painting serves to pose the issues at stake and to explore them in a visual context in a way that a text will not allow. Indeed, in some ways it suggests avenues that are not frequently traveled by philosophers.

SOURCES

Alcoff, Linda. "Introduction." In *Visible Identities*. Oxford: Oxford University Press, 2006.

Anderson, Benedict. *Imagined Communities: Reflections on the Origins and Spread of Nationalism*, ch. 3. London: Verso Editions, 1990.

Corlett, J. Angelo. *Race, Racism, and Reparations*, chs. 1–3. Ithaca, NY: Cornell University Press, 2003.

Gracia, Jorge J. E. *Surviving Race, Ethnicity, and Nationality: A Challenge for the Twenty-First Century*, chs. 3–5. Lanham, MD: Rowman & Littlefield, 2005.

Weber, Max. "What Is an Ethnic Group?" In *The Ethnicity Reader: Nationalism, Multiculturalism, and Migration*, ed. M. Guibernau and J. Rex. Cambridge: Polity Press. 1997.

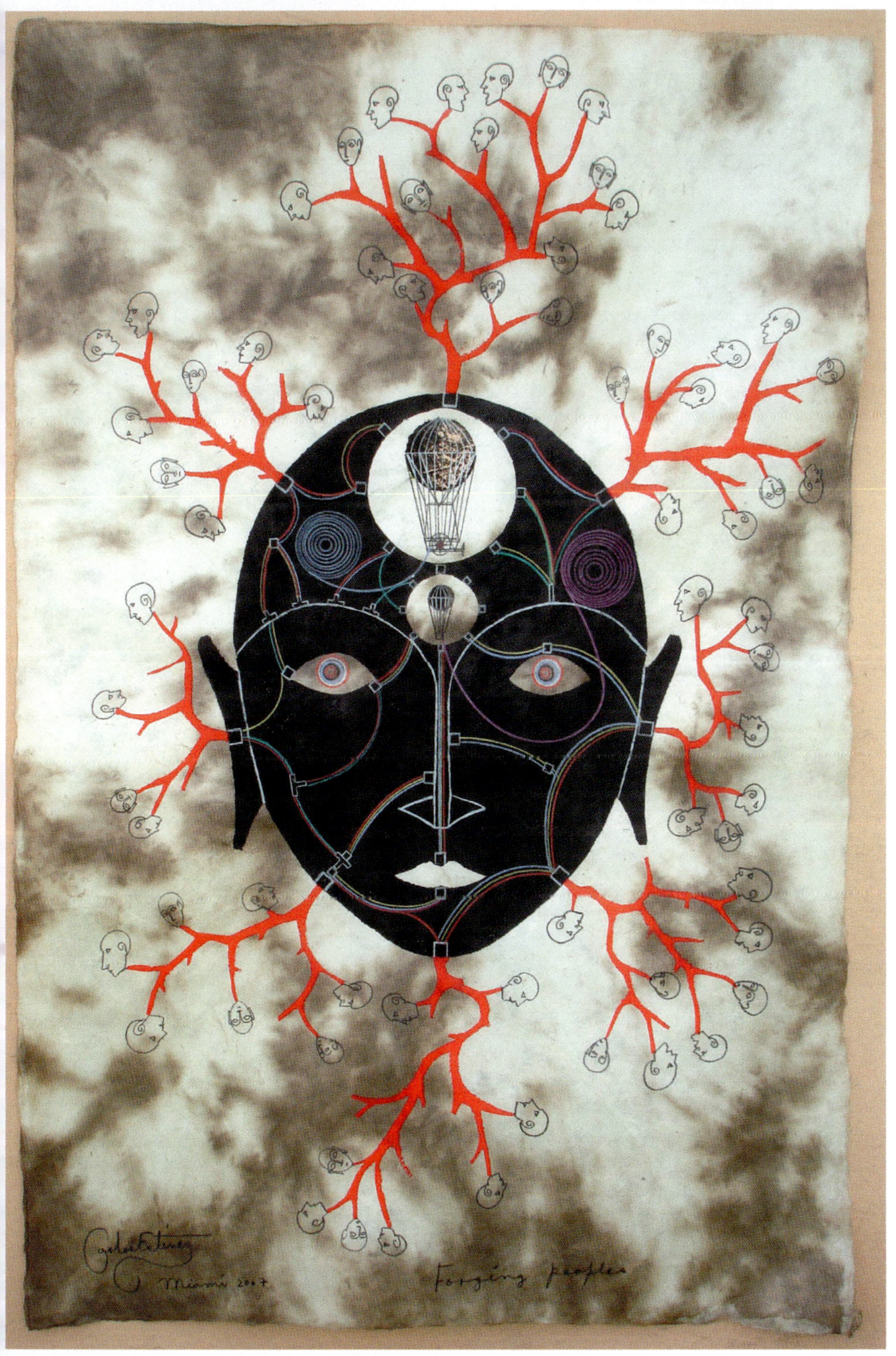

Plate XII. *Forging People,* 2007, 30" × 20", pencil and gouache on Nepal
paper

15

I-Thou

Martin Buber

Martin Buber's famous expression, "I-Thou," and the title of Estévez's painting, *Distances between Our Neighborhoods* (Plate XIII), suggest two interesting philosophical lines of speculation: identity and communication. In the case of Buber, the identity in question is between the self and the other; in the case of Estévez, it is the identity of the groups to which we belong. Because I discuss the topic of individual and social identities in other essays in this book, I turn here instead to communication.

Communication presents us with one of the most puzzling problems we encounter. It may be formulated in a general question: How is it possible? Or, we could put it more concretely by asking: How do I know what you think, and how do you know what I think? We use language to communicate with each other. I know that you think having a high-cholesterol diet is bad because you have told me so. The problem is to explain how I know this from the sounds you utter when you tell me, for the utterances themselves do not appear to have any obvious or natural connection to the thoughts they are used to convey. How can I know, then, that they convey those thoughts and not others? The same applies to you and your knowledge of what I think.

One formulation of this puzzle is known as the Hermeneutic Circle. This conundrum suggests that we are trapped in, and cannot escape, language, thus we can never get at the thoughts that the use of language is supposed to convey. The meaning of language can be conveyed only through language. To explain what I mean by a linguistic term, I must use other linguistic terms. And to explain what I mean by these other linguistic terms, I must in turn use some other terms, and so on, *ad infinitum*, or back to the original *explanandum*. To convey what I mean by "cat," I need to use some other expression, such as "feline mammal that meows." But this itself, as a piece of language, requires an explanation, which again must be linguistic, and so on. In short, we are linguistically trapped and can never get to meanings or to thoughts.

This difficulty was identified by Augustine in *On the Teacher*, where he put it, with his characteristic simplicity and clarity, as follows: "If I am given a sign and I do not know the thing of which it is the sign, it can teach me nothing. If I know the thing, what do I learn from the sign?" Signs by themselves do not have the power to communicate, for either I know what they mean, and then their use tells me nothing that I did not already know, or I do not know what they mean, and then they do not communicate anything at all to me. Language by itself is helpless; it has no power to do what we need it to do. So how do we communicate?

This kind of puzzle can be raised in the context of Estévez's work. The figures in the painting are male and female, so one would think that the painting can be interpreted only as posing the problem of communication between the sexes. But the matter need not be restricted to masculine and feminine difficulties in communication. The title of the work suggests something more. The use of "neighborhoods" in it can be a metaphor for each of us, or for the masculine neighborhood as opposed to the feminine one, but it also can be taken as an indication of the problem of communication posed between any two human beings, regardless of the sex or gender, and between any two groups of people, whether ethnic, national, or racial, to name just the ones that have elicited more discussion in recent years.

The two figures in the picture—puppets, as is frequent for Estévez—are drawn on a black background. Clearly they are male and female, not only because of the genitalia but also because Estévez has given each a certain look associated with the sexes. The male figure has a wider chest and is less rounded in form than the female figure. Both are standing, with their hands and feet hooked to lines that disappear at the top of the painting. They are looking at each other and appear to be trying to reach for each other's hands, but the hands are not touching. The connection between the two figures occurs at seven levels, but not directly through their bodies. All but one of these levels consist in bridges of various sorts, in which we see vehicles, again of various sorts, crossing them: automobiles, trucks, and trains.

The bridges metaphorically overcome the gap between individuals, the sexes, and different groups of people by carrying vehicles from one place to the other. The question is what these bridges symbolize, what they support, and whether this constitutes effective communication. So let us look again at philosophy and see what the philosophers have come up with.

The philosophical response to the Hermeneutic Circle has often been to argue that there are nonlinguistic ways to explain communication. The vehicles of Estévez's painting, if this view is right, would have to be not linguistic, and they would not entail a need to communicate through language.

This point seems to be made in the work, as we shall see immediately. But let me first note that the most often nonlinguistic means of communication proposed by philosophers have been intuition and ostension. I know what you mean when you tell me something, because either the meaning is intuitively revealed to me in a kind of epiphany, or it is made plain by your pointing it to me.

Neither of these, however, can defeat the Hermeneutic Circle. An intuition is something too private to be able to do this; it is for me alone and cannot explain how communication happens between two or more persons. Besides, the claim that intuition serves to communicate is contrary to our common experience, for we do not always agree on meanings, and this implies that only some of us are privileged to intuit whatever the proper or real ones are. This entails that intuition cannot serve to establish what each of us means when we speak. Intuition does not take us beyond the realm of privacy, and hence it cannot help us solve the hermeneutic conundrum.

Ostension is not more helpful, for it suffers from many well-known problems, three of which are particularly serious: imprecision, indeterminacy, and circularity. When I want to communicate the meaning of "cat" ostensibly to someone who does not know what the term means, I proceed by pointing to a cat. But this is not very helpful, for the person in question cannot tell whether I am pointing to the whole cat, a part of the cat, a property of the cat, or something in the neighborhood of the cat, to mention just a few of the most obvious possibilities involved. Clearly, pointing is a very imprecise procedure.

But let us assume that none of this constitutes an insurmountable problem, and that I have succeeded in getting the person for the benefit of whom I am pointing to see that I am pointing to the cat as a whole. Still, this is not enough, for the person cannot tell how it is in particular that I want her to think about the cat. Do I have in mind a substance, a series of states, a bundle of properties, or an event? This is a problem, because if one cannot determine how one is thinking of something, then it might not be clear that one is actually thinking about it. Ostension is not sufficiently determinate.

Finally, pointing itself is a sign, and this entails that it has a meaning on which we must agree for it to be effective in communication. But if this is true, then what was said about linguistic terms applies to it, and in using it I have only succeeded, in the best of cases, in substituting one term, "cat," for another, the act of pointing. So the Hermeneutic Circle kicks in, for now I must communicate the meaning of the act of pointing, and how is this to be accomplished? Ostension involves circularity.

The fact that the bridges in Estévez's painting connect different parts of the bodies, associated with different experiences and behavior, suggests that they may not be linguistic. One bridge goes from a red dot located in the brain area of one figure to another located in the brain area of the other figure. Here there is a kind of communication by thought, and perhaps a form of intuition. But there also are several bridges of a very different kind, more like the kind of hanging bridges used for individual persons to cross ravines in jungle areas, but which in this case contain no objects going across. Four of these go from eyes to eyes and from mouth to mouth, and two from nose to nose, suggesting that seeing, smelling, and tasting are ostensive means of communication that work directly, without intermediaries. I know you mean something because I have tasted it, seen it, or smelled it.

The painting also has a bridge between the hands, indicating the most commonly associated means of ostension, that is, showing. And there are bridges tying the genitals, the hearts, the knees, and the feet. Legs, feet, and knees, can bring us together; the heart is the place of feelings and empathy and seems to work effectively; and genitals are the seat of sexual desire, a powerful source of attraction and exchange. The hands themselves appear as if reaching for each other, even though they are not touching.

We could, then, understand Estévez's painting as an attempt to point to the ways in which the Hermeneutic Circle may be bridged by noting that language is not the sole means of communication we have. We communicate through sex, intuition, ostension, and so on. This interpretation is supported by another work of Estévez, *Vasos comunicantes* (Communicating Vessels, 2006), in which he presents us with the outlines of a nude figure of a man running with circles on the brain, heart, navel, and groin. From these circles issue many lines that connect parts of the body and seem to fly away, moved by an invisible wind generated by the running, through the body and beyond, changing color at the body surface from red-orange to blue-green. The man is running, but it leaves all kinds of traces, lines that can be picked up by those who come behind, and which originate not in the mouth, the organ of speech, but in more vital centers.

Still, this seems not to be enough, because there is always the possibility that what I communicate is something different from what I am trying to communicate. The receiver might read what I do inaccurately. This is why elsewhere I have proposed that we need to include something else in an account of communication, namely, expected behavior. I expect certain behavior from those with whom I am trying to communicate, and when this behavior takes place, I know, with various degrees of certainty, that someone has understood what I have said, or that I have understood what someone else has said to me. Consider the following exchange in a Mexican restaurant in Milwaukee:

I say: "Do you have *tamales*?"

The waiter responds: "Yes."

I: "What kind do you have?"

Waiter: "*Chiapanecos, de bola*, and with *chipilín*."

I: "Are the *chiapanecos* any good?"

Waiter: "Yes, but I especially recommend the ones with *chipilín*. They are delicious."

I: "I haven't had those. What kind of filling do they have?"

Waiter: "Chicken or cheese."

I: OK. Bring me some with cheese."

Waiter: Yes, sir. Would you like something to drink with the *tamales?*"

I: "Yes, bring me a Corona. Thanks."

At every point in this conversation, there are certain behavioral expectations for both of us, and the satisfaction of these expectations is essential to understanding the speakers and the continuation of the dialogue. When I ask the first question, there are three answers I expect: "Yes," "No," or "I don't know." All three suggest to me that the waiter understands me. If instead of these, the waiter says something like, "The weather is fine," "You are stupid," or "Life is a dream," for example, I would surmise that he does not understand me, he did not hear me, he understands me but does not want to answer my question, or some such reason. And something similar can be said about the subsequent exchanges in the dialogue. When I ask about the kinds of *tamales* available, I am given a list of names, some of which I recognize and some of which I do not. And even when I do not know exactly what an answer means—say, about the kind of filling—the response is within parameters that make sense to me. If the waiter says the filling consists of diamonds, dirt, or water, then I would immediately suspect a breakdown in communication or some other anomaly. So let us assume that behavioral expectations help explain how communication happens. Even then, it should be obvious that it is not enough to explain it, for a key question remains unanswered: Where do the expectations come from?

Estévez's painting has some leads in this direction. An obvious one is that although the two figures in the painting are different, their differences are not significant. The figures are composed of the same elements, the same number of limbs, the same structure, and so on. Yes, there are differences of sex, constitution, and shape, among others, but they also share much in common. In particular, there is something inside them that seems to be structurally the same: buildings with windows. The one in the torso of the male figure is narrower and taller and has only one door and three rows of windows organized vertically. Its color is a kind of greenish-yellow. The building inside the torso of the female figure is wider and shorter and has three doors and five rows of windows organized vertically. This could be read in at least two ways. In one, they could be suggestions about human nature. Both male and female are of the same kind, even if of different sexes. But one may wonder why Estévez chose buildings rather than, say, organs. Buildings are human artifacts, so does Estévez mean that humans are the result of human constructions? Perhaps in this sense much of what we are is the result of culture, of our history, and of how we respond to the events that surround us. We could speculate that the message of the work is that culture creates the expectations that confirm communication. But now let us return to philosophy.

Philosophers have come up with many answers to the source of our expectations in terms of behavior. For example, some claim that expectations are part of human nature. But this does not seem to work in the case we are considering insofar as the exchange described has to do with culture, not nature—language is a cultural product, not an exchange of fluids. That a restaurant has or does not have *tamales,* and a waiter answers my questions about *tamales* in a certain way, depends on cultural conventions.

One also could answer that expectations are grounded on intuitions. However, again this seems unsatisfactory in that such intuitions would themselves require an explanation unless they were common to all humans. But it is clear that they are not. The expectations that govern my exchange with the waiter cannot be explained in terms of anything that is common to all humans, for they are peculiar to the culture in which the exchange takes place, and the elements that make up culture are not generally common to all persons, even if some may be. This should be rather obvious when we consider that the expectations of the participants in the dialogue are linguistic and concern a particular language, namely, English. This dialogue could not have taken place in Mexico among non-English-speaking Mexicans. There I would not have begun by asking in English, "Do you have *tamales*?" Rather, I would have begun by saying: "¿Tiene tamales?" Expectations belong to the realm of culture and as such are governed by practices belonging to particular cultures. This is tradition and what Estévez's painting seems to suggest.

Broadly speaking, we could say that it is traditional that when one asks a waiter whether he has *tamales,* he will understand this to be a question as to whether the restaurant for which he works has *tamales* to be served, and he also will understand that there are only certain answers that he is supposed to use in his response if he wishes or intends for me to understand him. And the same goes for the answers he gives, as well as for the questions I pose. Traditions teach us to expect certain behavior when there is common understanding and communication is achieved. Tradition is a way to surmount gaps. Traditions serve as bridges between language and thoughts, past knowledge and present awareness of it, and the differences that separate individual members within social groups. This is the moral that one can surmise from Estévez's painting.

SOURCES

Augustine. *On the Teacher*, x–xii. In *Augustine: Earlier Writings*, trans. J. H. S. Burleigh, vol. 1. London: SCM Press, 1953.

Eliot, T. S. "Tradition and the Individual Talent." In *Selected Essays 1917–1932*. London: Faber and Faber, 1932.

Gadamer, Hans-Georg. "On the Circle of Understanding." In *Hermeneutics versus Science? Three German Views*, ed. John M. Connolly and Thomas Keutner. Notre Dame, IN: University of Notre Dame Press, 1988.

Gracia, Jorge J. E. *Old Wine in New Skins: The Role of Tradition in Communication, Knowledge, and Group Identity*, chs. 1, 5, 7. Marquette University 67th Aquinas Lecture. Milwaukee, WI: Marquette University Press, 2003.

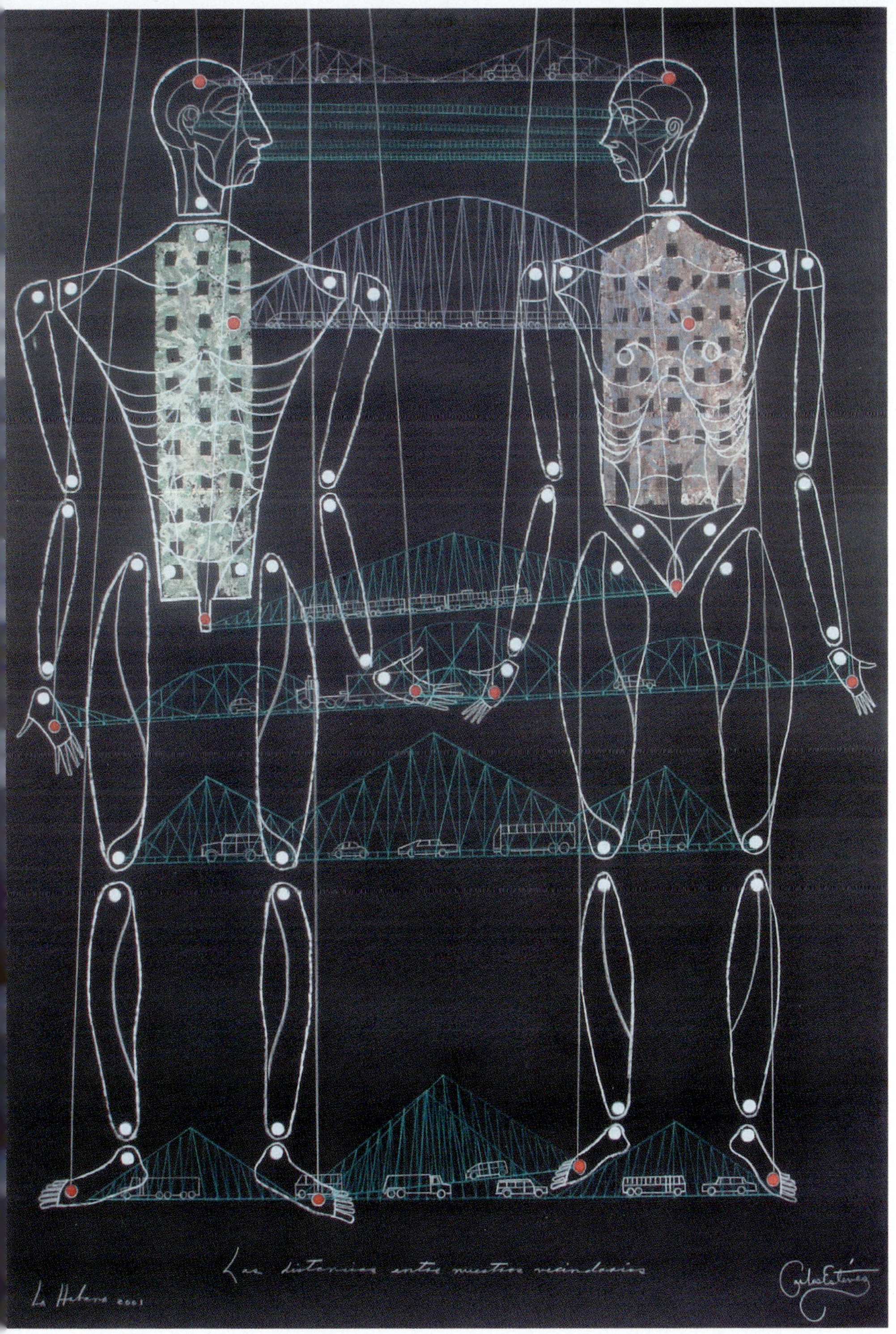

Plate XIII. *Las distancias entre nuestros vecindarios* (Distances between Our Neighborhoods), 2001, 44" × 30", watercolor and watercolor pencil on paper

16

Male and Female

Parmenides

At the center of *Shared Kingdoms* (Plate XIV) are two figures, in profile, very similar to each other except for understated male genitalia on the left one and a female breast on the right one. The female is slightly more plumb than the male, and the red tracings that mark their bodies are also different, although the spotted, fleshlike color of the bodies is similar. The figures are placed in the same position: standing on a foot, leaning against each other's backs, bending over some peculiar instruments through which they are looking with intensity and concentration. The instruments are different but neither is solid, and traces on them suggest idiosyncratic forms. Are they microscopes, periscopes, astrolabes, or something else? It is not clear, but the two figures look through them in opposite directions. The background is mysterious and indeterminate; a hint of mesh, wiring, or curtain suggests unidentifiable objects. A straight line crosses the painting horizontally, touching the shoulders, backs, and heads of the figures and serving as a kind of platform for a complicated maze of structures in an outline that resembles churches, buildings, towers, and a dome.

Men and women are the foundation of human society. On this it is easy to agree. But it is more difficult to decide what distinguishes them and how this influences society and male and female views of the world. These issues have been a battleground in contemporary philosophy and can be raised in the context of Estévez's painting. The first is as old as the Greek controversy over *physis* or *nomos*, nature or culture, except that here it is applied to men and women. Are the distinctions between men and women a matter of nature or of culture? On the one hand, and obviously, there are differences of nature. Men and women are physically different in perspicuous respects, perhaps more importantly in the areas that have to do with reproduction. On the other hand, some differences are clearly cultural and vary from society to society. In Western society, women often wear makeup, whereas contemporary men generally do not, and women are assigned roles that are different from those of men. Again, in Western society, men have been traditionally described as family breadwinners, whereas women have been in charge of household chores and of raising children.

One way to deal with these differences is to say that one kind of difference between men and women is genetic, call it sex, and another cultural, call it gender. Sex is a matter of biology and therefore is more stable than gender, which is a matter of history and context. A woman can become a man and a man can become a woman in terms of sex, but the process is complicated and takes considerable interference; there is plastic surgery and hormone therapy to contend with. But the roles prescribed by gender are more easily exchanged. Context or circumstances can be manipulated in various ways. Matters of dress and behavior are less difficult to modify than biological features. But not everyone agrees with this way of thinking about men and women. Here is where the controversy begins.

For some, sex is so permeated with cultural and social concepts that it is never possible to separate it from them. Even biology is not just a matter of laws of nature independent of human input; it is influenced by society and culture. So to think that masculinity and femininity can in any way be independent of social and cultural influences is wrongheaded. Matters are not so simple or hygienic; nature and culture are inextricably intertwined.

Others, however, hold that these categories can be kept separate, even if in fact it can be difficult to separate them in certain contexts. For some of these authors, cultural differences are often rooted in nature and respond to nature, whereas for others they are not so rooted, even if they may depend on particular contexts and circumstances.

Another issue frequently comes up concerning this matter. It is possible to think that nature is always the determining factor and culture always dependent on nature. But it is also possible to think that culture influences nature, so that often what is considered natural or part of nature is a response to culture.

Finally, regardless of the emphasis placed on nature or culture, men and women seem to know and feel differently. Apart from whether they deal with problems, and act, differently because their perspectives on the world are determined by nature or culture, still the perspectives appear to be different. This leads to a rather startling conclusion: science and philosophy, as primarily male products to this day, may be in fact one-sided, having ignored the contribution of the female perspective. And if men and women are different and see the world differently, then any one-sided perspective, whether male or female, is insufficient to give an account of human experience.

If the male and female perspectives are the result of culture, then it is possible to alter them, bringing them together to produce a better picture of the universe. But if they are products of nature, then it is questionable whether we can in fact do this, for men will always see the world through masculine eyes, and women will always see the world through feminine eyes. Neither will be able to see what the other sees or to understand the other in a meaningful way.

Estévez's painting is a locus where these questions can be posed more than a place where we find answers to them. Most of the points made so far can be traced to the painting, beginning with the view that men and women are the foundation of society. The two figures in the work support on their shoulders and head a whole structural complex of buildings, clearly social and cultural products. Neither figure stands alone in the effort to support these buildings. Each figure stands on one foot and leans against the other, so that the weight is supported by both. Men and women need each other, and culture needs both.

However, there is little difference between the figures; they are almost androgynous. The shape of their bodies, their coloring, and the internal lines that seem to indicate blood vessels and structures appear quite similar. Clearly these figures are of the same species. Their differences, when compared to their similarities, are small: the markings of sexual differences are understated. And although these physical differences could be called biological, they appear insignificant in context.

Still, there are important contrasts in the depiction of the figures, albeit external to them, such as the two peculiar instruments through which they intently observe the world. Even here, there are similarities: the instruments are microscopes, periscopes, astrolabes, telescopes, or something like these, and they are drawn in the same sort of way, with similar lines and colors. But they look in opposite directions and are not quite alike, suggesting that the views they reveal to their observers are different, and that men and women do not see the same things.

But are their views diametrically different, and even opposed? Do men and women ever see the same things? One could argue that they do not, because their views are precisely the result of differences between them, even if in fact the differences do not appear serious. Moreover, one also could argue that instruments of vision can be exchanged insofar as they are not part of the bodies in the painting, opening lines of communication between the man and the woman. If the instruments are not part of the bodies and are part of culture instead, then they are interchangeable and transferable.

But even if this is so, one could point out that the horizon of the views the instruments reveal is at the opposite end and in a different direction. Perhaps, after all, men and women cannot see the same things. Perhaps they are epistemically estranged, and there is no way to bring them together into a coherent, harmonious whole. And what if they changed positions? For one, this would not be possible without jeopardizing the whole structure of society—the buildings resting on the shoulders of this couple, would come tumbling down. And even if the exchange were possible, would the figures be able to see what each other sees at the time he or she sees it? If, as Aristotle held, time is the measure of change, then this would not be possible.

But is this what Estévez's painting is about? Perhaps the epistemic dilemma posited by the painting points to a deeper divide in nature and society than that between men and women: two forces different and ever opposed to each other but essential to the integrity of the whole. The ancient Greeks played with this idea, and so did the ancient Chinese with their principles of yin and yang, which make up a whole, represented by a circle. Indeed, it might be possible to draw a circle around the two figures in Estévez's painting, making up a similar whole. If this is so, then it is reasonable to begin the discussion with Parmenides.

SOURCES

Butler, Judith. *Gender Trouble: Feminism and the Subversion of Identity*, ch. 1. New York: Routledge, 1999.

Code, Lorraine. "Voice and Voicelessness: A Modest Proposal?" In *Philosophy in a Feminist Voice*, ed. Janet Kourany. Princeton, NJ: Princeton University Press, 1998.

de Beauvoir, Simone. "Introduction." In *The Second Sex*. Translated and edited by H. M. Parshley. New York: Alfred A. Knopf, 1993.

Ortega y Gasset, José. *Man and People*, ch. 6. New York: Norton, 1957.

Parmenides. *Way of Truth*. In *An Introduction to Early Greek Philosophy: The Chief Fragments and Ancient Testimony, with Connecting Commentary*, ed. John Mansley Robinson, ch. 6. New York: Houghton Mifflin, 1968.

Plato. *The Republic*, Bk. VI. In *The Collected Dialogues of Plato*, ed. Edith Hamilton and Huntington Cairns. New York: Pantheon Books, 1961.

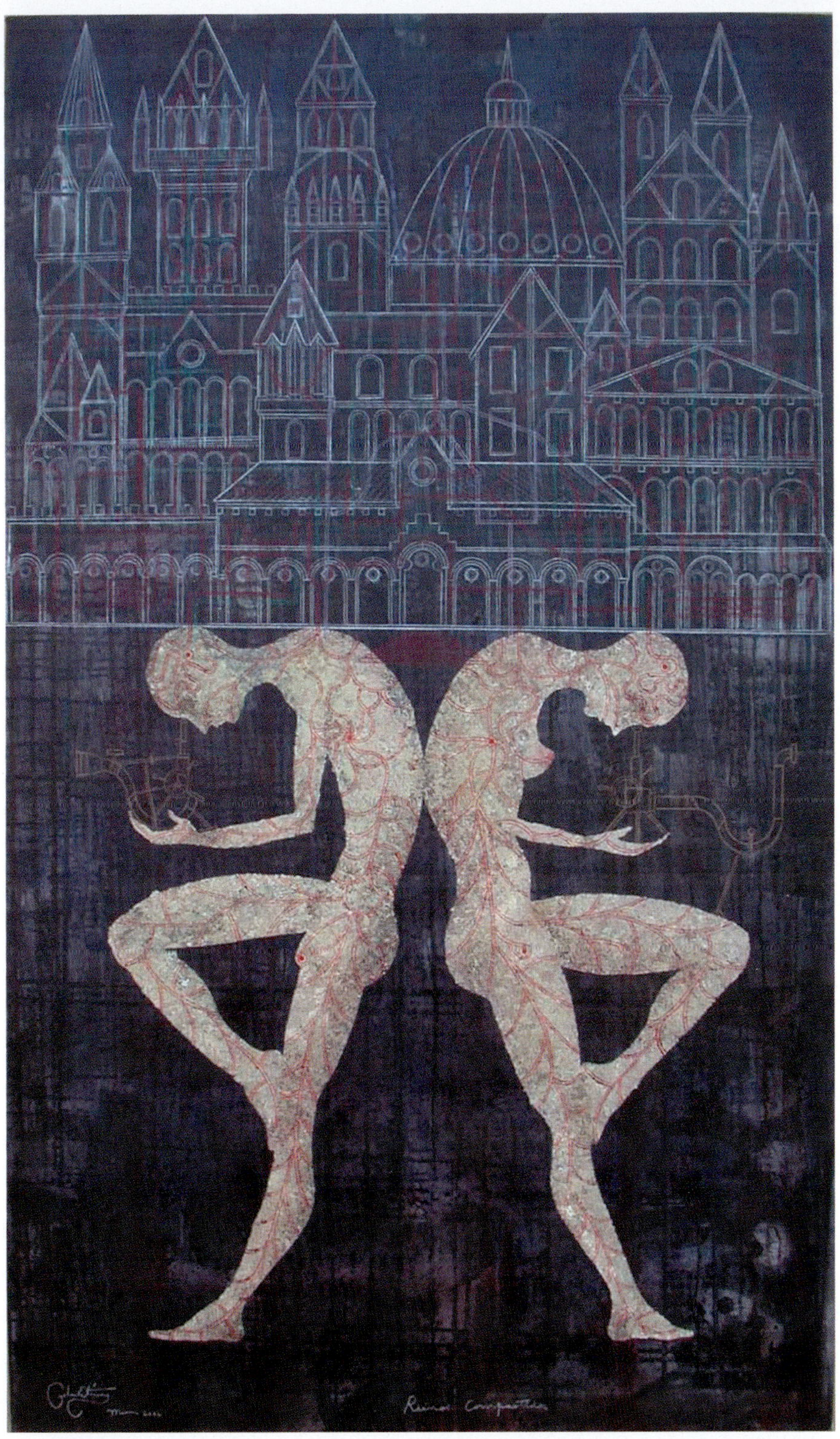

Plate XIV. *Reinos compartidos* (Shared Kingdoms), 2006, 64" × 42", oil and pencil on canvas

Destiny

17

The Will Does Not Desire of Necessity

Thomas Aquinas

In the *Summa theologiae,* Thomas Aquinas takes up one of the most thorny issues concerning human action, the question of whether the human will necessarily desires whatever it desires. Am I bound to want the bag of pork rinds I know is in the cupboard waiting for me? Or, to put it differently, am I determined to want it, and even perhaps to eat it? This seems to be, in part, the theme of Estévez's *Irreversible Processes* (Plate XV). The painting appears to be about processes that cannot be otherwise than they are, suggesting that once we are involved in these processes we are, of necessity, bound by their rules. What kind of necessity is it depicting?

Before I turn to the painting, let me say something about the philosophical problem that can be raised with it. It would be very comforting for most of us to think that we are determined to wish and do what we wish and do, because that would absolve us of responsibility. If the killer cannot but kill the victim, in spite of the moral repugnance of the act, and if I cannot but desire to eat and actually eat the bag of pork rinds, in spite of the fact that it is reeking with saturated fat and cholesterol, something that at my age I do not need, then we can do away with the struggle not to do certain things that we know we should not do but crave doing.

In this way, we could achieve what the Stoics called *ataraxia,* a fancy name for peace of mind. If we know we are determined to desire and do what we desire and do, then the only course for peace and tranquility, perhaps even happiness, is to be content with the realization that this is so. The killer can kill the victim and feel no remorse because he cannot be held accountable for what he cannot avoid. And I can eat the pork rinds in perfect delight, because I know that I cannot do otherwise. And if the killer goes to jail or is put to death for his crime, then he can be satisfied in thinking that an injustice has been committed against him, since he could not help himself. And if I have a heart attack as a result of my eating the bag of pork rinds, then I can also feel content in knowing that I could not have avoided it. This is a very comforting philosophy of life in that it solves many problems for us, particularly for those of us who want things we know we should not want.

The view Aquinas proposed concerning this matter is different, because he was intent on saving moral responsibility, for at least two reasons. One is that intuitively we seem to be able to control our actions and desires, at least sometimes. The killer might not be determined to kill, and I might not be bound to eat the pork rinds, which means that the killer deserves the punishment and I should feel guilty. A second reason behind Aquinas's view is that he was a Christian and took seriously the Christian doctrine that we are free and responsible for the actions we take, even when we have certain desires and inclinations to do certain things. Sin requires moral responsibility. For us, however, the theological reason Aquinas held this view is not important insofar as here we are interested in philosophy, not theology.

In his usually orderly fashion, Aquinas addresses this issue by making some important distinctions. He points out that the term *necessity* can be used in two ways, each of which is in turn divisible into two others. The first of these two pairs of uses concerns intrinsic principles. Materially, something is said to be necessary because it follows from the matter out of which it is composed. For example, when something is composed of incompatible materials, the thing in question is unstable and falls apart. By vigorously stirring oil and vinegar together, I can achieve a certain homogeneity in the liquid, but this homogeneity quickly disappears when I stop stirring, because oil and vinegar are incompatible. Their separation follows necessarily from the materials. And there can be a necessity of what Aquinas calls form, that is, the nature of a thing. It is in the nature of triangles to have three and only three angles, so it is necessary that the sum of these angles be equal to two right angles. Material and formal necessities are absolute, according to Aquinas.

However, there is another kind of necessity. This is extrinsic and does not have to do with what things are made of or with their nature. This kind breaks again into two other kinds. One concerns the end. For example, food is necessary for life, because without it organisms cannot survive, and some means of transportation (a horse for Aquinas) is necessary for a journey, because without it I cannot get to where I propose to go. This necessity, which Aquinas calls necessity of the end, is contingent on the end in question, life in one case and a journey in the other. I can certainly stop eating food, although this means that I will die; and I can decide not to undertake a journey, which means that I will not need any means of transportation.

The second relative necessity concerns coercion. This happens when an agent imposes on another a certain course of action that the other cannot avoid. If I stop eating, I can be force-fed. And if I decide not to undertake a journey, I can be tied and bound and put on a cart and be taken to wherever the agent forcing me wants. In both cases, I am being coerced.

For Aquinas, none of the first three kinds of necessities interferes with the actions being voluntary. Only the fourth does, a reason it is called violent. This is also why we are exonerated from moral responsibility when we are coerced. If the killer is forced to kill, and I am forced to eat pork rinds, then neither one of us is responsible for our actions. But if the killer kills while he is not forced, and I eat the pork rinds without coercion, then we are not absolved from responsibility.

Someone might object that this scheme does not work to the extent that I may have a natural desire to eat pork rinds and therefore cannot be held responsible when I eat them: I eat them out of necessity. Aquinas's response is that we are not bound by this necessity, because the natural necessity in humans is to desire our ultimate end, which is happiness, and this leaves room for the free choice of means. That I love pork rinds is not enough for me to be excused in eating them, because my happiness is more complex than eating pork rinds. Eating pork rinds is not part of my natural desire but an acquired taste. There are many things I like, and what I ultimately will do is subject to negotiation among these various means. Certainly if I think a bit, I realize that eating pork rinds might kill me, thus defeating the overall purpose of making me happy, since I would not enjoy happiness being dead.

And what does Estévez's painting have to tell us about all of this? The work depicts an amusement park with three rides: a Ferris wheel, a roller coaster, and a merry-go-round. Dominating each of these is a black figure. On the left, occupying roughly half of the canvas, is a bust in profile resting on a structure that supports the Ferris wheel, whose center is in the head. At the edges of the wheel spikes are buildings of various sorts. On the right, at the top of the painting, there is a second figure, standing, with its head coming down the slide of the roller coaster. The movement is suggested by the outline of various other heads, eventually returning toward the figure. On the right-hand side, at the bottom, a stylized human figure, with extended arms, rests on the platform of the merry-go-round supported by wheels. The seats of the merry-go-round are sea horses, and inside the torso of the black figure at the center of the merry-go-round several wheels and mechanisms are tied to the wheels under the platform.

All three figures are involved in motion. The first is stationary but seems to be at the center of the Ferris wheel and thus of its motion, perhaps controlling the motion, the speed, and the places where it stops. The second figure has a stationary body, but its head is moving forward and around, all the way back to its place at the neck. And the third is like the first, at the center of the movement, and in the same place, although turning around and around as the ride requires.

The head of the first figure cannot change its position at the center of the wheel, the nature of the wheel, or the range of its possible actions—it cannot walk away or even turn. In Aquinas's term, it is bound by its intrinsic makeup, whether the material out of which it is made or the nature of the contraption of which it is a part. If it is the source of the wheel's motion, then it can only move it in a circular fashion. Yet it also can not move the wheel, and it appears that it can stop it at any point, choosing to stop at any of the buildings that surround it. There is, then, no coercion in Thomistic terms, although there is both a natural necessity and a necessity of the end. The head can produce only circular motion, and if it wants to stop at a certain point, it needs to turn the wheel.

The second figure, with the head sliding downward on the roller coaster, seems bound by nature and by the end—by nature, because the body is fixed in place, and the head moves only in the way prescribed by the incline of the roller coaster, and by the end, because the head is bound to return to its body when the ride is finished. Again, we could interpret this as we did the first figure: there is necessity of nature and end but no coercion. It does not seem at all necessary for the head to move, although if it decides to take a ride, it will have to follow the path laid out by the roller coaster. It is bound both formally and by its goal.

The third figure gives us a more ambiguous picture of the situation. Like the other figures, it seems to be bound by its nature, and one could argue that the ropes that tie it to the wheels of the merry-go-round suggest that perhaps it has something to say about whether it moves, and thus that it has the power of decision, even if not the power to choose the end. The end does not seem to be a matter of choice, because the motion suggested goes only one way (as indicated by the figures of the sea horses), and around. But then one also could think of this figure as symbolizing coercion, where the will ceases to be free because an agent or agents impose a certain course of action on it. How? Because the figure appears to be helplessly carried by others—the sea horses that determine both direction and motion.

Estévez's painting seems to have covered the theoretical possibilities outlined by Aquinas and to be concordant with Aquinas's position. From a philosophical standpoint, however, we still face the question of whether the position is right, and this we can ponder through further analyses of the work.

SOURCES

Epictetus. *Discourses and Enchiridion.* Roslyn, NY: Published for the Classics Club by W. J. Black, 1944.

Marcus Aurelius. *Meditations,* Bk. XII. Translated by John Long. Mineola, NY: Dover, 1997.

Thomas Aquinas. *Summa theologiae,* I, q. 82. Edited by Thomas Gilby. Garden City, NY: Image Books, 1969–.

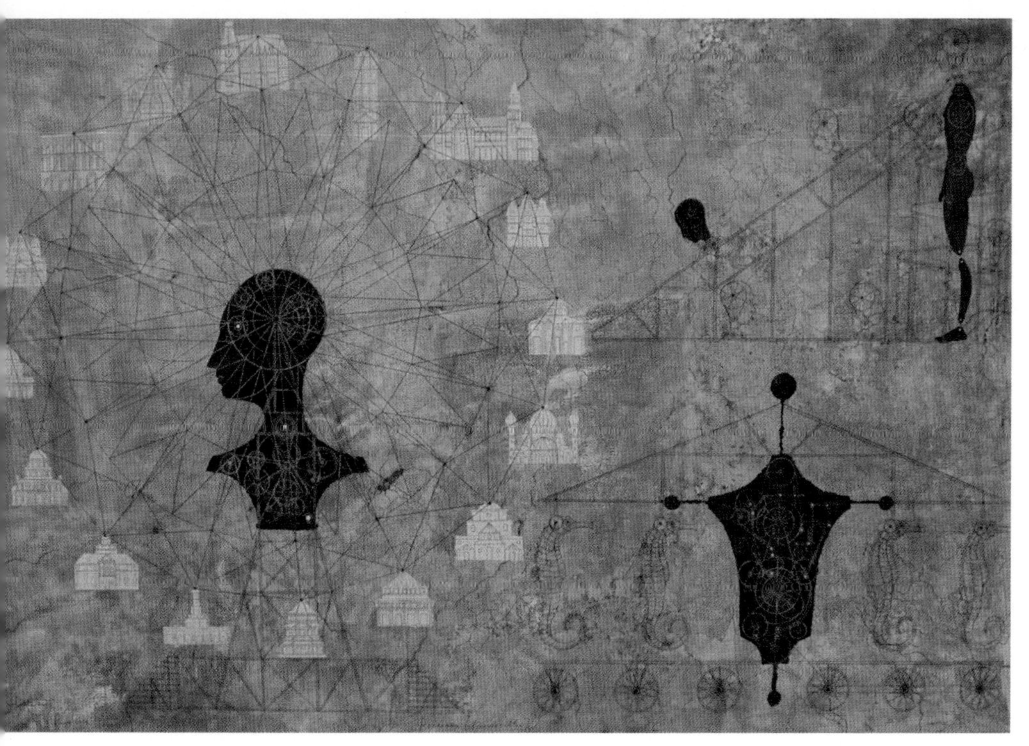

Plate XV. *Procesos irreversibles* (Irreversible Processes), 2004, 51" × 77", oil and pencil on canvas

18

____

The Very Hairs of Your Head
Are All Numbered

The Gospel according to St. Matthew

On a spotted red background, a puppet sits in a version of the traditional Yoga lotus pose for meditation, with the arms bent and the palms of the hands facing the audience. The puppet is enmeshed in a web in the loose shape of a heart that ties the arms, parts of the legs and feet, the torso, and the head to a large hand above it coming from somewhere and perhaps belonging to the puppeteer. The hand seems to control the strings that lead to the puppet, but the strings extend beyond the hand. The puppet's body has a color that mimics flesh, and in it there are niches, containing either hands or figures, some of which in turn have other niches with hands or figures within. The arch of the niche in the head is a semicircle, but the ones in the torso, the hands, the feet, and the genitals are Gothic. The painting's title is *Infinite Will* (Plate XVI).

An obvious philosophical problem posed by this painting concerns the relationship between divine and human wills. Does human freedom make sense in light of God's infinite will, his omnipotence? Although the notion of an infinite God was not developed in the Middle Ages until the thirteenth century, from the beginning of the Christian era theologians and philosophers accepted the doctrine of God's omnipotence: God's power has no limits. This is one of the three properties that traditionally has been assigned to God in Christian theology, along with omniscience and omnibenevolence. God is all powerful, all knowing, and all good. The problem with this idea is that it seems to leave no room for human freedom. And the matter does not rest there, for Christian doctrine goes farther by holding that, in addition to these attributes, God also has a plan for human beings and human history, which usually is referred to as Providence. How can all of this be reconciled with human choice and freedom?

The matter becomes critical when sin is considered, for this produces a rather startling dilemma. Either sin is the result of human freedom, or it is not. If it is not, then this fits nicely with the idea of God's infinite will, but it does not sit well with his goodness or with human freedom. The first is unacceptable to Christians because it takes away one of the most important of God's properties, and the second because it eliminates the possibility of moral responsibility for humans. The other alternative, however, that sin is the result of human freedom, does not accord well with God's infinite power, knowledge, or goodness, for how could a good God knowingly allow evil to happen? How could he permit that we, beings he is supposed to have created and love, sin? This horn of the dilemma also is unacceptable.

Augustine was the first Christian thinker who addressed this issue in depth. His solution involves two doctrines. The first is a distinction among three types of goods: great goods, lesser goods, and intermediate goods. Great goods are absolute and include such things as happiness and virtue. These are good in themselves and can never be used to do bad things. Lesser goods and intermediate goods differ from these in that they can be used badly. An example of a lesser good is physical strength, for although it can be used to save someone, which is good, it also can be used to kill someone, which is bad. The will is an intermediate good because it is primarily an instrumental power and as such can be used for different ends, some good and some bad. I can will to be virtuous, which is good, or to sin, which is bad. Still, the will is in itself a good, and therefore the freedom that it gives humans is desirable, for it is better to have a will that is free than not to have free will at all.

The second foundation of Augustine's solution is the view that someone who can control and limit his power has greater power than someone who cannot. If God is able to limit his power in order to allow humans freely to decide for themselves what they do, then his power is greater than if he were not able to do it.

Augustine's solution has not been found satisfactory by many, but it is still defended by some philosophers interested in this issue. What does Estévez's painting suggest about this matter?

The puppet is trapped in the web controlled by the large hand painted at the top of the work. From this, one could surmise that the puppet is not free: whoever controls that hand can make the puppet do whatever he wants. But several other aspects in the work leave some room for human freedom. One is the complicated structure of the web. The hand has five fingers and controls five strings, but these strings disappear in a mesh of connections. This means that the movement the hand produces in the puppet is difficult to predict and possibly to control. Of course, one could argue that an omniscient being could easily figure out what to do under these circumstances and, being also omnipotent, he could be always effective. But it may be that the ways things are, their natures, for example, and the circumstances in which they are found impose certain parameters on divine action, even when God is the ultimate source of power. Just as our past imposes constraints on our future, God's actions and designs impose constraints on him, even if these might be regarded as self-imposed to some extent. Indeed, few theologians have gone so far as to say that God can violate the laws of logic. And not many would agree with Peter Damian, who argued that God is so powerful that he can bring it about that a past event did not happen.

But there also is another factor, for the web does not extend to all of the extremities of the puppet. It is tied to the hands and feet, but it is superimposed on the rest of the body, just as is the case with puppets in a circus. No web lines seem to be tied to the legs, arms, torso, or head. And its loose shape as a heart hints that perhaps the connections are not mechanical and fixed but like anything that has to do with feelings, complicated and indeterminate. This opens up the possibilities that the web may not be touching all parts of the puppet's body, and that it may not control the puppet as effectively as first thought. The situation may allow some movement independently of the one produced by the big hand on top.

Another hint of freedom comes from the figures within the niches on the body. These consist of images of puppets and hands which seem to be reproductions of the puppet and his hands. This introduces an element of reflexivity: the puppet thinks and feels himself and his parts and is aware of himself and his powers; he can objectify his situation, which is a first step toward creating an awareness of it and of possible courses of action to change it. Indeed, if it were the case that, as the Stoics believed, the only freedom we have is our awareness of our determination, then this is still more than no freedom at all. But the painting suggests something more, for this self-awareness, combined with the limitations of the web, indicates that there may be room for human free will in God's scheme.

There is even more in that the lines that control the puppet extend beyond the hand. Could this be suggesting that something higher than the hand cancels some of the hand's action, making even more room for the puppet's choice? Is the infinite will to which the title of the painting refers symbolized by the hand, or is the hand a mere instrument of that will? Does the will belong to some other being not present in the work? Is God subject to someone or something other than his will? Is he bound by other beings, the laws of logic, the laws of nature, or even the laws of history? As some have put it, is what God does good because he does it, or does he do it because it is good? As usual, with Estévez's work, this painting provides no answers but instead leaves us with questions that entice us to further reflection.

SOURCES

Augustine. *On Free Will*, Bks. II and III. *The City of God*. 2 vols. Indianapolis, IN:
     St Maur Theological Center, 1979.
Thomas Aquinas. *Summa theologiae*. I, q. 22. Edited by Thomas Gilby. Garden City,
     NY: Image Books, 1969–.

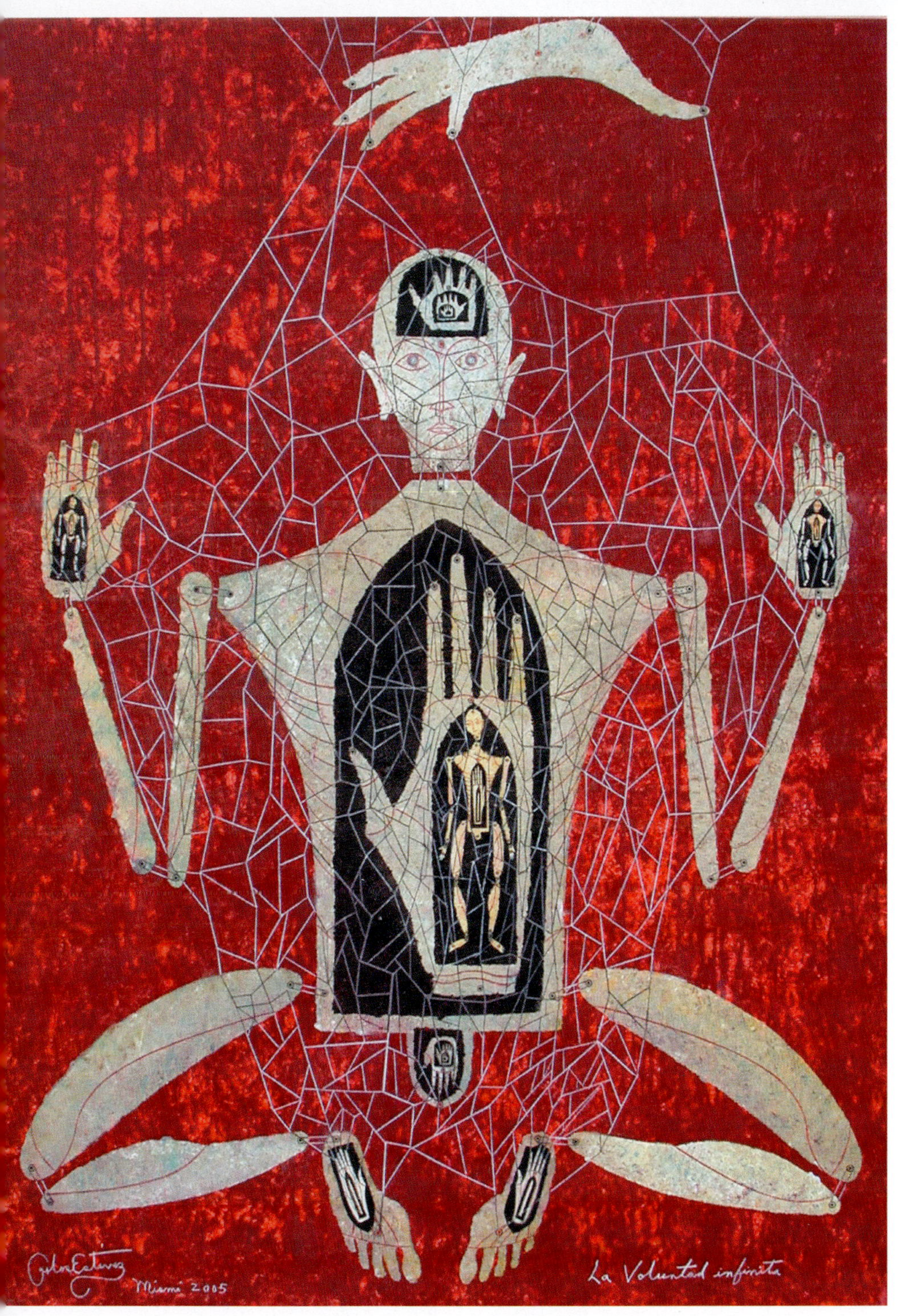

Plate XVI. *La voluntad infinita* (Infinite Will), 2005, 55" × 39", oil and pencil on canvas

19

God Has Predestined His Elect

Augustine

The doctrine of predestination is central to much Christian theology. It is grounded in the Bible, and many major Christian theologians accept it, although they differ on the details of interpretation. Apart from the obvious directive of accepting the Bible as the word of God and what it says about predestination as undeniable, there is another motivation for this doctrine: it tries to make sense of the present condition of human beings and of their inability to merit salvation.

According to the story of Genesis, Adam and Eve were expelled from the Garden of Eden because of their disobedience to God. God had given them everything good, including free will, and instead of appreciating it and obeying his command not to eat the fruit from the tree of knowledge of good and evil, they did. This elicited God's wrath and their appropriate punishment. Redemption was impossible, in that their nature became contaminated in various ways, preventing them from doing the right thing. Even in cases in which their actions could be construed as good, their motives, and their status as rebels against God, devalued their actions, making it impossible for humans to earn salvation.

Yet God still loved his most cherished accomplishment in creation, made in his image and likeness. He could not abandon humanity. But how could he be a just God if he forgot what Adam and Eve had done and made it possible for them and their descendants to enjoy a life of eternal happiness they did not deserve because of their sin? Only if a ransom were paid, and it was made patently clear that the ransom was not deserved, could God's justice be harmonized with his love and compassion for humans. The ransom was the sacrifice of Christ on the cross, and the undeserved nature of this sacrifice was made plain by the doctrine of predestination. According to this doctrine, we are not saved because we deserve salvation in any way, but only because God has chosen some of us to join him in Paradise in exchange for Christ's sacrifice, which ironically is God's own insofar as Christ is God.

Predestination should not be confused with either predetermination or condemnation. Predetermination is the view that God preordains what humans will do. This has been maintained by some theologians, but it is a marginal interpretation of the pertinent biblical texts. Predestination does not entail that the elect are predetermined to act in any particular way. They remain free to do as they wish, although they are assured of salvation.

Predestination should not be confused with condemnation, because the latter view holds that God damns some human beings to eternal suffering in Hell. Most Christian theologians oppose the idea that God condemns anybody in the sense that he decides who will not be saved. Beginning with Adam and Eve, we, as humans, are responsible for our punishment, for our damnation. God is not. God gave us free will to do as we wish, and we should follow his injunctions. But our foreparents did not, and since then we have done even worse. God does not determine who will be damned; he only determines who will be saved.

The doctrine of predestination generates problems, because it does not seem to be just for God to choose some to be saved simply because he wishes it. Indeed, is it not against justice that the chosen would be saved no matter what they do? Christian theologians have been divided about this issue from the very beginning. On one side, Augustine argued that the solution to this problem is to be found in divine grace. God gives those he wishes to save a special, gratuitous gift in virtue of which they are brought back into God's favor. This gift produces a change in them so that they bear the fruits of God's spirit, but those fruits come only as a result of grace and do not count for salvation.

At the opposite end was Pelagius, who argued that Augustine's proposal does not solve the problem at all. In fact, it makes it worse, because it demonstrates that God is the sole cause of human salvation. God gives grace to whomever he wishes, unrelated to his or her merits. According to Pelagius, the only way to make sense of human salvation is to realize it is contingent upon merit, the result of effort, rather than unilateral divine action.

Estévez's *Doctrine of Predestination* (Plate XVII) explicitly addresses the doctrine of predestination. On a light background he has painted four players around a game of dominoes, a favorite pastime in Cuba. The players are puppets who have points of power on the head, the heart, the hands, the feet, and the penis. They are presented in different poses, one sitting and the others standing. The one in the background looks like a priest, opening his arms and hands in the welcoming gesture used during Mass: "The Lord be with you."

The dominoes have been placed in the jagged way they usually follow on the table after a game is under way. But clearly the game is unusual, because the places of some pieces violate the rules of the game. Blank pieces sometimes follow pieces with positive values, and pieces with particular values sometimes follow pieces with different values. To complicate matters, the hands and feet of the puppets are tied to strings that disappear at the upper border of the painting, and each puppet holds a last piece on its hand, whose value is hidden.

Is there a particular message about predestination in Estévez's painting, and if so, how does it mesh with Christian doctrine? The answer is not obvious. Perhaps the game of dominoes is the game of life, and we are all engaged in it. There is an element of luck, which perhaps for the puppets is not luck so much as something determined ahead of time, namely, that God has given them the particular pieces of dominoes they hold. This, however, does not ensure that anyone in particular is going to win, which is probably the end game, namely, salvation. The players need to play, and to do so effectively, but what ensures that they will do so?

Here is where the positions of the pieces that violate the rules of the game become significant, for clearly they are allowed, and they have been placed in strategic locations. Does this mean that it does not matter what the players do? This would seem to reflect the Augustinian view that human actions have no bearing on salvation. Or does it mean that the puppets are being controlled by the divinity, even to the point of violating the rules of the game? If so, does predestination become more a matter of predetermining actions rather than of predetermining the result? Is predestination a kind of predetermination after all? In this, one cannot help but ask whether there is an element of irrationality involved: Does predestination make sense? How do we answer these questions, particularly when the positions of some pieces make no sense in the game?

One way to look at this is to view the actions and the right or wrong choices that puppets make as irrelevant to the game or its end. There is a point at which one of the puppets will win, the one slated for salvation: he will be able to play the last piece. We may surmise from this that Estévez's painting falls on the side of Augustine and not Pelagius. The person who is saved is saved by the grace of God, who somehow manipulates things to bring that person to the right place at the right time, for not only are violations of the rules allowed, but God himself distributes the pieces among the players. This does not necessitate that the actions of those who are saved be predetermined, although the question lingers as to whether they are. And this makes us ponder what this portrayal of the doctrine of predestination ultimately means. Does it show that predestination is irrational? Does it show that it is in fact a kind of predetermination in which humans are not free? Does it mean to endorse a leap of faith untainted by reason? Or does it suggest that such a leap is to be rejected? The painting leaves us wondering, and that is perhaps its most effective philosophical function, although one thing is certain: we do not know who will be saved and who will be damned, for we do not know how the game will end, and this is quite concordant with Christian doctrine.

SOURCES

Augustine. *Retractations*, Bk. I, ch. 9. In *Saint Augustine: The Problem of Free Choice*, trans. Dom M. Pontifex. London: Longmans, 1955.

Pelagius. *Letters of Pelagius and His Followers*. Translated and edited by B. R. Rees. Rochester, NY: Boydell Press, 1991.

Thomas Aquinas. *Summa theologiae*, I, q. 23. Edited by Thomas Gilby. Garden City, NY: Image Books, 1969–.

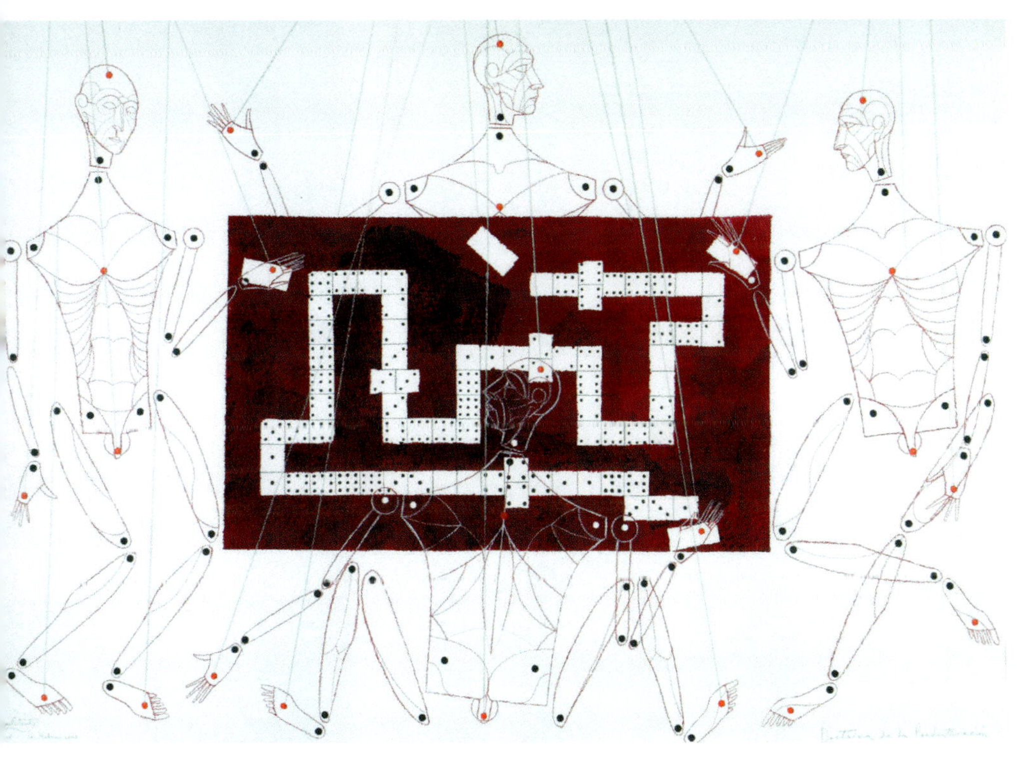

Plate XVII. *Doctrina de la predestinación* (Doctrine of Predestination), 2002, 29.5" × 41.5", watercolor on paper

Part 2

Philosophical Interpretations and Art

Interpretation

In the interpretations of Estévez's work presented in Part 1 of this book, I have used philosophical perspectives to which I am partial. I have emphasized the work of ancient and medieval authors as well as that of existentialists to whose views I am particularly drawn. And I have looked at some pieces through the lenses of recent controversies concerning social identities and the views I have developed elsewhere about them. For example, in *Self-fishing*, I saw a metaphor for the Socratic dictum "Know thyself" and all that it implies. I used Aquinas to discuss the significance of *Irreversible Processes* because he presents a view of the role of necessity in human action that is clear and, to this day, a serious contender in philosophy. Ortega y Gasset came to mind to think about *No One Can See through My Eyes,* because of the effectiveness with which he articulated the perspectivist point of view in the Hispanic world. I saw in *Forging People* a way of posing the problem of how social groups are formed and an opportunity to examine various contending positions on this, including my own. Plato's theory about the origin of numbers was an obvious choice for the interpretation of *Numerical Thoughts.* The opposition between Aristotle's essentialism and Sartre's existentialism came to mind in the understanding of *Undetermined Being.* Augustine's theological use of the Principle of Plenitude made sense to think about *Horror vacui.* And race theory seemed a well-suited topic in the context of *Difficult Loves.*

These interpretations of Estévez's works reveal something about his art, the society in which we both live, various philosophical theories, and my own thinking, helping to make explicit views and assumptions that might otherwise remain implicit and safe from analysis and criticism. But are the interpretations I have provided legitimate, and if so, why? This is the question that a philosophical analysis should answer, and this is the aim of Part 2 of this book. I begin with interpretation.

INTERPRETATION

The notion of interpretation is quite contested. Two particularly important conceptions of it are in use, even though they are seldom explicitly acknowledged or distinguished.[1] According to one, an *interpretation* is a certain understanding that someone has of something.[2] We speak of my interpretation of the first line of Aristotle's *Metaphysics*, "All men by nature desire to know," of your interpretation of the accident you witnessed yesterday near your home, or of someone else's interpretation of Picasso's *Guernica*. In this sense, an interpretation consists of the acts of understanding that persons entertain when they think about the line of Aristotle's text, the accident, or *Guernica*. Someone might understand Aristotle's text as referring exclusively to males, whereas someone else might think of human beings in general. You might think that the person responsible for the accident you witnessed was the driver of the red car, whereas another witness might think it was the driver of the blue car. When we come to *Guernica*, I might think of it in terms of something particular about the brutality of the Spanish Civil War because of my familiarity with that historical catastrophe, whereas others might think of the horrors of war in general. In all of these cases, we are dealing with understandings of the objects under interpretation—the text, the accident, or the painting.

Another way to conceive an interpretation is as something through which an interpreter aims to cause an understanding of an object in an audience. This is perhaps what Lamarque and Olsen have in mind when they say that part of the function of "the interpretative vocabulary is that it should bring the subject of the work under descriptions that clarify it by categorizing it for the reader."[3] Call this *instrumental interpretation*. This kind of interpretation, just like the object of interpretation, can be anything. It can be a text, a picture, or an action, although some means are more frequently favored than others: actions, texts, events, and human artifacts in general are often the instruments used in interpretation.[4] Aquinas's *Commentary on Aristotle's "Metaphysics"* is an instrumental interpretation of Aristotle's *Metaphysics*, but so is the drawing you make on a piece of paper of the accident you witnessed in order to show me what you think took place. And the same applies to the image you or I construct in our minds when considering Picasso's *Guernica*. In all cases we have an instrument to help create understanding: Aquinas's *Commentary* is supposed to help us understand Aristotle's text; your drawing of the accident is intended to make me understand what happened; and the mental images we construct are tools we use to think about and understand *Guernica*.

Obviously an instrumental interpretation of the sorts mentioned, with one exception I shall identify, is not an understanding but rather something that presupposes an interpretation in the first sense, that is, an understanding on the part of an interpreter who then proceeds to create the instrumental interpretation to produce a further understanding in someone else. The exception is the image, for a mental image I have in my mind also may be considered a kind of understanding of what happened, say, in the accident. If so, it also would be an interpretation of the first sort. I can use the picture of the accident I have in my mind to think about the accident and its causes, for example. In this case the image would be an instrument of understanding. But the image also can be considered a kind of mental act, a certain grasping, which then would function not as an instrument of understanding but as a kind of understanding itself.

For our purposes, both senses of interpretation, as understanding and as instrument of understanding, are important. Indeed, three items are pertinent for us:

1. Object of interpretation, which in our discussions consists of Estévez's art.

2. Interpretation as understanding, which here refers either to my understanding of Estévez's art or to readers' understandings of Estévez's art.

3. Instrumental interpretation, which for us consists of the essays accompanying the images of the art.

Just as we need to be able to talk about Aquinas's understanding of Aristotle's famous treatise as his interpretation of it, so we need to be able to talk of the text of Aquinas's *Commentary* as an interpretation of the treatise. The first consists of Aquinas's acts of understanding, the second of a text he produced to help an audience understand Aristotle's treatise. In our case, we should keep in mind Estévez's art, the notion of an understanding of it, and also the texts of the essays included here, whose intention is to cause understandings of the art in the readers of this book.

Apart from these, there are other objects of interpretation and instrumental interpretations involved in the first part of this book. Each piece by Estévez can be taken as an instrumental interpretation of whatever prompted Estévez to produce it, intended to cause an understanding of it in audiences. And the very essays included here about Estévez's art can themselves become objects of interpretation, whether each in turn is regarded as an understanding or as an instrumental interpretation. However, our concern is primarily with Estévez's pieces as objects of interpretation, and so I will dispense with these other items.

We also need to keep in mind that just as we have access to Aquinas's understanding of Aristotle's *Metaphysics* only through what he wrote about it, that is, through the text of his *Commentary*, both the readers of this book and I, as interpreters, have access to Estévez's understandings only through the art he has produced, unless he tells us something about them (as he does in fact in the interview in the Appendices). Moreover, the readers of this book have access to my understanding of Estévez's art only through the texts of the essays I have written about them. This is why the notion of interpretation in the second sense mentioned earlier, namely, as the text of Aquinas's *Commentary*, or in our case as the text of the essays presented here, is useful; both texts are instruments for producing understanding.

KINDS AND AIMS OF INTERPRETATIONS

One of the greatest sources of misunderstanding concerning interpretation is the belief that all interpretations have, or should have, the same aim.[5] This belief extends both to those who judge the value of particular interpretations and to those who engage in the production of interpretations. Before evaluating, or even setting out to develop, particular interpretations, it is helpful to have some clarity as to the most common aims that are pursued in interpretations. Before I list these, I should note that very seldom do interpreters pursue one and only one of the aims I list, even when they explicitly acknowledge that they are doing so. There is often a gap between the theory and the practice of interpretation. Moreover, most interpreters are not clear about the aims they pursue, except in a vague and an indeterminate way. With this in mind, let me now list some of the most common aims pursued in interpretation.

They break down into two general categories: interpretations that seek an understanding of *the meaning* of the object of interpretation, and interpretations that seek an understanding of *the relation* of the object of interpretation, or its meaning, to something else brought into the process by the interpreter.[6] The distinction Foucault makes between resemblance and similarity in the case of art may be useful in understanding part of what I have in mind here. For Foucault, according to the Principle of Resemblance, an interpretation is conceived and judged in terms of something else to which it is subordinated, whereas similarity is open and relational and has no particular direction that it must follow.[7] When an interpretation is based on resemblance, Foucault thinks it is tied to the object of resemblance, and therefore it is not completely open and free. If my aim is to understand how an object resembles another, then I have to stick to whatever is involved in that resemblance as dictated by that other object. But the situation changes when I am concerned with an interpretation based on similarity.

Consider an interpretation of Estévez's *Doctrine of Predestination*. This work is clearly about a Christian belief. In Foucault's language, we could say that if the interpretation is based on the resemblance between the painting and the belief, then the interpretation needs to consider the painting only insofar as it says something about predestination. Because of this, my interpretation cannot be the product of free associations—it must stick to the theological belief that inspired the work. However, if the interpretation is not based on resemblance, but on a similarity between the painting and the doctrine of predestination, then matters are different in that there is no subordination of the painting to the doctrine, only a relation between the two, which can be explored in a multiplicity of ways. The similarity between the painting and the doctrine can lead the interpretation in many directions, because similarity will depend on context and how the interpreter considers it. In the language I have introduced here, and using Foucault's insight, we could say that meaning interpretations are ruled by their objects of interpretation, whereas relational ones are not.

MEANING AND INTERPRETATIONS

The key to meaning interpretations is the meaning of the object of interpretation. But meaning is a controversial notion that breaks down into at least five categories, depending on how it is conceived: significance, reference, intention, ideas, and use.[8] The conception of meaning as significance is very general and applies easily to all sorts of things. The conceptions of meaning as reference, intention, ideas, and use apply particularly to language, although they also are used in other contexts, including art.

Meaning as Significance

Sometimes meaning is taken to involve importance, relevance, and consequences.[9] We speak of a particular event as having meaning because it has important historical repercussions, and we refer to something as being meaningful when it is considered relevant to something else. On the contrary, we dismiss the meaning of certain events because they have no important consequences, or we consider them irrelevant in particular contexts. Anything can have meaning or be meaningful, or lack meaning or be meaningless, in this sense, and so can art. The meaning of Picasso's *Les Demoiselles d'Avignon* (1907), for example, can be the historical fact that this painting initiated the most important twentieth-century art movement, namely, Cubism. And the meaning of Picasso's acquaintance with African masks accounts for the kinds of images he uses in some of his works.

Apart from speaking about meaning in the general sense of significance, which is easily applicable to all sorts of phenomena, we also use meaning in the context of language in particular. We speak about the meaning of words, sentences, or texts, although there are important differences in the views that have been proposed to account for the meaning of these, and not every theory applies to all of them. For example, the so-called Causal Theory, according to which meaning is explained in terms of a causal chain going all the way back to the first time the bearer of meaning was used, is intended to apply to names rather than sentences.[10] And the Verificationist Theory, proposed by the members of the Vienna Circle, according to which the meaning of a sentence is given in the account of the conditions under which it would be true, is not intended to account for the meaning of words.[11] Because of space limitations and our primary focus on art, I ignore the differences between theories of meaning applicable to words, sentences, or texts in particular and address meaning generally as it applies to all linguistic entities as well as to nonlinguistic phenomena.

Meaning as Reference

Sometimes meaning is used to indicate the reference of a bearer of meaning, or as it is often put in the case of words, the extension of a word.[12] The meaning of "Paul" is Paul, and the meaning of "human being" is the group of human beings. In the case of declarative sentences, their meanings are thought to be the facts expressed by the sentences. The meaning of "Estévez was born in Havana" is the fact that Estévez was born in that city. In this sense, meanings are neither in the mind (psychologism) nor in the head (physicalism) unless they happen to be mental or neurological entities, as is the case with the meanings of "thought" or "neuron." The referential view also is used in art.[13] The meaning of a portrait, for example, is the person of whom the portrait is the likeness. The meaning of Goya's *Portrait of the Duke of Alcutra* is the Duke of Alcutra.

The referential view of meaning appears to work well when applied to proper names that refer to existing persons. Something similar can be said about definite descriptions, such as "the current President of Bolivia" whose meaning is Evo Morales, or certain declarative sentences such as the one given earlier. But it is more difficult to apply it when the referents are fictitious characters such as Don Quixote or abstract entities such as justice, because it is not clear that such referents exist. Don Quixote is not a real person but a fictional character in a novel, and justice is an abstraction. The case of sentences also poses difficulties, for the status of facts has never been established convincingly. Other troubling cases are commands and exclamations insofar as these have meaning, and yet there seem to be no things to which they refer. What could be the reference of "Be kind in your judgment when you read this" or "Heavens!"?

In the case of art, it becomes difficult to use this theory for works in which fictional events are portrayed, such as one of Goya's Caprichos. But it is easier when the works depict events that actually took place, such as

Goya's *The Executions of the Third of May 1808,* whose referential meaning is the very executions supposedly depicted in the painting. Much contemporary art and thinking about art has been directed toward undermining both the referential view of meaning in art and also the primacy of the object that art is supposed to interpret.[14] Artists such as Klee and Kandinsky, according to Foucault, have claimed that painting, for example, has nothing to do with anything but itself.[15] Indeed, Foucault has argued that "the death of interpretation is to believe that there are signs. . . . The life of interpretation, on the contrary, is to believe that there are only interpretations."[16] For Foucault, interpretations should not assume that their objects, in this case, works of art, consist of signs with reference. Art is not composed of signs of things, and any interpretation that assumes that it does turns out to be a dead end.

Finally, there are cases in which two different bearers of meaning have the same reference but nonetheless appear to have different meanings. Consider "the painter of *Guernica*" and "the most famous artist of the twentieth century." Assuming that Picasso was the most famous artist of the twentieth century, the reference of these expressions is the same, but still the meanings of the two expressions seem to be different. In art, different works often refer to the same event or person, such as the many portraits of Thomas Jefferson, but again what they mean seems to be different, so here also there are difficulties.

Meaning as Intention

This view of meaning reduces meanings to the intentions users have to produce beliefs in listeners through the recognition of those intentions.[17] In this sense, meanings are regarded as states of mind. If I do not know English well, and in the morning I say to you, "Good evening," then it is clear that I do not mean what I say: I mean to wish you a good morning. This seems to make considerable sense, although there are difficulties. For example, it is not clear that anyone but the user of the language knows its meaning, which would make meanings private affairs, contrary to some of our most basic intuitions.

The matter becomes even more difficult when this view is applied to art. Consider *Guernica.* Does it make sense to say that the meaning of this work is the intention Picasso had when he painted it? Some would say that it does not, for at least three reasons. First, the meaning seems to have to do with the work itself, regardless of any intention Picasso may have had. Second, how can anyone but Picasso have access to his intention except through the very work in question? And third, the meaning of the work does not seem to be anything in Picasso's mind, whether an intention or any other state; the meaning of *Guernica* is a certain event and the horrors involved in it, and this does not appear to be anything mental.

Meaning as Ideas

Others adopt an ideational view of meaning, according to which meaning consists of ideas, although some of these authors would object to the use of the terms *idea* and *ideational* to refer to their views. Philosophers generally talk about this understanding of meaning as "intensional" when used in the context of texts or words, because the meaning is regarded as the intension of a linguistic term or expression. The meaning of "triangle" is "geometrical figure with three angles," and the meaning of "human being" is, say, "rational animal." Those who hold versions of this position differ in particular in their understanding of what these ideas or entities are, and whether they are nonmental forms, abstract objects, mental concepts or images, or the result of mental or neurological states.[18]

This view of meaning encounters various difficulties, depending on how ideas are conceived. For example, if they are taken to be forms or abstract objects independent of the mind, questions arise as to their status, origin, and relation to the mind. And if they are interpreted as mental concepts or images, or as mental or neurological states (or their results), it is not clear that they account for meaning, as was evident in the intentionalist view. It does not seem to make sense to say that the meaning of "cat" is the idea of cat when this is understood as a mental or physical state, for the mental or physical state whereby I think of cat is something very different from a cat.[19] Indeed, the language I would use to refer to it would be "the mental state whereby I think of cat" or "the physical state whereby I think of cat," rather than "cat."

In art this position is difficult to maintain across the board, for what do we make of abstract art? What is the idea behind a Jackson Pollock painting? But even not going to this extreme, it is unclear that the meaning of a work of art is an idea. The sensible dimension of a painting, for example, militates against this view. Indeed, even with literary works, the forms of the works seem important, as I have argued elsewhere using the example of Borges's *Pierre Menard, Author of the Quixote.*[20]

Meaning as Use

Some philosophers propose a conception of meaning as use,[21] and this is sometimes taken to entail that to understand the meaning of a sentence, say, is to know the conditions under which it can be asserted.[22] One way to understand this view is in relation to what Austin called an illocutionary act.[23] Consider an example. When I *say* to James, "James, apologize to your sister Clarisa," I utter a sentence. The act of uttering the sentence is a locutionary act. Apart from this act, the sentence may cause certain other acts, such as the act of *getting* James to apologize, which is also an act I perform. This is called the perlocutionary act. Finally, I also perform the act of *ordering* James to apologize, and this is an illocutionary act. Now the meaning of a text may be expressed in terms of the notion of an illocutionary act as follows: The meaning of a term is that in virtue of which one who performs a locutionary act also performs a certain illocutionary act. Unfortunately, there is no agreement on what this is exactly.[24]

One important disadvantage of the view of meaning as use is that it does not seem to work well with long texts or complex meaning bearers. It is difficult to think of all the illocutionary acts that take place when the locutionary acts involved in reciting or writing *War and Peace* are performed, and this raises questions of indeterminacy. Another is that in an effort to pinpoint the limits of meaning, some philosophers appeal to rules, but the status of these rules themselves and their source becomes a point of contention. In art, maintaining the use view of meaning becomes particularly difficult when one considers abstract art. Can we treat the abstract designs on a canvas as we do uttered words? Clearly there has been a performance, but it is questionable whether we can speak of a locution as such, let alone an illocution.

The views of meaning as significance, reference, intentions, ideas, and use have interesting implications for the particular case of the meaning of artworks, and some of them pose special problems. Consider, for example, the view that meanings are ideas, whether in human minds or outside of them. If they are abstract objects separate from human minds, then the question arises as to the existence, location, and eternity of these objects. Do they exist, and if so, where and since when? If they are eternal realities, are they caused or uncaused? The view that meanings are states of mind leads to the questions of what exactly they are in the mind and their relation to the brain and brain processes. And if meaning is taken to be use, then the matter of what use is, and the status of the rules governing it, becomes prominent. Is use a set of practices, or does it consist in certain dispositions? And if it consists in dispositions, then where are we to find them?

MEANING INTERPRETATIONS AND DETERMINANTS OF MEANING

Meaning can be further divided in four ways, depending on what determines it and what is included in it, as follows:

1. determined (i.e., understood or intended) by the author(s)

2. determined (i.e., understood) by a particular audience(s)

3. considered independently of what the author(s) or particular audience(s) understand(s)

4. including the implications of the meaning (taken in any one of the previous three ways in which the meaning is understood)

In (1), the interpreter seeks an understanding similar to the understanding the author(s) of the object of interpretation had of, or intended for, it—say what Aristotle thought he meant, or intended to mean, when he wrote "All men by nature desire to know," or what El Greco had in mind when he painted *The Burial of Count Orgaz*. Although there are various versions of this kind of interpretation, most of them are gathered under the general label "intentionalist."[25] These interpretations generally try to reveal what is often called "the mind of the author," that is, what the author thought the work meant, or what he or she intended to convey through it.[26] Note that I leave open the matter of the singular or plural nature of the author. The reason is that even in cases in which there is supposed to be only one author of a work or text, it turns out that often many other persons have had some input into it. Editors, for example, are certainly responsible for much that is present in a text as published, insofar as they add things and delete others, thus changing the identity of the text in the process.[27] And publishers sometimes crop images of artworks or place them next to others, and this has an impact on their meaning. The example of *The Burial of Count Orgaz* illustrates this point well, for the painting is located in a chapel, on top of the tomb of Count Orgaz. The body of the count portrayed in the painting is being lowered into its actual sarcophagus. Any depiction of just the painting, therefore, changes its impact, insofar as the setting is essential to it for a certain effect, and yet the setting is not part of the painting.

In (2), the interpreter pursues an understanding similar to that which a particular audience(s) had of it. For instance, interpreters might want to capture what Greeks contemporary with Aristotle understood by the opening sentence of his *Metaphysics*, what Basques contemporary with Picasso thought about *Guernica*, what scholastics understood by Aristotle's text, or what the forces loyal to Franco understood through *Guernica*.

In (3), the interpreter aims at an understanding of a work regardless of what its author(s) or any particular audience(s) understood it to mean—what "All men by nature desire to know" or *Guernica* means, independent of anyone's understanding of it, including the author(s). Whether there is such a meaning has been a matter of debate among philosophers, but the issue does not need to be settled here, because the notion of a meaning of a work apart from both audience and author meanings is common.[28]

In (4), the interpreter wishes to achieve an understanding not just of the meaning of the work in any of the particular ways mentioned but also of its implications—the issue is not to understand, say, just what Aristotle and Picasso understood when they produced the items to which we are referring but also the implications of what they understood and of which they may or may not have been aware at the time. This assumes that meaning does not necessarily include implications. The meaning of "Humans are animals, and animals are material" may, or may not, include that humans are material, even if that is a logical consequence of it. Some authors argue it does, whereas others claim it does not. The matter hinges in part on whether one approaches meaning logically or psychologically. If meaning is approached logically, then logical implications must be included, but if meaning is approached psychologically, then they do not. The meaning of "Humans are animals, and animals are material" logically includes, because it implies it, the meaning of "Humans are material." But to be psychologically aware of the first does not carry with it an awareness of the second.[29]

RELATIONAL INTERPRETATIONS

So much for interpretations whose aim is the understanding of the meaning of an object of interpretation. The other general aim of interpretations involves understanding the relation of an object of interpretation, or its meaning, to something else. Because this something else can be practically anything, the possibilities are vast. Interpreters may seek to understand the relation between an object of interpretation and many kinds of things. If, for example, the object of interpretation is a text, then here are some possibilities: a text and another text—Aristotle's *Metaphysics* and Aristotle's *Physics*; a text and a date—Aristotle's *Metaphysics* and the date of his birth; a view expressed by a text and the view expressed by some other text—Aristotle's view of forms put forth in the *Metaphysics* and Plato's view of them as presented in the *Parmenides*; the meaning of a text and one or more historical events—the meaning of Plato's *Apology* and Socrates' trial; a text and a person, whether the author or someone else—Plato's *Crito* and Socrates; and so on.

The same applies to art. One thing is to try to understand the meaning of a work, in any one of the four senses discussed, and another is to understand the relation of the work, or its meaning, to something else. In the case of Estévez's *Difficult Loves,* I have interpreted the painting as a springboard for the philosophical understanding of race. But other interpretations are possible. Carolyn Korsmeyer tells me that when she first looked at the painting, she thought it had to do with a yearning for knowledge of the species, desire for perfection, or a projection of a fantasy. Other audiences, I am sure, would have other understandings of it. And all of this will depend on context and what interpreters aim to do and bring with them.

Of course, interpreters may intend to produce an understanding of the meaning of a work, and not of its relation to something else, but nonetheless may hold that the only way to produce such understanding is through something outside of the work that they bring into the process. A Freudian interpreter of Bram Stoker's *Dracula* may want to understand the meaning of the novel but also hold that the only way to understand it is in terms of Freudian theory: Freudian theory is the means necessary to get at the work, just as Greek is a necessary means to get at Aristotle's *Metaphysics*. In this case, the interpretation intended is the meaning kind, but the interpreter has a view of the world or of the method of producing interpretations that makes it necessary to relate the work to Freudian theory. This meaning interpretation comes with certain baggage, and the relevance of the baggage can be put into a question: Does Freudian theory really make sense in relation to a particular work? Is Freudian theory necessary to understand *Dracula?* In cases such as this, we have several issues at stake: the interpreter's commitment to a certain theory, the interpreter's commitment to a certain theory as a proper means of interpreting a work, and the accuracy and effectiveness with which such a theory is applied. It is important to keep these in mind when judging an interpretation.

Most interpreters engage in the interpretative process without a clear distinction between meaning and relational interpretations in mind and often mix different kinds of interpretations and objectives. Meaning interpretations often contain relational elements. Most interpretations of Aristotle's *Metaphysics* refer to historical facts that are not part of the text, and thus are brought into the interpretive process by interpreters. The point to keep in mind, however, is that the establishment of the relation of these facts to the work need not be the primary function of the interpretation. And, indeed, if what we aim to have is a meaning interpretation, whose function is to understand the meaning of the work, then the relations the work has with these facts can be used merely as ways to enhance that primary function. Only when these facts are brought in to produce some other kind of understanding, such as the relation of the work to a historical period, does the interpretation become relational.

Most relational interpretations of a work do not ignore the work or its meaning, but they are mediated through the primary aim of causing some other effect or achieving some other end, such as relating the work to a historical event. Still, although meaning and relational interpretations are seldom found in isolation from each other, and there are relational elements in meaning interpretations and meaning elements in relational interpretations, it is useful to preserve this distinction in order to facilitate the understanding of interpretations and their connection to the works they interpret.

The factors interpreters bring into relational interpretations are too numerous to list here. They may involve the discipline in which the interpretation is provided, personal experiences, ideological agendas, conceptual assumptions, sensory constraints, and so on. Many of these are commonly used, but when conceptual schemes are applied to the views presented in a text, these interpretations are singled out sometimes by referring to them as theory-laden.[30] What kinds of conceptual schemes are these? Here are some examples: feminist, Freudian, Marxist, Thomist, sociological, psychological, theological, and literary. One may, for instance, attempt to understand Aristotle's "All men by nature desire to know" in terms of a feminist scheme. Under these conditions, it becomes important to relate Aristotle's text and its meaning to feminist principles and to see how Aristotle's thinking as revealed by this sentence includes a particular view of women. The same can be applied in other cases, as happens in art. We could look at Goya's *The Executions of the Third of May 1808* and interpret it through certain political lenses, a Marxist critique, or even a certain view of art. And we could interpret Estévez's *Shared Kingdoms* in feminist terms, or as referring to the ultimate nature of the universe, or as a social commentary, and so on. In my essay on Estévez's *Waverings of Faith,* I provided two ways of understanding the identity of the puppet, as faith itself, or as the believer who has faith. Both seem possible.

In order to achieve the various ends pursued in interpretations, it is necessary to adopt particular procedures. So we need to turn next to some of the ways in which interpreters approach their task. Before I do this, however, let me make sure we understand that the notion of meaning as significance is not confused with the notion of a relational interpretation. Superficially they would seem to be the same thing: the significance of X amounts to relating X to Y—the significance of Picasso's *Les Demoiselles d'Avignon* is its relation to Cubism. However, this is not quite right, in two respects. Recall that an interpretation is either an understanding or an instrument of understanding. The significance of something is neither an understanding nor an instrument of understanding. Significance is a relationship that something has to something else. There is an important ontological difference here: these are two different entities. Second, the understanding of the significance of something can qualify as a meaning interpretation, as long as the aim is the significance of the meaning of the work and not the significance taken as the understanding of a relation to a term the interpreter brings in. Again, these are two different things. One is the understanding of the significance of *Les Demoiselles d'Avignon* and another the understanding of the relation of this work to Freudian theory.

Still, someone might object that the understanding of the meaning of Picasso's work as the significance it had for Cubism (i.e., a meaning interpretation) is not really different from the understanding of the relation the work had to Cubism (i.e., a relational interpretation). And the answer is that there is an important difference, even if in fact the interpretations appear to be the same. The difference is in the aim, because the different aims (i.e., the understanding of the meaning of the work vs. the understanding of the relation of the work to something brought in by the interpreter) create a different interpretive dynamic that may give rise to other understandings, even if, in fact, in certain cases the understandings coincide. Something may have two functions, but this does not entail that the functions are the same, just as it happens with a proper name that elicits two different understandings. For some people "Jorge Gracia" means "the philosophy professor at the University at Buffalo who was born in Cuba," and for others it means "the grandfather of Sofia and Eva."

FACTORS IN INTERPRETATION

The approach to be used in interpretation directly depends, quite naturally, on the aim pursued, but certain factors seem to be conditions of all interpretations. For example, it is essential to any interpretation that the object of interpretation be identified, and to make clear that it is regarded as falling under a certain description.[31] Let me begin by distinguishing between general and specific factors that affect interpretation in the case of texts and then turn to works of art. The reason I begin with texts is that these are often taken as paradigmatic objects of interpretation.

At least four factors stand out when we are dealing with the interpretation of texts: linguistic, logical, historical, and cultural. As groups of signs used to convey meaning, texts are linguistic entities, and for interpreters to deal with them effectively, they are required to know the languages of the texts (i.e., the meaning of the words used and the rules according to which the words are put together). This kind of linguistic information is essential to the interpretation of any text. Without it, interpreters are powerless to understand texts.

Logic also is essential. Most texts are intended to convey meaning, and this generally includes concepts and their interrelations. Philosophical texts in particular often contain claims and arguments to support those claims, and logical analysis is necessary for the understanding of these, in that it is in logic that we learn the rules that reveal the structures of both arguments and complex claims.

Historical facts are indispensable for interpretation, although this is sometimes disputed. Some philosophers claim that an interpreter is not required to know anything historical about a text, particularly a literary one. Interpreters need only be interested in what a text tells them and not in anything surrounding its history, including the identity of the author or the audience of the text at the time of its composition.[32]

But can we even know that something is a text if we do not have some historical information about it? Some texts from past cultures look like artistic or decorative designs (consider Mayan and Egyptian glyphs), and it is only through the historical facts that surround them that we are able to tell they are texts. Some of these facts, such as dates, places, and the identity of authors, seem at least important, if not indispensable, for their understanding. In certain interpretations these factors play more substantive roles than in others, but in most they play at least some role.

A fourth factor involved in the interpretation of texts is culture. Language is part of culture, but I have already singled out language, so now I am concerned with other cultural factors. Culture has to do with practices in which groups of people engage and views they have. Among other functions, these practices serve to give meaning and significance to what members of these groups do and make. And these groups produce texts that make sense only when considered in the context of the groups' practices and views. We cannot judge that something is a text when it is taken out of its cultural context, insofar as the latter provides us with the criteria to identify it. Figures and lines arranged on a wall are a text only if they are used as signs to convey meaning, and this is possible only if there is an actual draftsman and one or more actual or potential recipients that share some practices and views. Otherwise, there could be no communication and therefore no text. In a Wittgensteinian twist, one might say that texts are the products of ways of living or forms of life, so that knowledge of those ways or forms is essential for their identification and understanding. To play the textual game, one must know the rules, and the rules are supplied by culture.

The exclusive consideration of any of these four general factors yields a different approach to interpretation: linguistic, logical, historical, and cultural. But none of the approaches is by itself methodologically complete; all four factors need to be taken into account if interpretations are going to be accurate and sensible and not fall into anachronism. Imagine for a moment that logic is emphasized to the detriment of the other factors mentioned. How could the interpreter guard against linguistic mistakes, anachronisms, and cultural inaccuracies?

Apart from general factors that apply to all textual interpretations, there are specific factors that need to be taken into account for particular kinds of interpretations. Because the number of the possible kinds of interpretations is indeterminate, there is no point in even attempting to list them. A couple of examples should suffice.

Consider the case of theological interpretations. If interpreters seek to provide a theological understanding of a text, then it is essential to presuppose the theology.[33] This supplies all kinds of principles, some of which are hermeneutical. A Roman Catholic interpretation of the Bible presumes that no interpretation of it can contradict established Roman Catholic doctrine. Texts that speak of Christ having brothers must be understood to be referring to cousins. Something similar applies to Freudian interpretations. In this case, Freud's theories about the unconscious, the libido, and so on are presupposed, for the task of the interpreter is to understand the text in relation to them.

Visual art poses different challenges than texts. The relation of this art and texts is complicated. On the one hand, the titles of the works are texts. The title of Estévez's *Doctrine of Predestination* indicates that the work is intended to address a certain theological doctrine. But, on the other hand, some titles are not descriptive. The common "untitled" is a case in point. Moreover, some works of art include texts. Estévez's *Undetermined Being* has an inscription on a column that reads: "The meaning of life is its lack of meaning. The essence of being consists in its incompleteness." Still, most works of visual art do not include texts. Most paintings have no texts in them, and it is only in certain periods that texts are more frequently part of these works. Most of Estévez's works discussed in this book have no texts in them, except for the titles, and some others contain mostly numbers, such as *Numerical Thoughts. No One Can See through My Eyes* has no texts, numbers, or linguistic signs of any kind, and this makes a great difference for the interpretation of the piece and particularly its philosophical understanding. The interpretative requirements of textuality do not generally apply to art, and even when they apply they do not do so in the same way that they do with texts that have no visual illustrative context.

In addition, much art that carries a conceptual message uses symbols to convey it, but much art is nonsymbolic. Generally, abstract art is of the latter sort. Still, symbolism is a common feature of art and has been popular in certain historical periods. One need think only of medieval art to illustrate the point or of Bosch's *The Garden of Earthly Delights.* And the puppet in Estévez's *Waverings of Faith* seems to be a symbol for the control to which humans may be subjected. The procedures involved in the interpretation of symbols play an important role in the interpretation of some art. This entails the recognition of symbolic meaning and the tools to unravel the messages conveyed. In early Christian art, where a fish was an important symbol for the identification of the Christian community, art that integrated it required that the interpreter be aware of the symbol and how it was supposed to be understood. The image of the fisherman has been a symbol of the search for information and knowledge from ancient times. Augustine uses it, for example, in *The Teacher*, and Plato repeatedly refers to it in his Dialogues. It is not surprising, then, that we find it in Estévez's *Self-fishing*. The way some symbols are used is not unlike the way words are used, which is a requirement of textual interpretation, although symbolism has different rules.

Finally, the interpretation of art is heavily influenced by two other factors: changes in medium and interpretative traditions. The first is obvious when we consider three of Estévez's works. *No One Can See through My Eyes* functions differently than *Stationary Journey;* one is a sculpture/installation, whereas the other is a flat painting. And both of these pieces work differently than *Bottles to Sea,* because the last one involves drawing, performance, and the element of chance.[34] The three-dimensional character of the first piece makes it easy for observers to become integrated into the installation's space and to identify with the central sculpture. In the painting, we more easily become detached observers, both because of the two-dimensional quality and the machinelike, artifactual character of much of the images in it. And in the performance, we participate in the event.

The second factor that heavily influences the interpretation of art is interpretative traditions, for symbols and motifs are part of these traditions. The connection between fishing and knowing, mentioned earlier, is a good example of this in Estévez's art. Another is the use of puppets, which suggests the control to which humans are subjected, or the depiction of balloons, with the implication of flights of the imagination.

In sum, the way one approaches an object of interpretation and the method one uses to interpret it will depend on the aim pursued, but general requirements also apply to all interpretations and make certain hermeneutical procedures indispensable, which have to do, among other things, with language, logic, history, and culture. In addition, the character of interpretations depends on specific factors related to the kind of interpretation; one thing is to provide film interpretations of a novel and another is to do a philosophical interpretation of a work of art. Finally, changes in medium and interpretational traditions cannot be ignored. The passage from image to discourse is significant, and past interpretations prepare the way for present ones.

SOME QUESTIONS ABOUT INTERPRETATION

This leads us to some general questions that the philosopher interested in the interpretation of art might ask:

1. What are the aims that interpreters have pursued in interpretation?

2. How have interpreters pursued these aims?

3. How successful have interpreters been?

4. What do answers (1)–(3) tell us about interpreters themselves and
    the period in which they lived?

5. What do these answers reveal about the objects of interpretation,
    if anything?

Answers to these questions call for careful attention and the exegesis
of particular interpretations to yield hermeneutical information. The first two
questions require historical answers. The third question aims at a value judgment, which can take place based on two different sets of criteria, depending
on whether the criteria are those according to which interpreters themselves
would judge their interpretations or are criteria brought into play by others
who seek to judge the success of the interpretations. The answers to the last
two questions are particularly important historically and philosophically, for
they are supposed to uncover not only significant aspects of the philosophy
of the interpreters but hopefully, in our context, something about art itself
that otherwise might not be noticed.

The tasks, however, required for answering (3)–(5) involve different
approaches from those needed to answer (1) and (2). The answer to (3)
requires the application of evaluative criteria to conclusions concerning aims
and procedures previously established. And the answers to (4) and (5) entail
drawing generalizations about the conclusions reached in answer to the first two
questions, exploring relations between particular conclusions and the pertinent
phenomena of the period and comparing what these interpretations propose with
the standard or prevalent understandings of the objects of interpretation.

Answers to (4) and (5) are facilitated and can potentially yield more
rewarding results if interpretations of the same objects of interpretation by
interpreters from different philosophical traditions and historical periods are
compared. Each person, each philosophical tradition, and each age will view
objects of interpretation from unique historical vantage points. This is to
say that they see them through sets of presuppositions, biases, and interests.
Moreover, individual perspectives are affected by traditions embedded in the
age of the interpreters, but the reverse also takes place. Some of the work of
Estévez appears to have an archaic quality to us because of its Renaissance-
like drawings, but it would not look archaic to a sixteenth-century audience.
Indeed, it would probably look futuristic.

Interpreters live in houses with different windows. Some houses have
large windows, some small; some have windows only on one side, others have
windows on more than one side; some have windows covered by blue glass,
and some by pink glass; some have square windows, others have rectangular,

octagonal, or circular ones; and some have windows located high up, near the ceiling, and others have them located way down, near the floor. Those who dwell in these houses may have very different views when they look out through the windows. Some see more than others; some see a landscape tinted by a certain color; the sight of some is framed by an octagonal shape but that of others by a square one; and so on. All of these perspectives yield information about what is outside of the house, even if only fragmentary and affected by a vantage point.

The same is true of the interpretation of art. The understanding that interpreters get from artworks is always mediated by their own individual, cultural, philosophical, and historical perspectives. When we examine these and compare them with ours, we discover something about the artworks themselves. But perhaps even more important, we discover something about ourselves. Perhaps the greatest benefit of the study of art is precisely that it gives us a deeper understanding of ourselves through the understanding we have of others. This same benefit is found in the study of the various interpretations to which artworks have been subjected, except that the benefit is even greater in this case, insofar as the focus on particular works and their understanding by others through history reveals more clearly and easily the perspectives from which others, and consequently ourselves, view them.

We can learn more about who we are by looking at how we, and others, look at something else. Self-reflection is a difficult thing because of the obstacles we encounter to observe ourselves objectively and directly. Indeed, we cannot; we always need a mirror to do so. But even when we examine our interpretations and compare them to those of others, we can indirectly and objectively become the objects of reflection; we understand ourselves through the understanding that others and we have of something else. To put it in Danto's eloquent statement: ". . . the Brillo Box . . . does what works of art have always done—externalizing a way of viewing the world, expressing the interior of a cultural period, offering itself as a mirror to catch the conscience of our kings."[35] And, I would add, of ourselves.

The study of the interpretation of art has an important role to play in doing philosophy, for it opens the way to self-knowledge and this is, as Socrates knew only too well, the beginning of wisdom. Without self-knowledge, we are not very different from nonhuman animals. The morals to be learned from the interpretations contained in this book, then, belong to philosophy and not just to history. This lesson is quite obvious from Estévez's *Self-fishing*, where it is suggested that wisdom is within us, but that we have no access to it unless we objectify it by fishing it out, as it were, or, as Socrates would have us do, by engaging in a process of self-discovery.

Still, one may ask, do not some interpretations create obfuscation rather than enlightenment? Are there limits to the interpretation of art, particularly its philosophical interpretation? In short, what is the boundary between the use and abuse of art by philosophers?

USES AND ABUSES IN INTERPRETATION

To paraphrase Nietzsche, the use or abuse of art by interpreters depends very much on the kind of aim interpreters pursue and the hermeneutical assumptions they make.[36] Consider the common view mentioned earlier, according to which the aim of an interpretation is to discover or reveal the intention of the author. Obviously if one adopts this kind of interpretation as paradigmatic, then any other kind will appear inadequate. An interpretation that provides an understanding of what an audience understands, makes explicit a meaning independent of the author's meaning, or includes in it implications of which the author was unaware would constitute an abuse. Even more inadequate and illegitimate would be interpretations that seek to relate a work or its meaning to factors the interpreter brings into the picture that were not considered by the author. Indeed, these are the grounds on which many oppose feminist, Marxist, or Freudian interpretations, for example.

If we were to adopt the authorial point of view and apply it to the philosophical interpretation of art, then we would be limited in trying to understand what the artist, and only the artist, understood by the work. What did Estévez have in mind when he painted *Shared Kingdoms?* Was he concerned only with his marriage, for example? If so, the interpretation I have provided, which sees in the painting a general philosophy about male and female perspectives, would be abusive.

On the other hand, one may adopt Foucault's view, according to which the author of a work is a mere fiction invented by an interpreter, a view explored with subtlety by Borges in *Pierre Menard, Author of the Quixote.* If so, interpretations that seek to determine the mind of the author are illegitimate and spurious and for this reason should be considered inappropriate.[37] In these terms, Estévez's understanding of the significance of *Shared Kingdoms* would be irrelevant to the interpretation of the work. What would matter is merely what *I* or *you* understand by it.

Obviously a legitimate interpretation of a work, that is, what is considered its legitimate understanding, depends on the aim pursued. There are no absolute criteria to judge the legitimate use or the illegitimate abuse of a work. Criteria of interpretation vary and depend on aim. A common mistake is to assume the opposite, namely, that there are absolute standards of interpretation that apply in all cases and contexts. Many of those who defend the value of authorial interpretation adopt this point of view. They fail to see that interpretations may have many different aims, and this affects the rules they need to follow and the criteria that should be used to evaluate them.[38]

The dependence of legitimacy on the end pursued does not mean that there are no criteria to determine legitimacy, that anything goes, so to speak. Indeed, often the end will establish parameters of legitimacy. If the aim is to discover the mind of the author, then it is obvious that relational interpretations will not generally do. If the aim is to understand what Aristotle meant in the *Metaphysics*, then any attempt to relate this text to Christian principles would appear abusive. In this context, Aquinas's understanding of Aristotle's Unmoved Mover as the Christian God would be illegitimate and abusive. But if the aim of the interpretation is not the mind of the author, that is, what Aristotle thought, but rather the relation of Aristotle's thought to Christian principles, then Aquinas's interpretation is not ipso facto illegitimate.

Something similar applies to art. If the aim of the interpretations of Estévez's work given earlier were to find out Estévez's views about the significance of his art, then much that is included in the first part of this book may be taken as abusive. But if the aim pursued is not Estévez's mind, then this judgment is inappropriate without the appropriate consideration of that aim. Keeping in mind the relevance of the aim to judge legitimacy, readers can look at the interpretations included in this volume and place them more easily within a perspective that will allow them to understand and judge their legitimacy and value.

One more point needs to be made before I turn to art in the next chapter. Our present context is the interpretation of art, not its use, and interpretation must be distinguished from use, even if use may entail interpretation in some cases, and vice versa. An interpretation is supposed to be focused on an object, its meaning, or its relation to something else that is intended. The focus of use is not an object of interpretation but something else for which the object becomes an example, illustration, or something along those lines. The use of literature in philosophy, for instance, takes this form when a philosopher refers to a fictional story or character to make clear the value of a philosophical thesis, such as happens with Plato's use of the Myth of the Cave in *The Republic* to illustrate the epistemic condition of humans. And the use of Estévez's *Forging People* on a poster for the conference "Forging People: Race, Ethnicity, and Nationality in Latin American and Latino Thought" was intended to draw audiences' attention to the topic of the conference rather than to make them understand anything about the work.[39] If this is so, then one might want to argue that some of the texts I have provided earlier in the context of particular artworks by Estévez are not in fact interpretations, but rather uses of the works for philosophical purposes. And I am not sure this claim is without grounds, which points to the difficulty of being able to draw a clear line between interpretation and use.

21

Art

The nature of art is one of the most disputed topics in aesthetics. Several accounts of these developments in the twentieth century have been produced, including well-known studies by Noël Carroll and Stephen Davies.[1] The controversy has taken many turns. Some of it has to do with an effort, under the influence of Wittgenstein, to question the very possibility of defining art.[2] The success of this enterprise, as Carroll has pointed out, culminates with the publication of Monroe Beardsley's *Aesthetics* (1958), which in contrast with previous books of this sort contains no definition of art. Subsequent work, however, has moved in a different direction, coming back to efforts to define art in various ways in terms of aesthetic qualities, society, and history. Among the most salient have been the institutional understanding championed by George Dickie, Joseph Margolis's conception of artworks as culturally emergent entities that are identified and individuated in historical contexts, Arthur Danto's notion of art as the embodiment of the meaning of something else, Marcia Muelder Eaton's emphasis on communities, and Stephen Davies's introduction of a transcultural aesthetic of universal appeal to humans. To this must be added recent discussions of the social dimensions of art that try to take into account gender, race, and ethnicity, among other social phenomena.

Obviously this is not the place to examine these many and complex views, let alone evaluate their relative merits. Within the confines of the present project, I can consider only a more modest task. I propose to use a position I have defended elsewhere to address our general topic, beginning with the distinction between art objects and aesthetic objects.[3]

ART OBJECTS AND AESTHETIC OBJECTS

Let us begin with a working definition of an art object:[4]

An art object is an artifact capable of producing an artistic experience.

177

Art objects are artifacts rather than natural entities, the latter being objects that do not fulfill all the conditions of artifactuality. But what is an artifact? Here is my understanding of it:

> An artifact is an object that is either the product of intentional activity and design or, not being the product of intentional activity and design, has nonetheless undergone some change or its context has undergone some change, the change in either case is the product of intentional activity and design and the object is considered in the context where the change has occurred rather than apart from it.[5]

A sunset, a valley, a rock, and a tree are examples of objects that result from processes in which intention and design play no role. Examples of artifacts are such things as a chair, a house, a computer, and a piece of paper. None of the latter is necessarily an art object, even though all four are products of intentional activity and design. This is why a second condition is necessary.

For something to be an art object, it also must be capable of producing an artistic experience. Everything that is both an artifact and capable of producing an artistic experience is an art object. Chairs, tables, and piles of bricks can be art objects, provided that they are capable of producing an artistic experience, a point that was dramatically made in the last century by Marcel Duchamp with his urinals, wine bottle racks, and other ready-mades.

This leaves open the question of what makes an object capable of producing an artistic experience. This is an important question for philosophers of art, because an answer must be given to it if the possibility that all artifacts qualify as art objects is to be precluded. To provide a satisfactory answer here is quite impossible, but I nonetheless clarify the matter in a way sufficient for our limited aims.[6] I propose to understand an object capable of producing an artistic experience in the following way:

> Something is capable of producing an artistic experience just when it is regarded by someone both as an artifact and as capable of producing an aesthetic experience.[7]

The category "artistic" is included within the category "aesthetic," but it is limited both by the recognition of the artifactual nature of the object that gives rise to the experience and by the historical character of the experience.[8] The object of an artistic experience must be regarded by someone as an artifact at some time and place and capable of producing an aesthetic experience.[9] This way of unpacking the notion of the artistic allows us to exclude all sorts of artifacts from the category of art object, namely, those artifacts that have not been regarded as artifacts by someone at some time and place or have not been regarded as capable of producing an aesthetic experience. It also allows us to make room for changing historical perceptions of what an art object is. The nineteenth century did not consider a pile of bricks, a urinal, or a crucifix dipped in urine artistic because they were not regarded as being capable of producing an aesthetic experience but examples of these objects have been considered artistic in the twentieth century, as the work of Duchamp and Serrano demonstrates. Finally, this understanding of artistic also permits us to ignore the intention, or lack thereof, of the artist. Artifacts not intended as art by their authors may become art as long as they are regarded as artifacts and capable of producing an artistic experience by someone else. Much folk art produced in the nineteenth century, for example, was not regarded by their authors as art, yet some of it is considered art today.[10] A case in point might be the work of Martín Ramírez, whose drawings were made while he was a patient in a mental institution and bypassed the art establishment.

I have not addressed the question of the identity and number of the regarding persons to which I refer because it is largely irrelevant to the issue at hand. As long as an object is regarded as an artifact, capable of producing an aesthetic experience, it must be considered capable of producing an artistic experience. This does not mean that it is good art; for that, some other conditions are required. The condition so frequently assumed, that all art must be good, is surely mistaken. No car needs to run well in order to be a car, and no person needs to be moral in order to be a person. Bad cars are cars, and bad persons are persons, and the case of art should not be different. The degree of the value of an entity does not enter into its nature, although many have thought it does, at least in some cases, as Anselm argues about God in the *Proslogion*.

The difference between art objects and aesthetic objects can be gathered from what has been said. Aesthetic objects do not need to satisfy either of the two conditions that art objects have to satisfy. Aesthetic objects can be products of nature.[11] This is the case, for example, with a sunset. But this does not mean that aesthetic objects cannot be the product of art. Botticelli's *The Birth of Venus* is a product of human art, and yet it is certainly an aesthetic object. Furthermore, aesthetic objects need not be regarded as capable of producing an artistic experience. That is, they need not be recognized as both artifactual and as capable of producing an aesthetic experience.

The sole condition of an aesthetic object is its capacity to produce an aesthetic experience in a subject. An object may be an aesthetic object whether someone actually thinks of it as such or not, and whether it has actually produced an aesthetic experience or not, and, finally, whether it is an artifact or not.

At this point the question may be raised as to what makes an experience aesthetic and what in an object can cause it, which are certainly important questions for the philosopher of art.[12] Indeed, to preclude the possibility that all objects qualify as aesthetic objects, these questions must be answered, and some criteria of demarcation must be found. But I do not need to answer them for my present purposes, because my concern in this book is not with aesthetic objects as such but rather with the philosophical interpretation of whatever is taken to be an art object.

Art objects are aesthetic objects because they are capable of producing aesthetic experiences in subjects, and aesthetic objects can be art objects if they are regarded as artifacts capable of producing aesthetic experiences, although they need not be so. This leaves open the possibility that there may be aesthetic objects that are not art objects in addition to objects that are both art objects and aesthetic objects. A sunset is an aesthetic object that is not art, and Botticelli's *The Birth of Venus* is both an aesthetic object and a work of art.[13] Whether there are objects that are neither depends on how the notion of aesthetic experience is unpacked.

The notion of object I have been using is broad and includes properties and actions. Much art consists of objects considered in a narrow, Aristotelian sense of substance, in which they are not properties of anything else. Aristotle defined a substance in *Categories* as what is neither predicable nor part of something else. Such is the case with sculptures, for example. But much art consists of entities that exist only parasitically in other entities, as parts or properties of them, for example, drawings and dances. Art objects, like artifacts, can have diverse ontological status.

Having adopted a way of distinguishing between art objects and aesthetic objects, we can now turn to the question of what distinction, if any, there is between these objects and texts. This is important here for two reasons. One is that the notion of interpretation often is developed in the context of texts, and many have argued that there is no clear distinction between the two. Another is that one of the difficulties noted earlier to the philosophical interpretation of visual art is that philosophy is generally expressed textually, whereas visual art is not.

ART OBJECTS, AESTHETIC OBJECTS, AND TEXTS

Let me borrow the following view of texts I have defended elsewhere:

> A text is a group of entities, used as signs, which are selected, arranged, and intended by an author in a certain context to convey some specific meaning to an audience.[14]

From this conception follows, on the one hand, that texts can be aesthetic objects. There is no reason a physical text, for example, either as a result of its physical appearance or of the images that its meaning may give rise to, cannot produce an aesthetic experience in a subject. Calligrams may produce an aesthetic experience even in those who do not understand the meaning of the words of which they are composed, because of the peculiar shape they have. And some Egyptian hieroglyphs are quite beautiful, and beauty is one of the properties associated with the aesthetic. Moreover, the meaning of a text may produce an aesthetic experience in a reader resulting from the images it conjures up.

On the other hand, the production of, or the capacity to produce, an aesthetic experience in a subject is not a necessary or sufficient condition of a text. Someone could argue that all texts may, in principle, be objects of aesthetic experience at some point and in some context, although I very much doubt that anyone could derive an aesthetic experience from reading Kant's *Critique of Pure Reason*, *The Chicago Manual of Style*, or the list of items I needed to buy when I went to the grocery store last Friday.[15] But that would not make texts particularly aesthetic in nature; indeed, to say that would be to say no more than what one could say about any other object, whether natural or artifactual. In either case, the production of, or the capacity to produce, an aesthetic experience in a subject is not part of what makes something a text. Aesthetic objects and texts do not necessarily share any characteristics.

The relation between art objects and texts is different, in that they do share some fundamental properties. The most obvious one is that both are artifacts, that is, products of intentional activity and design. This property, although essential to both, would not be sufficient to identify texts with art objects, or vice versa. However, another element seems to tie them more strongly: texts and art objects are intended to produce some changes in subjects. In the case of texts, it is understanding, among other things, and in the case of art objects, it is the artistic experience. Indeed, the language used to talk about texts and art objects is sometimes interchanged. We frequently hear art critics speak of an art object, such as a painting or a sculpture, as subject to "reading." They ask, for example: What is your reading of that work of art? And language normally applied to art objects also is frequently associated with texts. We often talk about "seeing" something in a letter, for example.

The two properties common to art objects and texts that have been noted indicate also that they have something else in common; both have authors and are meant for audiences: the first, because they are products of intentional activity and design, and the second, because they are intended to produce a change in someone. All of this is further supported by the existence of texts that also are generally accepted as art objects, and vice versa. Entire literary genres fall into this category, such as poetry and the novel.

Bearing in mind that, first, some properties of art objects and texts overlap and, second, some art objects are unquestionably texts, we may ask whether all art objects are texts, whether all texts are art objects, or whether these categories simply overlap. The view that classifies all texts as art objects is neither viable nor popular. In ordinary discourse, we regard many things as texts that are not art objects, as the examples already given illustrate. I have not yet encountered anyone who would claim that the texts of Kant's *Critique of Pure Reason* and *The Chicago Manual of Style* are artistic. Undoubtedly, some texts are not art objects.

But the converse position is not so clearly counterintuitive, and some philosophers speak as if all art objects were texts. If we wish to argue that the extensions of "art object" and "text" do not coincide, then we must find some feature common to all texts that is not necessarily shared by all art objects, or alternatively, some feature of all art objects that is not necessarily shared by all texts.

One could, in principle, argue that not all texts are art objects, because somehow the entities that constitute texts are different sorts of entities from the entities that constitute art objects. However, that will not do, because any sort of entity whatever may function as a text, and the same seems to apply to art objects. The reasons for distinction between texts and art objects must be found elsewhere.

Three possibilities look promising. Texts are composed of signs, but signs themselves have meaning, so texts are composed of entities that are themselves meaningful. Some art objects are, like texts, composed of signs that have meaning. Novels, poems, and even paintings can have parts endowed with meaning. The words in a poem by T. S. Eliot and the pictorial symbols in Bosch's *The Garden of Earthly Delights* have meaning and function as signs, but not all art objects are composed of signs. It would be difficult to find any signs in a painting by Pollock, for example. Abstract art in general seems to be composed of shapes that by themselves do not express anything, and only the complete work of art may be said to have meaning (if it has any at all). Here, then, we have a property common to texts that not all art objects share.

A second factor also separates art objects and texts: although art objects share with texts that they are intended by authors for audiences, they are meant to do different things. Texts are always intended to convey meaning, even if the authors have other and even more fundamental intentions as well. Now, we do speak of meaning as purpose, significance, relevance, and the like, as we saw earlier, but the meaning that texts qua texts aim to convey includes the sort that results in propositional understanding. In contrast, art objects are not generally intended to convey meaning of this sort to audiences.

Thus although both art objects and texts are intended for audiences, art objects need not be texts. For an object to be classified as art, it must have more than a propositional meaning—it must be regarded as capable of producing an artistic experience. It is not the propositional aspect of an object at all that makes it art but whatever artistic experience it is thought to be capable of producing. Many art objects produce understanding; didactic art, political art, and so-called representational art fit this bill. The famous Romanesque sculptural ensemble, *Pórtico de la Gloria*, in Santiago de Compostela, clearly contains a lesson; Mexican muralists often used art as a political instrument to undermine what they considered corruption and oppression, as José Clemente Orozco did in *Hispano-América*; and Jacques-Louis David's *Coronation of Napoleon* ideally represents Napoleon's coronation and makes a point about his legitimacy and power. But even these works differ from texts in that, in addition to what they might propositionally say, there is also a nonpropositional effect they are thought to produce, or to be able to produce, in their audiences.

I should make clear at this point that I do not mean to hold that the criterion of meaning is verifiability, and least of all empirical verifiability. If verifiability were the criterion of meaning, then commands, questions, and requests would not have meaning, and yet it seems difficult to argue that they do not. Moreover, if that were the case, then texts composed of them would not be texts, which obviously they are. Indeed, one could very well imagine a whole text covering several pages and composed of only one sentence that ends with a question mark. Moreover, if the verifiability in question were of the empirical sort, then most or perhaps all theological and metaphysical treatises would have to be excluded from the category, again something few would be prepared to do. Meaning need not entail empirical verifiability or even verifiability at all.

A third factor that distinguishes art objects and texts is that texts need not be recognized as being both artifacts and capable of producing artistic experiences. This does not imply that they may not do so. There are ample cases of texts that are recognized both as artifacts and as capable of producing artistic experiences, but no text, qua text, is required to be so recognized, and many are not. To repeat, neither the texts of Kant's *Critique of Pure Reason* nor that of *The Chicago Manual of Style* is so recognized.

Attempts to reduce texts to art objects, and vice versa, are misguided. The distinction between them in terms of, first, the character of the entities that compose them, second, the intended function of texts, and, third, the recognition of the capacity of art objects to produce artistic experiences allows us to understand how the same object can be a text and an art object without the implication that to be one is the same as to be the other.

Consider an art object that is also a text, say St. John of the Cross's *Spiritual Canticle*. This poem, among the best ever written in Spanish, is both a text and an art object. It is a text because it consists of entities that function as signs, which St. John selected and arranged in a particular way to convey a specific meaning to an audience. But it also is an art object, because it is regarded as affecting readers in ways that go beyond the ways in which a nonartistic text could affect them. Indeed, St. John himself wrote an extensive commentary on the poem in which he laid down in nonpoetic language the views he took the poem to express. Yet the poem is much more to the attentive reader than what St. John says in his commentary; there is a world of difference between St. John's poem and his commentary. One is a work of art that never ceases to move those who read it; the other is a nonartistic presentation of what the poem meant to the author in a language that fails to move the audience in the same way.

Perhaps another more controversial example will help clarify the view I am proposing. Consider Beethoven's *Fifth Symphony*. Is it a text, an art object, or both? The example is controversial because what is meant by Beethoven's *Fifth Symphony* is complex; once its complexity is exposed, however, it can easily fit into the scheme I have presented.

The expression "Beethoven's *Fifth Symphony*" is used to refer to two different things: a score and a group of sounds. The score is a group of entities used as signs, selected, arranged, and intended by Beethoven to convey two different meanings to two different audiences. One audience is composed of performers. For them the meaning of the score is a set of rules that they have to follow if they wish to perform Beethoven's work. The other audience is composed of those persons who, looking at the score, can imagine in their minds the sounds that the performers are supposed to produce if they interpret the score correctly. (Naturally there is no reason the same persons may not be both performers and imaginers.) From this it follows that the score of Beethoven's *Fifth Symphony* is a text, and that it has two meanings.

Apart from the score, we also talk about the set of sounds produced by performers when they correctly read the score and follow the rules it stipulates as Beethoven's *Fifth Symphony*. This group of sounds can be one of the meanings of the score, which is a text, and therefore in that capacity the group of sounds is not itself a text. However, as an artifact it could be in turn a text if the entities that compose it were used as signs by Beethoven to produce understanding.

The answer to the question posed earlier is that the score of Beethoven's *Fifth Symphony* is without a doubt a text, but the group of sounds making up Beethoven's *Fifth Symphony* is a text only if the sounds are taken as signs intended to produce understanding. Frankly, I do not think that Beethoven had in mind to produce understanding with the group of sounds composing the *Fifth Symphony*, and so I believe those sounds are not a text. Herein lies the main difference between the sounds of Beethoven's *Fifth Symphony* and the sounds produced when someone speaks. But one may want to ask: What about singing? Are songs texts or art objects? Insofar as they are intended to produce understanding, they are texts, but insofar as they are artifacts capable of producing artistic experiences, they are art objects.

Still, it is clear that the group of sounds that make up Beethoven's *Fifth Symphony* constitutes an art object when measured by the two criteria indicated earlier. But the case of the score of the symphony is not clear. It is an artifact, but is it in itself capable of producing an artistic experience? More precisely, is it regarded as both an artifact and as capable of producing an aesthetic experience? It is generally accepted that the score of Beethoven's *Fifth Symphony* is an artifact, but I doubt very much that anyone regards it as capable of producing an aesthetic experience—at least I do not know anyone who regards it as such. For this reason, I do not believe it is an art object. But then someone else may have a different view, in which case it would have to be considered an art object, even by me.

In sum, the understanding of texts and art objects I have provided allows us to include some art objects within the category of texts but also allows us to maintain a distinction between art objects and texts. This distinction is useful in preventing some conceptual confusions when discussing texts and art objects. However, the distinction between texts and art objects might seem to support the view that the philosophical interpretation of art makes no sense. If texts and art are as different as I have claimed, and philosophical interpretations are generally provided through texts, then is it not questionable whether these interpretations are viable? This is the view against which I argue in this book, but to complete my argument I need to turn next to the philosophical interpretation of art.

22

Philosophical Interpretations of Art

The working conceptions of interpretation and art presented in the previous two chapters allow us to turn to the heart of our topic, the philosophical interpretation of art. But there is still a loose end we must tie up before we do so, for although I have used the notion of philosophy throughout the previous discussions, I have not pinpointed explicitly what I take philosophy to be.[1] This is necessary insofar as, like art and interpretation, philosophy is a contested notion.

PHILOSOPHY

We speak of philosophy in many different ways, but they all tend to fall into two broad senses. In one, we speak of it as something we have, hold, study, develop, adopt, commit ourselves to, discover, admire, believe, formulate, or state. In another, we speak of it as something we do, practice, engage in, or carry out. When we speak of philosophy in the first sense, generally we are thinking of it as a view, that is, as a set of beliefs, although there may be differences with respect to the beliefs in question. Sometimes these beliefs concern anything an ordinary person may hold. We speak of the philosophy of a gardener with respect to pruning finicky wisterias: doing heavy pruning in the autumn. Or we speak of the philosophy someone has about feeding dogs: feed them only once a day.

These examples are rather pedestrian, but we also speak about more lofty cases of having a philosophy in this sense. We speak about someone's philosophy of life, for example, or even about one's philosophy of God. Someone might say that she believes one must be virtuous in life, and that God is an all-powerful being. The quality of the particular examples is not important in understanding this use of the term *philosophy*; the important point is that for a view to qualify as philosophy in this sense, it is sufficient that it be a belief someone holds or may hold, although usually one expects such a belief to be about ways of behaving and doing things. Indeed, someone might find it odd to say that the belief in water being composed of hydrogen and oxygen, or the belief in the existence of a tree in a forest, constitutes a philosophy in this general and ordinary sense. But others have disagreed. After all, have not some philosophers questioned the existence of the external world? And views about the composition of the world also have been thought to be philosophical. Is not Thales's claim that the world is made up of water regarded by many as philosophical, even though it is not, as a view, very different from the position that regards water as composed of hydrogen and oxygen?

Note also that I say "may hold" because there are beliefs probably no one would hold, or could consistently hold, and yet they would nonetheless qualify as philosophy in this sense. There is no reason we cannot think of a philosophical view that not only has never been held but will never be held by anyone. We might examine such a view, consider why it is untenable, and argue against it, even though it will always remain unsubscribed.

Apart from the conception of philosophy as a view in general, philosophy may be conceived, more narrowly, as a view of the world, or any of its parts, that seeks to be accurate, consistent, and comprehensive, and for which evidence is given as support. The object philosophy studies does not seem to be restricted to any individual thing, such as a cat or a dog, or any particular kind of thing, such as space or mind. Philosophy is concerned with everything subject to human experience, whether morality or matter. In this sense, there is no difference between this conception of philosophy and the first one mentioned: both are views of the world or its parts. The differences arise only because philosophy, in the second sense, seeks to be accurate, consistent, comprehensive, and supported by sound evidence. I do not say that it is or must be so. Indeed, I do not yet know of any philosophy that is generally regarded as having satisfied these conditions. If these conditions were to be applied as the criteria of what constitutes a philosophy, then, based on what we know, we could not call philosophy any of the things that are generally called philosophy. And this makes no sense.

In order to qualify as philosophy, a view need not be accurate, but its aim must be accuracy in the sense that it must strive to be faithful to experience understood broadly to include both empirical sensation and nonempirical intuitions. It must be intended to achieve consistency, because it must attempt to avoid contradiction. It must seek to be comprehensive in that it must try to present as complete a picture of what it describes as possible. And it must aim to be supported by evidence that is thought to be sound, because it strives to achieve the status of knowledge, and views without sound support are matters of opinion, not knowledge.

In the first two and the last specified conditions, philosophy is not very different from science. The differences between them rest on factors involved in the third condition: particular sciences do not aim at comprehensiveness and are restricted to certain aspects of things, areas of study, and modes of inquiry. Human psychology investigates the mental dimension of humans; astronomy studies heavenly bodies; and chemistry the composition of bodies. Moreover, they are concerned only with certain aspects of these objects and use specialized methods to do so. Indeed, even if all the sciences were put together into one super science, the picture of this would not be comprehensive, insofar as there would be epistemic, ethical, logical, metaphysical, and aesthetic dimensions that would be missing from it, which this super scientific view would not cover or be intended to complete. For example, it would not include claims about the general condition of certainty, whether moral obligations based on convention, the rules of sound reasoning, the number of most general categories, or the nature of art. Only philosophy aims to be fully comprehensive. Philosophy seeks to produce a big picture, even of partial aspects of the world; it is not content with partial pictures of the world, as are most other knowledge enterprises.

Consider, for example, a philosophy of human beings. Surely this would include claims about the chemical composition of the body, the functioning of the brain and the mind, human behavior, and similar views proposed in the social and natural sciences. But philosophy would in addition make metaphysical claims, such as "the body is extended and the mind is not," epistemic claims such as "the human senses are unreliable," ethical claims such as "humans should not end human life purposefully," and aesthetic claims about the beauty of the human body.

Philosophy takes into account the knowledge provided by social and natural sciences, although it excludes the details involved in its acquisition and goes beyond it in two ways. First, it aims to integrate this knowledge into an overall coherent conceptual picture of the world and, second, it complements it with metaphysical, epistemological, moral, logical, and aesthetic claims, among others. In short, philosophy is more and less than the sciences, playing a unique role in the human pursuit of understanding and interacting with and feeding from the results of scientific research.

One might object that this conception of philosophy is not generally in agreement with the use of the term. One reason is that this view conflicts with at least one widely accepted understanding of philosophy as the attempt to do away with views of the world of the sort mentioned.[2] What do we make of philosophers such as Gorgias, Nietzsche, and Derrida, who have considered themselves, qua philosophers, engaged in a primarily critical function, rather than as offering substantive descriptions of the world?

Two ways out of this difficulty suggest themselves. The first is to reject the credentials of these philosophers and to say that what they do is not philosophy, because their aim is not appropriate for philosophers. But this strategy would be liable to the charge that this view is not sufficiently inclusive, for what these critics of philosophy do has been traditionally called philosophy, even though there have been repeated attempts at disenfranchising them. One cannot adopt this answer without having also to abandon the pretense of doing at least some justice to the way the term *philosophy* is used in the classroom, and that is not sensible.

A second way out is to argue that, in spite of initial appearances to the contrary, critics do fit the mold of philosophers. But, we may ask, how can this be when they explicitly strive not only to undermine views of the sort described but, more significantly, to question the whole process of production of such views? One way to include critics in the conception of philosophy proposed here is to point out that those who aim to undermine noncritical philosophers do in fact have a view of a part of the world, namely, of philosophy, which they believe to be accurate, consistent, comprehensive, and supported by sound evidence.

Their view must be regarded as concerning a part of the world, because philosophy, apart from one's conception of it, is part of the world when one understands the world to include everything found in our experience or capable of being experienced. And by experience I do not mean only empirical experience but anything that can be sensed or thought. The view of the critics of philosophy, moreover, must be thought of as seeking to be accurate, because these authors hold philosophy to be the way they believe it is, namely, not a view at all, or if a view, one that is always flawed. It must be considered as seeking to be consistent, because these authors believe it applies to all philosophies, including their own. Indeed, they aim at undermining all views that claim any kind of universality or certainty. This view must be thought of as comprehensive, because it seeks to apply to the whole of philosophy, not just to some of its branches, and in fact it does often extend to all knowledge, not just philosophy. Skeptics, for example, reject certainty in all knowledge, not just philosophical knowledge. Finally, it must be regarded as seeking support in sound evidence, because it is claimed to be effective in reaching its conclusions.

So much, then, for the understanding of philosophy as a view. Now we must turn to the second, although related, understanding of philosophy. This is as something one does, practices, or engages in rather than something one has, holds, or believes. In this sense, philosophy is an activity rather than a view, although the activity in question is not just any kind of activity. Running is not the same as doing philosophy, although one may do philosophy while one runs, and the same goes for digesting or for scratching oneself.

It appears at first that the activity in question may be of two sorts. One is the activity whereby a view of the sort described earlier is produced. Another is the activity whereby one seeks to develop the formulation, explanation, and justification of rules according to which the production of such a view must proceed. But clearly the latter activity also involves the production of a view that itself seeks to be accurate, and so on. This sort of activity concerns the development of a view of proper philosophical method and, therefore, strictly speaking, it should be subsumed under the general heading of philosophy. In essence, there is no fundamental distinction between these two sorts of activities.

This discussion brings to the fore another conception of philosophy, namely, philosophy as a view of philosophical method. In this sense, philosophy consists of the set of rules (e.g., "contradictory claims are not allowed") to be used to guide the activity that yields philosophical views. Philosophy is often called a discipline in that it consists of a set of procedures that must be followed to achieve philosophical knowledge, although its disciplinary character also is associated with the activity involved in the implementation of the rules to do so. Understood as a set of rules, philosophy can be subsumed under the notion of philosophy as a view, although it may be convenient to keep it separate in order to prevent confusion.

We have, then, three different conceptions of philosophy:

1. a view of the world, or any of its parts, which is intended to be accurate, consistent, comprehensive, and supported by sound evidence

2. the activity whereby (1) is developed

3. the rules that are to be followed in the formulation of (1)

Obviously (1) takes precedence over the others, insofar as it is the aim of all the others and presupposed by them. None of the others makes sense apart from it, even if (1) cannot be developed without the others. In Aristotle's language, (1) is the *telos* of (2) and (3). The view expressed in (1), therefore, is the notion of philosophy that we need to keep in mind here.

Philosophy breaks down into many branches, depending on the subject matter and the way that subject matter is dealt with. The core of philosophy is usually thought to include disciplines such as metaphysics, epistemology, logic, ethics, and political philosophy, to which the history of philosophy is added sometimes. Metaphysics is concerned with fundamental categorization; epistemology with knowledge and the conditions under which certainty can be achieved; logic with correct and incorrect ways of reasoning; ethics with human behavior and morality; political philosophy with social organization and government; and the history of philosophy with the way in which philosophy, and its branches, has developed throughout the ages.

Apart from these general subfields, philosophy includes specialized areas that sometimes combine some of its more general branches as well as some subfields of them. The philosophy of science, for instance, involves elements of metaphysics, epistemology, and logic when it presents views aimed at the understanding of the nature of science. The philosophy of mind includes aspects of metaphysics, epistemology, and logic in its understanding of mind. Hermeneutics is concerned with the interpretation of texts, but in order to present a view of this task, it sometimes develops metaphysical views about texts and delves into epistemology.

The philosophy of religion is a very telling case of a field that integrates many branches of philosophy. It includes epistemological views when it deals with human knowledge of God; metaphysics when it explains the nature of God; ethics when it attempts to reconcile moral behavior with the rules prescribed for it in religion; philosophy of mind when it presents views about the nature of the soul; and philosophy of science when it compares the conclusions of science with the doctrines regarded in religions as divine revelations. Finally, it concerns itself with hermeneutics when it tries to find appropriate principles for interpreting revelation.

Aesthetics or the philosophy of art also is a field that integrates various other branches of philosophy. It deals with epistemology, insofar as it tries to establish the mechanisms of aesthetic and artistic recognition; with metaphysics when it seeks to determine the ontological status of works of art; with philosophy of mind when it develops theories about the cognition of the beautiful and the ugly; with hermeneutics in that it attempts to establish rules about the correct interpretation of art; and so on. Moreover, as happens with other branches of philosophy, it tries to integrate the insights of scientific research.[3]

A philosophical interpretation of art must take into account the various conceptions of philosophy presented here as well as the way philosophy breaks down into fields and subfields. In some cases, an interpretation will concern only one of these, but in other cases there will be cross-fertilization among them. All of this affects the interpretation.

PHILOSOPHICAL INTERPRETATIONS

I have adopted a conception of philosophy as a view of the world, or any of its parts, which seeks to be accurate, consistent, comprehensive, and supported by sound evidence. I also distinguished between two senses of interpretation: meaning interpretations and relational interpretations. Moreover, I distinguished between interpretation as understanding and interpretation as an instrumental object that is used to cause an understanding in an audience. These distinctions yield the following possible conceptions of philosophical interpretations:

A. Meaning Interpretations

1. Philosophical understanding of the meaning of an object of interpretation when that meaning is understood as determined by the author(s), a particular audience(s), independently of author(s) or audience(s), or as including its implications.

2. An object that can be used to produce a philosophical understanding of the meaning of an object of interpretation determined in the ways mentioned (instrumental interpretation).

B. Relational Interpretations

1. Understanding of the relation of an object of interpretation or its meaning (determined according to the mentioned possibilities) to philosophy.

2. An object that can be used to produce an understanding of the relation of an object of interpretation or its meaning (determined in the mentioned ways) to philosophy (instrumental interpretation).

Meaning interpretations of the philosophical sort are either philosophical understandings of objects of interpretation or instruments that can produce philosophical understandings of objects of interpretation. Whether one or the other, the key is that the object of interpretation is looked at as a locus of philosophical views. If the first (A-1), a philosophical interpretation of the object aims to clarify and make explicit the philosophy in the object of interpretation, that is, what we might call its philosophical meaning as determined in the various ways mentioned earlier. An interpretation of Aristotle's sentence "All men by nature desire to know" will attempt to explain the philosophical view the sentence expresses, that is, its philosophical meaning as judged by Aristotle, a particular audience, independent of what Aristotle or any audience thought, or including its implications. If the second (A-2), a philosophical interpretation will be an object such as a text that helps produce understanding of the philosophical meaning of the object of interpretation in some audience. In the case of a literary work, such as Borges's *Pierre Menard*, the job of a meaning philosophical interpretation would be to understand or produce an object that in turn causes an understanding of the philosophy in Borges's story.

Relational interpretations (B) of the philosophical sort differ from meaning interpretations in that they are not concerned with the philosophical meaning of the object of interpretation but with the relation of the object or its meaning to a philosophical view. So it is not necessary for these interpretations to assume that the object or its meaning is philosophical. The objects of interpretation or their meanings need not be philosophical for them to be the subjects of philosophical interpretations of the relational kind. In this sense, one could provide a philosophical interpretation of one of Jackson Pollock's paintings which, because of its abstract nature, makes no philosophical claims. This would be no different than giving a philosophical interpretation of a historical event, or of any particular object in the universe. Anything can be the object of philosophical investigation, insofar as it is used to develop a philosophical view. And this applies when the interpretation is an understanding (B-1) or an object that produces understanding (B-2).

That philosophy is divided into many general and specialized branches also affects the nature of interpretations. It is one thing is to produce a metaphysical interpretation and another to do an epistemological or a social one. The first is concerned with views that have to do with the categorization of reality, the second with issues of knowledge, and the third with society. The interpretations of Estévez's works presented in the first part of this book fall into four different areas, dealing, respectively, with epistemology (knowledge), metaphysics (reality), social philosophy (society), and eschatology (destiny). So how is all of this applicable to art?

PHILOSOPHICAL INTERPRETATIONS OF ART

If James Elkins is right when he claims that "seeing is irrational, inconsistent, and undependable," then it is clear that interpretation in visual art is inevitable.[4] The question for us, then, is not whether the interpretation of art is possible but whether philosophical interpretations of it make sense.

In meaning interpretations of the philosophical sort, the interpreter considers an art object in order to determine whether there are traces of philosophical views in it. Relational interpretations of the philosophical sort differ from these in that their object is not the philosophical meaning of the object of interpretation but rather a relation of the art object or its meaning to some philosophical position. It is not necessary for relational interpretations to assume that the objects they interpret present philosophical views. In both cases, meaning and relational, the interpretations can be understandings or instruments of understanding in audiences. Let us now see how this applies to art.

The general conditions that apply to art are: artifactuality and the capacity to produce an artistic experience. The first is cashed out in terms of intentional activity and design, and the second is analyzed in terms of artifactuality and the capacity for producing an aesthetic experience. In no case is there anything that has to do with philosophy. Philosophy does not play a part in making something an art object. Art may be philosophical,

or it may not. If the art is not, then the only kind of philosophical interpretation that can be given of it is relational. In this kind of interpretation,
the art object or its meaning is related to some philosophical view. And the
interpretation is either an understanding of such a relation or an instrument
that can be used to produce such an understanding.

When an art object is philosophical, it is possible to provide for it both
relational philosophical interpretations and meaning philosophical interpretations. In a meaning interpretation, the meaning is philosophical in the ways
mentioned before, and the interpretation may consist of an understanding or
of an object that serves to produce such an understanding.

In short, all art can be the subject of relational philosophical interpretations, but only art that is philosophical can be the subject of meaning
philosophical interpretations. This is important, for several reasons. First,
the interpretations of art are frequently meaning interpretations in which
the meaning is determined by particular audiences. This often leads to judgments of abuse on the part of those who evaluate interpretations, whereas in
fact this judgment is not always justified. Meaning interpretations in which
meaning is determined by persons other than the artists are not for this
reason illegitimate as long as they are not passed as authorial.

A second reason this is important is that very frequently interpretations
of art are relational, and popular and personal interpretations often fall into
the relational category—they tend to be understandings intended to relate
a work of art to factors extraneous to it. This allows the interpretations to
develop in ways that otherwise would justify a different characterization of
their nature while maintaining a connection to the original work. Again, these
do not need to be considered ipso facto abusive. When looking at Alberto
Rey's *El Morro*, for example, I might become sentimental and nostalgic
because the painting portrays accurately what I last saw when I left Cuba,
my native land, whereas someone else will not have any such feelings. But
my interpretation need not be considered illegitimate, as long as it is taken
for what it is: a relational interpretation of a very personal sort.

A third reason it is important to understand that all art can be
the subject of relational philosophical interpretations, but only art that is
philosophical can be the subject of meaning philosophical interpretations, is
that this accounts for the popularity of the former kind of interpretations.
Relational interpretations can follow socially contextual leads that draw the
attention of the public at large in ways that other kinds of interpretations
do not. They can easily adapt themselves to the interests and needs of new
audiences and social contexts. For example, film interpretations of Stoker's
Dracula have become progressively more sexually explicit. Morrisey's *Dracula*
(1974) contains erotic material that would have been unthinkable fifty years
earlier. Meaning interpretations in which an audience is not the determiner
of meaning are often too scholarly, historical (even archaic), and stuffy to

be of interest to the general public. Their emphasis is on the understanding of the work in itself, and often on its authorial meaning, so they tend to lose audiences whose interests are the here and now. Most contemporary audiences could care less about what Stoker meant in *Dracula*. That would tend to be of interest primarily to historians and literary critics.

A fourth reason is that the view presented allows us to formulate better criteria for judging the value of philosophical interpretations of art. This is significant, because it is one thing to consider essays such as the ones contained in this book as independent works whose relation to Estévez's art is irrelevant, and another to think of them as interpretations of that work. If the first, then their value is completely divorced from a relation to Estévez's art, but if they are considered interpretations of it, then it is not. It is one thing to think of, and judge, them on their own and another to do so as interpretations of the artist's work. But if they are regarded as interpretations, then it also is important to keep in mind the kind of interpretations they are, for relational interpretations should not be judged by the same criteria as meaning ones. Unfortunately, some critics adversely judge some interpretations of art because they fail to meet the standards one would expect certain meaning interpretations to meet. Moreover, we find responses to these that opt for the artificial separation of relational interpretations from works on which they are based in order to provide favorable evaluations.[5] Neglecting to take into account the distinctions I have introduced leads to charges of interpretative abuses that are groundless when one considers the kind of interpretations at play.

This brings up the controversial question of definitive interpretations. Can there be definitive interpretations of works of art? I doubt it, although it is always healthy to keep this notion as regulative. One thing is clear, however—the kind and object of interpretation are of the essence when thinking about this issue. But that discussion has already taken place elsewhere.[6]

We now have an account of the various ways in which philosophical interpretations of art may be conceived, as well as some conditions that must be satisfied for some of them to apply. Relational interpretations do not require artworks to be philosophical, but meaning interpretations do. This leads to the question: Is it possible for art, and particularly visual art, to be philosophical, and if so, how? To answer this question, we need to turn briefly to the distinction between philosophy in art, philosophy and art, and philosophy of art.

PHILOSOPHY OF/AND/IN ART

The relation between philosophy and art is commonly broken up in three ways and expressed by "of," "and," and "in": philosophy *of* art, philosophy *and* art, and philosophy *in* art.[7] This way of looking at it is not unique to art; something similar is done with literature, for example. These expressions refer to very different things, two of which are only indirectly related to the task of this book.

Philosophy of art is a subdiscipline of philosophy that explores the nature of art and its relation to other phenomena in our experience. Its primary function is to produce a view of art. Questions about what makes something art and how this is to be distinguished from things that are not art enter into this discussion. The very discussion on the philosophical interpretation of art in which I have engaged here falls within the purview of the philosophy of art, because in it I present views of interpretation, art, and philosophy, and of how they are related. This branch of philosophy is similar to such fields as the philosophy of science or the philosophy of mind. Its aim is to produce an understanding of art that follows the requirements of a philosophical understanding.

Philosophy and art differs from the *philosophy of art* in that in it philosophy is not conceived as a discipline whose object of investigation is art. In this case we have two items that are put side by side without one being subsumed under the other. In the philosophy of art, art is the object that philosophy studies and about which it constructs views. In philosophy and art, neither is explored in terms of the other.

There are two ways of thinking about philosophy and art, depending on what one means by "philosophy" and "art." If what we have in mind by the first is a view and by the second certain works, then the pertinent question is the following: What is the relationship between philosophy and art? But, of course, once we pose this question, we must identify the perspective from which it is asked. If the perspective is sociological, for example, then we would be engaged in a kind of sociology. And if the perspective is philosophical, then we would be doing philosophy of art.

Let us look at an example. Say that I consider the relation of philosophy and art from a sociological perspective. If so, I might entertain questions about how philosophers look at art. And this might lead us to the examination of the views of philosophers from certain societies to the art produced in them. For example, we might consider why Plato was such a harsh critic of art in ancient Greece, concluding that it had to do with elements in Greek society that affected both him and Greek art.

But one could look at the relationship between philosophy and art purely in philosophical terms, ignoring social factors as such, except insofar as they contribute to philosophical understanding. In this case the pertinent questions have to do with, for example, whether art should or should not be philosophical in order to be good art. This would lead us to questions about the nature of both philosophy and art.

We also can look at philosophy and art as disciplines, enterprises engaged in the production of philosophical views in the first case and of works of art in the second. The issues then turn to how these disciplines are related, whether they are compatible, and if so, how. Again, questions arise, and these questions will have to be posed from a disciplinary perspective. If this perspective is sociological, then we get a sociology of the relation between philosophy and art. And if the perspective is philosophical, we end up with a philosophy of art after all.

In short, the difference between the *philosophy of art* and *philosophy and art* is that in the first we are restricted to the philosophical understanding of art, whereas in the second that understanding could be philosophical or not. If that understanding is not philosophical, then it opens the door to other disciplinary perspectives.

Both the *philosophy of art* and *philosophy and art* must be distinguished from *philosophy in art*. This last involves the philosophical views presented or expressed in works of art. If the question that arises is, say, whether in fact art can be philosophical or whether it can express philosophical views, then we end up with something not very different from the *philosophy of art*, provided that the issues explored are philosophical; but the result is *philosophy and art* if the issues involve other disciplines. It is only when we look at works of art with the aim of providing philosophical interpretations of them, either meaning or relational, that philosophy in art comes up. So whereas this very discussion is part of the philosophy of art, the essays about the works of Estévez included in this book fall within philosophy in art. One might still want to argue that the philosophical speculations the essays contain are not part of Estévez's philosophy, insofar as his philosophy amounts to the philosophical views present in his works, and nothing more. However, if the interpretations given in the essays are relational, then one could argue that they qualify as philosophy in art, insofar as they have been prompted by the consideration of works of art in relation to philosophical views. This matter cannot be settled easily, and in fact it might not have a solution at all but might be a matter of context and emphasis.

PHILOSOPHICAL INTERPRETATIONS OF ESTÉVEZ'S ART

The interpretations of Estévez's art presented in this book are instrumental and take the form of essays whose aim is to produce philosophical understandings in the readers of this book. The essays rely in turn on my own philosophical understanding of Estévez's art, themselves interpretations, but as far as readers are concerned, the interpretations are the texts of the essays.

Meaning interpretations depend on who determines the meaning and what is included in them. We saw that there are three possibilities concerning who determines meaning: authors, particular audiences, or the works themselves considered independent from authors and audiences. If we aim to give meaning interpretations of Estévez's art, then each piece may have four different philosophical meanings: what Estévez thought it means, what particular audiences think it means (including the interpreter), what the piece means independent of any meanings thought by Estévez or audiences, and any of these, including their implications.

Not all of these options make the same sense here, however. Why bother with the artist's understanding when in fact the artist sought to present that understanding through the work and regards that as its best expression? I have not emphasized this dimension in my interpretations. In addition, to seek what a historical audience understood by a work seems to run the risk of undermining the philosophical nature of the interpretations, turning them into history, so this also I did not emphasize. That leaves only two possibilities concerning meaning interpretations: the understanding of the meaning of the work, considered apart from the author or any particular audience, and of that meaning and its implications. Both were viable, insofar as Estévez's works contain clues as to their philosophical meaning, both in the titles and in the configuration of the art.

But why not go beyond these and try to explore the art in terms of philosophical ideas that have been frequent in the history of philosophy? Why not ask questions that philosophers have asked and see how the work of Estévez can be related to them? This is the kind of interpretation that I have called relational. And this is, indeed, the kind I have sought to present in the essays contained in this volume, although I also kept in mind an understanding of the philosophical meaning of the works, when this was possible, of their implications, and of the artist.

This also helped to buttress the overall thesis of this book, namely, that philosophical interpretations of art, and even of visual art, are possible; philosophy and art are not incompatible.

To make the procedure I chose to follow in my interpretations more explicit, I began each essay with a well-known quote and developed essays that refer to the views of famous authors who have addressed pertinent topics. Of course, the essays were written by me and therefore often contain my particular take on these issues, but this should not undermine their legitimacy, if what I have argued in this book is sound.

BACK TO THE BEGINNING

I began this book with a problem, the presumed incompatibility of philosophy and art and the obstacle this poses for the philosophical interpretation of art. Philosophy and art, and particularly visual art, seem to be essentially different in medium, means, end, as well as practitioners. Philosophy aims at an understanding of the world; it uses language and arguments to achieve it; it results in a comprehensive view claimed to be supported by sound evidence; and its practitioners are persons who engage in discussion, conceptual analysis, and criticism. Visual art for its part aims to construct sensible images and artifacts of various sorts; it uses materials such as paints, wood, and paper; it produces physical and observable objects; and its practitioners are more like artisans who manipulate substances in various ways. These differences between philosophy and visual art would seem to make any attempt at putting them together impossible. They appear to be like oil and vinegar; there is no way to mix them. No wonder that some authors argue that it would be wiser to give up the effort and regard them as two separate ways of approaching the world that should remain independent of each other. Philosophy cannot become art, and art cannot become philosophy. Any attempt at putting them together turns philosophy into art or art into philosophy, destroying the other in the process. The idea of developing philosophical interpretations of art should be abandoned.

My response to this problem has been to challenge it by claiming that it is based on a misunderstanding of interpretation and its relation to art and philosophy. My argument has two parts, corresponding to the two parts of this book. The first consists of an illustration of philosophical interpretations of art in the context of Estévez's visual work. The second is a theoretical analysis of the concepts at play in the philosophical interpretation of art.

The theoretical analysis began by adopting two conceptions of interpretation, depending on whether it is conceived as an understanding of an object of interpretation or as an instrument to cause an understanding of that object. These were further distinguished into meaning and relational interpretations. Meaning interpretations seek to provide the understanding of the meaning of objects of interpretation when these are taken to be determined by the author(s), a certain audience(s), independent of what the author(s) or audience(s) think(s), or including the implications of any of these. Relational interpretations seek to provide understandings of the relation of objects of interpretation or their meaning to factors brought into the interpretative process by interpreters. The counterpart of philosophy conceived as a view is a work of art, which here is taken as an artifactual object that has the capacity to produce an artistic experience.

A philosophical interpretation of art consists in the development of philosophical understandings of art. If the interpretation is one concerned with the meaning of the work, then it can be philosophical only if the work itself is philosophical. In works that are not philosophical, only philosophical interpretations of the relational sort are possible.

This means that in order to argue persuasively that philosophical interpretations of art are impossible, one would have to hold that art can never express a philosophical view, and that only if it did would philosophical interpretations be possible. But this is not so, for we have seen that not all art is antithetical to philosophy. Indeed, Estévez's works contain much philosophy, making their philosophical interpretation possible. But even for works of art that are not philosophical, relational philosophical interpretations are possible, because they require only that an interpreter relate some philosophical view to the works.

In the first part of this book I provided evidence for these claims in two ways. First, I showed that meaning philosophical interpretations of Estévez's art are possible, insofar as many of his works have a philosophical intent. This is clear not just from the titles of the works but also from the images used and from Estévez's own statements. Second, I also provided examples in the essays that incorporate the philosophical views of various authors, including my own, and relate them to particular works by Estévez, resulting in relational philosophical interpretations.

In short, philosophy and art are not necessarily antithetical, and the philosophical interpretation of art is not only possible but enlightening. For some art, only relational interpretations are possible, because the art is not philosophical, but for all art relational philosophical interpretations are possible, because all art can be related to philosophical views. This should help open interpretative avenues that to this day are infrequently explored, without fear of accusations of illegitimacy and abuse.

Appendices

Appendix 1

Interview with Carlos Estévez

Conducted by Jorge J. E. Gracia in the home and studio of the artist, on January 10, 2006.[1]

Carlos, let me begin by asking how you got to where you are today; how did you begin your intellectual voyage?

I began studying art when I was eleven in the Amelia Peláez School in Vedado, Havana. I studied art for thirteen years, including four years in the Academia de San Alejandro and five years in the Instituto Superior de Arte.

When you were eleven, did you know you were going to be an artist?

I painted like almost all kids do. First, I was enrolled in a kind of library that had a workshop for children; the children went there to paint and I liked it. When I was in sixth grade there was a call for applications for a special school. The announcement stated that applicants had to show up for entrance exams. I went with a friend from the neighborhood. I took the test, and passed. I think a bit of luck was involved, even though I believe in destiny. Perhaps it was an accident, but it was more than an accident; there was a reason. In some way, it was in my destiny, because I did not have any special preparation and they passed me. At that point I began to gradually develop along the art path. I had very good professors in a happy period in Cuba. . . .

What period are we talking about?

The '80s. I started to study in that school, I think, in '81. At the time there was much hope. There was a very good social atmosphere; it was the period when Cuba was supported by the Soviet Union. There were some economic advantages, and people could live decently. Many of my professors were artists that earned a living as professors. To do this now is impossible. I was lucky that many of the important artists of that historical period in Cuba, such as Elso Padilla, were my professors. It was tremendous for me; it had significant implications in my life and was the beginning of my career.

This was in Cuba, but you traveled many times to foreign countries while you lived in Cuba, right?

205

Yes.

Where did you go? Europe, Mexico?

I started to travel in '95 when I went to a biennial event in Venezuela. In Cuba there is a kind of mythology about traveling, because Cubans don't have the opportunity to do it easily; travel turns into a deeper adventure than normal and has significant implications. In the world of art there is a famous phrase that no one is a prophet in his own land. The idea of traveling is a kind of legitimation. When you travel you are thought to be important and more interesting; it is the beginning of other things, other projects. After my first trip I kept on traveling.

How has your art evolved? Describe what you are trying to do and the stages through which your art has gone.

My work centers fundamentally on the human spirit. That central theme and preoccupation has not changed drastically throughout my career. It began to manifest itself by the time I was a student. It appears reflected in my sketchbooks, my writings, and my drawings. The process of creation gets stronger with exercise and practice. It is as if each artist has his own language or codes of communication that are new to the world, but practice helps to perfect them. The language becomes clearer; the message becomes clearer; and one gets to the essence of what one wants to say.

Your art is very different. When one looks at Cuban art, there are no other artists who are making things similar to yours. Many are interpreting the human spirit, but the way in which you approach this is different. One sees your works and says, "Oh yes, that is Carlos Estévez's." Where did that come from? It is so uniquely yours. Was this so from the beginning?

Without falling into stereotypes and generalizations, in the long history of Cuban art there have existed two fundamental currents. One is more visual, more archetypical in recognizing the Cuban as a visual identity—the folkloric part. The other, which I think is most important, has developed throughout history like a subterranean current and is permeated with philosophy; the thought of the Cuban human being. This last current to me is the most interesting. This idea is fundamentally a part of my work. I am constantly assimilating things that happen around me. I try to understand the things that happen inside of me, and I reflect on them. My work is a kind of personal existential philosophy translated into the world of images. Each piece is a reflection, a meditation focused on the topic of being human. And this apart from the fact that everyone has a style of language, a kind of recognizable calligraphy. So this belongs to so-and-so. But the most important thing in my work is not that, it is the thought behind it. Each work expresses a preoccupation that exhausts itself and then is related to others, but what interests me is that each has a unique touch that has to do with what I am living.

Much of what you do looks like machinery, wheels, and such things. When did you begin to go down that route?

I am very interested in this aspect of psychology in which the conduct of mature human beings is traced back to infancy. I am basing this on myself in order to explain to you that I always was a curious child and I liked to take things apart and see how they function. I was the typical child that would break toys in order to see how they work for the pleasure of discovering their secret.

A mechanical aspect.

Exactly, and I am also interested in the mechanical world as a metaphor or symbol of how things function. Perhaps they are not reproductions or representations of what really exists inside each material object, but they are metaphors, points for reflection on what is inside each thing.

It is interesting that, given this ability or interest, one would have expected that at a certain moment the child would be channeled toward engineering, architecture, or something that has to do with machinery, but this did not happen to you.

My dad is an engineer, and in my childhood I had to live a bit in the atmosphere of drafting tables and designed plans. My dad's dream was for me to become an engineer or ultimately an architect, but I was never really interested in that. Later, maybe to acknowledge a bit my father's wishes, I became interested in engineering from the point of view of the arts. When I started studying art, my dad thought that this would be useful for engineering, but it was the reverse. Engineering was useful for art. Still, as years passed, and with persistence, he became reconciled.

And did the art you produced in the beginning look like the art you are producing now? In Cuba artists were trained very academically, but I am not sure that when you arrived at school it was like that.

I had the luck of encountering renewed processes in education. But yes, I had an academic training. I was trained as a painter, one of the standard fields of specialization. At that time the fields were separate—painting, printing, and sculpture—but I was always interested in many things, and the instructors taught us a variety of things. Apart from the academic training, our professors put us in touch with the work of contemporary artists. They taught us to think, to do things that we wanted to do. It was a very profitable, conceptual training that was decisive in my career. In San Alejandro I experienced the most academic period. But when I entered the Instituto Superior de Arte I had the fortune of having instructors like José Bedia, Flavio Garandía, María Magdalena Campos Pons, Consuelo Castañeda, and José Franco, who rather than instructors were artists, and more than artists, were excellent creators who inculcated in us a process. At the time, academic programs had been set aside, and the approach was more creative. One had to present a proposal developed in consultation with an instructor. One could choose a particular course according to what one wanted to do, and take the courses in which one was interested. After leaving the Instituto, I started to take photography courses, film, and sculpture, and ended up graduating with sculpture as my specialty.

Obviously you do a lot of sculpture but you keep painting.

In the Instituto Superior de Arte, they taught me how to paint during my seventh or eighth year, but there came a point in which I got bored with painting. Painting was not an adequate medium for expressing what I wanted to say. So I started to experiment with three-dimensionalism, because I was interested in the symbolic and suggestive character of materials. I also started to experiment with sculpture in installations, and I abandoned painting for a long time. Later, after five or six years, I retook it, but I did not approach it with the same vision of the world, from the same point of view. I started incorporating objects and making fabrics. I think that even the feeling of my drawings is also a bit material, because I confront the paper as alchemists used their sketchbooks. It is a medium to obtain something, a means of reflection and knowledge.

And do you like using paper and drawing?

Yes, I have a kind of fetishistic relation with paper. When I enter a store that has materials and I see paper, it is like it is asking me to take it so I can do something with it. Paper is a very immediate medium. A work on paper is not like an installation or sculpture that requires a lot of time for elaboration. That helps me perhaps in the process because I need to visualize and materialize those ideas so they rise to the next stage. Working with paper is a process closely linked together in a chain, very narrowly tied; it is like stairs. If you do not finish with one step you cannot go to the next. In this sense, drawing is a very effective medium in order to realize an idea, I visualize it. And perhaps from a drawing another thing might come, be that an installation or a sculpture.

Drawing has lines, and that is a very essential part of practically all your work. Even in the semi-sculptures, what do you call the work we have back here [Gracia points to a work hanging on the wall]?

Hermetic Garden.

And how would you describe it?

A box.

So these are boxes of mix media, but. . . .

For me it is difficult to classify.

Because here you have drawing, sculpture, collage, many things.

A mixture.

But you incorporate lines in practically everything you do, even oil painting.

I have always made my work graphic. My oil paintings are very graphic, they are practically painted drawings.

Drawing in oil painting, exactly. In other words, drawing is the heart of your work and your art.

I think so, like writing.

I am fascinated by all this machinery in the art, because it reminds me of watches, the machines that our friend da Vinci used to draw. Artists who drew these objects came at the end of the Middle Ages and the beginning of the Renaissance, and they were artists as well as scientists. You are in that line, except that you are not really a scientist; you are an artist, but in some ways you are in the middle of it all. How did this develop? You started to read things from that time period?

Among my gods there is the one you mentioned: Leonardo da Vinci. But apart from that, I am interested in the work of Jesuits from the seventeenth century, like Kircher. It's a time when humans begin to discover the world, start to investigate, the pseudoscience, the poetry and personal perfection, where poetry influences a bit more that vision, and that interests me a lot as a methodology, that is, as a method to access reality. Art is a way of understanding life. It is a way of understanding myself. But it is like an object of knowledge. Papers and canvases are the fundamental instruments of my laboratory, and from there comes a repertoire of mechanisms, machines that are nothing but metaphors of functions and of things that perhaps I do not understand but that I intend to understand.

Then in the representation, the process of producing something, you are in a certain sense looking at yourself, and the product reflects who you are. You are coming to know yourself, objectifying yourself.

Exactly. What is inside me does not seem very clear because it is inside. Until I undergo this process of externalizing it, of taking it out, I cannot analyze it, as happens when you take things from reality and into a laboratory to study them. This happens a bit with the human spirit. Inside of us there is a vast darkness, because all our feelings and emotions are mixed there. And when you succeed in bringing them out, they become part of the world, and that is when you can reflect on them.

By the way, have you done self-portraits?

Sure, sometimes. The self-portrait is a theme that can develop in different ways, and in a certain sense my work in general is a self-portrait.

But not a self-portrait of you physically, but of your inner workings, as one might say.

Exactly, a portrait of my deepest identity.

And what part did Cuba play in this, because this art of yours is fundamentally universal. I do not see any particularity in it: the images do not have anything to do with Cuba; the themes are completely universal. Is there something in it that relates to the Cuban situation and the process that Cubans have gone through for the last forty or fifty years?

Human beings are like plants. We are born in one place and grow roots. We assimilate the nutrients from the earth, and that marks a fundamental guideline in life. I am Cuban. I was born in Cuba. My way of seeing life I believe is Cuban. I am aware that, compared to Europeans and Americans, I have a very definite culture, and that is like a sieve through which I filter all the information that comes to me from reality. However, the interaction with other realities continues to enrich that vision, and from the beginning I aimed as an idea for my work to discover the depths of humanity beyond the confines of a specific place, be it Cuba or Africa. There is a universal human concern, deeper than particular spaces and contexts, common to human beings: feelings, passions, and thought. In this sense, I am interested in how a human being from a particular latitude can make an experience an important event for another human being in another latitude. It is in that sense that my work goes beyond particular social, political, and cultural contexts. I cannot deny that many of my works had a local source at the outset, but with practice, when one starts to polish the work and outline the idea, I think it transcends to what I really want.

I can cite as an example a work that is in the Museo Nacional de Bellas Artes, entitled *The True Universal History*. It concerns the manipulation of history; the way history is a personal phenomenon that changes according to the contexts in which it functions. It can become two completely different histories. This idea is the topic of the movie *Rashomon* by Kurosawa, where different visions of the same event are presented. I became fascinated with it in the context of how the history of Cuba was before the triumph of the Revolution, and how it became something else in the Revolution, how facts and personalities became omitted. I was very interested in how negative events could turn into positive ones, and vice versa. So I did a work in which there were many personalities. This piece was a kind of toy, like an atemporal scenario, in which time periods mixed.

I realized that this was a universal phenomenon that happened all over the world. This is why I gave the work that title and changed the personalities into universal personalities from all walks of life: musicians, thinkers, philosophers, politicians. The piece is a mixture of dolls that are on the floor of a stage, and each member of the audience takes his or her character and finds a place for him or her. The piece worked very well because when it was exhibited for the first time in the Salon de Arte Contemporáneo in Havana, the Minister of Culture came and took Che and Lenin, and then other people came and took other characters. It is like a toy—you make history according to your interests and ideas.

This part of toy machinery, a sense of play, that is present in your work, is most intriguing. Have you made mobiles?

I have made puppets with a more sculptural and plastic feel, but I plan to make representations of puppets. I am describing the work that I want to do in the future, with these puppets and a visual feel that interact, dialogue, and have texts.

But would they be sculptures, or would they be painted?

They will be sculptures with movement.

Fascinating! Here is another question: These trips that you made overseas while you lived in Cuba, did they have a significant impact on your work, in the way you thought and worked as an artist?

Traveling is definitive for an artist. For me personally, it is something indispensable. It is like a book. If you do not go through a chapter, then you do not know what happens in the remaining pages. To be in different spaces, in different cultures, subject to completely different experiences from what is natural to you because you were born in a particular place, widens your vision as an artist. Later the process of creation is closely tied to external stimuli. Basically, one has what one needs inside of oneself, but these things get activated in reality, and you do not know where they are, and you have to go around the world to find them.

Did you spend a lot of time in France?

I lived in Paris for one year.

A year is a substantial amount of time. Did you visit other places for shorter times?

Three, four months.

Was there a difference? The French experience in particular, did it impact you?

There are places in the world that are exceptionally different from others. It is like when you enter a university or are passing through a school. There are courses that are essential and you have to take. Paris is a basic course. Living in the city one day, one week, or for a month is not the same as a year—I think it is still a short time to be in Paris—where you can identify with the city, make the neighborhoods your own, identify yourself in everyday life, penetrate into that culture and understand what is happening there or at least assimilate it in an unhurried fashion.

Did you make the effort to learn French? Was it difficult?

It really was not a great effort for me. I assimilate languages in a natural, spontaneous fashion. I think it was in my third trip, when I had a scholarship in London and I practically did not know English, because I had never paid much attention in English class in school, that I arrived there, but I went along learning by listening to television. In the beginning it was a bit difficult, but later the language formed a part of me and functioned perfectly. The French language I do not really speak perfectly, but I understand it and can communicate in it.

Apart from your travels, this change involved in settling in Miami is very drastic and happened in a short time. In a previous conversation you told me that the first months were very hard. Tell me about these experiences. In the first place,

*how did you decide to come here? In the second place, after you arrived here, were
you shocked?*

Since I am a believer in destiny, I think few things happen in a short
time. Everything involves a process of slow gestation for humans. Things
that happen, in some way, were already preparing themselves from the past.
I left Cuba for about three years for an exhibition in Switzerland. It was an
opportunity for me to go out with my family, which was very, very difficult.
Afterwards, I had this scholarship in Paris.

We did not plan on living anywhere in particular. In fact, I have a very
special understanding of this. My family is the territory where I want to live,
or, in other words, it is my country. As long as we are together, we are fine.
And it can be beyond political borders or ideologies. I think that feeling, in
which one really feels good, is really essential for life. Maybe it is also that
it is not important for anyone else, but it is personally important, and that
is what is most valuable. It is like one's region, one's own kingdom.

Then there was this opportunity to experience something together with
the family outside of Cuba. This made it possible for us to insert ourselves in
a different environment. The quality of our lives changed ostensibly, and we
decided to maintain it and continue forward and make it progressively better,
because we only live one life, and we want to enjoy it as much as we can.

After living one year in Paris we wanted to move to Spain, because
I had very interesting offers of work there. On top of that my grandfather
was Spanish, and he came to Cuba looking for help many years ago, and my
wife's grandfather was also Spanish, and he went to Cuba with the same plan.
So I, very innocently, went to request residency in Spain, under conditions
much more advantageous than my grandfather in Cuba—my grandfather
came as a stow on a boat, escaping the Civil War. But I had some money,
health insurance, and a bunch of things that the embassy demanded. In a
month they answered that because I was Cuban, there were only two ways
that I could stay in Spain: marry a Spaniard or find a job. This was absurd
because, as I said to them, I was already married and was already working.
Immigration laws are complicated, especially for Cubans, who are like the
last seat in the last car of the last class of the train—it is very difficult and
humiliating how one has to insert oneself into these spaces and is the last
in line. I believe that I might be digressing a bit from the matter at hand,
but I want to add a very interesting anecdote.

*This interview is an opportunity for you to say what interests you, so
go ahead.*

I am very proud of being Cuban. I admire many Cubans, because I
think we have a kind of spiritual training that others do not have. I began
to think for a moment that—and this is a bit egocentric—reality divides
into Cuba and the world. This anecdote is about how a Cuban is the last

one on line, even in Cuba.

I was in a barber shop with my two-year-old son. We lived in the Plaza de Armas, which is a tourist place. My son was sitting on the barber chair and a foreigner came in. The barber made my son, who had waited in line, get up in order to give his place to the foreigner. That hurt me a lot, because in the first place the barber was Cuban, like me, and secondly because I had already traveled enough to understand that one of the most important things for nations is the national feeling of protecting your own, having others come after—it's a bit the social idea of the family: my family is first, and everyone else gets incorporated into it insofar as they deserve to be. It made me very sad, not for me, or for my son, because there were other barbers and a haircut is routine business; it made me sad for that man. That because of historical circumstances and money he felt he had to privilege a foreigner—a man that he did not know and who maybe cleaned toilets in Istanbul. I was able to experience something similar elsewhere. In Paris, on top of that, Parisians think of themselves as the center of the world.

They call Paris the capital of the world.

They feel very superior, and I think one has to establish some measure in human feelings. There has to be a middle ground.

The terrible thing about your anecdote is that maybe that man was not an exception but a rule of the way many people think in Cuba.

Yes, sadly.

It is not that a certain priority was given to someone because of money. It is that the barber violated the rights of someone else. He violated the right of someone who already was in line and was sitting on his seat and ready to have his hair cut. From the beginning, no one made a regulation that stated that because a foreigner has money he will be given priority. If the barber had said to your son, "Look I am going to cut your hair, but if a foreigner comes in, you have to understand that I will give him priority because he pays money," then you would have understood that it was a pragmatic matter and that these were the rules of the game. But there was no such rule. No one consulted you, and he moved your son out of his place.

This brings to mind a very important phenomenon especially in Latin America, maybe in Cuba too. There is a kind of contempt for our own things and a certain valorization of things that come from outside, from what is foreign. This happens in many Latin American countries—Argentina, Peru, Mexico, in all the places. There is plenty of rhetoric about the nation and the national culture but at the same time, when it comes to the case of philosophy, for example, Latin American philosophers do not think well about Latin American philosophers. Everything has to be foreign—the imported is valued, and the native is not.

It is a somewhat distorted tendency concerning the direction of humanity. The world bosses are the countries supposedly more developed, such as the United States. They are the paradigms of human society. To me this is terrible, because wherever there are human beings there are thinkers, creators. All human beings are worthy of developing, expressing themselves, and having the place they deserve because of their values.

With respect to the Miami experience, it had to be a great shock, except that here we are in a certain way in a Cuban environment.

It is rather a pseudo-Cuban environment, because it's a derivation from Cuba in another context, in another place, in an American territory. But now let me go back to the thread of what I was telling you. We lived in Paris. We tried to go to Spain because we were interested in staying in Europe, but then I had various exhibitions there. I had worked with various galleries in the United States, and that was my principal source of income. So we decided to move here. Really it was at first very depressing—the confrontation of the two perspectives and more serious still for us who had lived in Paris, across from the Seine and the Church of Saint Louis. The place was *la creme de la creme* and, all of a sudden, coming to live here in Miami, in a suburb, it is a bit. . . .

Let me return to what I was saying before. The human being is like a plant. You can grab the plant and you can plant it on another soil, in another place, and in another climate, but the plant responds. You take your body where you want for personal reasons, but the soul is sensitive and responds. In fact, I fell into a deep depression for several months, but I was saved by some things one always finds. The human spirit is not that easy to crush and always has that impetus—I grabbed certain things, among them my work and some things I discovered here. I had come many times to the United States before, practically two or three times a year, because I had many projects at universities, and nobody had ever talked to me about the library system. They took me to the malls and to the stores to buy things. . . .

The intellectual part never played a role. . . .

I had never known that there were free libraries with an arsenal of movies and incredible books that one could get online. That was my point of salvation; there I began to see all the gaps I had. I am passionate about the movies, and I started to look for movies by Truffaut, de Vigo, films I had never seen before. I used to spend hours watching movies, and feeding myself with images and reading. That's how I spent that period. Until little by little I adapted because, as I said, where human beings live there is hope, there is a spirit of creation. Many interesting people live here. There are entire generations that have moved from Cuba and are here because of practical reasons. And interesting things happen in the art world. There are many art fairs, concerts, and exhibitions.

With respect to the way you work, do you have certain hours of the day that you work? Is your work something you do by habit, or is it something that you do sporadically?

For me the work is a necessity more than anything else. I work from an imperious desire to say things and to understand what is happening in my head. I work every day, absolutely every day.

Are you Aristotelian?

At every moment. The artist, the creator, is like a film camera that has to be constantly processing reality, constantly processing everything that is happening around us. From all of this information, at some point a work explodes. I get up in the morning, sometimes earlier, generally very early. I work until the afternoon or evening every day.

You were telling me before we began the interview that you collect all kinds of objects, things that you use for work and inspiration, that you go to flea markets. . . .

I am passionate about flea markets; especially European flea markets are very interesting; they are like antique museums. Suddenly you find objects of artistic, historical, and utilitarian interest. There are things that you do not even know what they are that you discover. I use them because I have a very big passion for knowledge. I love to collect things and use them for my work, which is something I am currently doing. The passion is old, the work new. I found this out also when I arrived in Miami; going to the antique shops helped me to distance myself from home activities. I enjoy going to flea markets, looking for things, strolling and entertaining myself, while also working.

Quite interesting, Carlos. I believe that we have covered the most important and pertinent milestones, but I wanted to ask you if there is something that you are interested in saying, something that you have in mind. . . .

I am more interested in journeys than in destinations. Many times I have put myself in a situation where I ask: What would I do with my life if I had one minute left to live? And my answer is that I would not do anything. Now I would respond the same, because I think one does *during*, not in the *end*, because the end already happened, and that is how life is: there is no body of work. I am not going to make a collection. What I have inside is developed and presented in the journey.

There is another thing I wanted to ask you. The life of an artist is not easy, and earning a living is not easy. Do you have a different job, besides art, to support yourself?

I have to help around the house.

And your wife, does she have a job or something of that sort?

Yes, my wife works.

Oh, so you have what is called a "brunette scholarship." She has black hair?

No, she has brown hair.

Well, then, you have a brown hair scholarship. In the United States this sort of expression is used to talk about men whose wives work and help to support them while they are being trained in the university. But in your case, do you sell? Your art seems easy to appreciate, right? For me, it is very easy.

I have had the satisfaction of presenting my work to people from different social and cultural groups, and it has been well received. I think maybe because the essence of my work is the human being, and in some form or another it touches everyone in the world, and everyone in the world feels that they identify with it in some way or another.

Before we end, we have to talk about this extraordinary project of the bottles that is incredibly original. How did this spring up? What is its purpose? In what does it consist?

It arose out of various things. First, it was a homage to Havana's *malecón.* I lived in old Havana, in the port, and I always used to pass by the seafront, and the confrontation between the sea beyond and where I was was always strong. I used to say, there is such a short distance between Miami and Havana, and yet there is so much distance in another sense—the families are separated, many relationships, so many separations. The *malecón* is an important place, where Cubans gather at night and jog in the day. For me it is a kind of metaphor for human limitations; also for Cubans it is an obsession to know how the world looks outside Cuba. The idea that people have of the outside, in Cuba, comes from the movies, from hearsay, and it is somewhat rosy. The world is not like that; it is very different. It is neither that beautiful nor that horrible; it is rather a reality that you have to live and assimilate in a personal way. And then my son made a bottle—I will show it to you. Now suddenly I do not see it. Oh, here it is . . . this is a relic for me. This is one of the inspirations of my work. My son was playing with his friends and he made this bottle with a message that said something like, "We need medicines," to send outside. Suddenly it occurred to me that when one threw the bottles to sea, one could put something about oneself on a piece of paper, and when one threw it, one would transcend human limitations. In other words, that very act is a metaphor for transcending our limitations.

Later I realized that this was not just a Cuban phenomenon. Some ideas arise locally and later transcend to a more universal form. Throwing the bottle in the sea is to go beyond the limits of the human spirit in any location in which I find myself. The project consists of 100 drawings made in a style of illuminated manuscripts that are a recapitulation of texts from my notebooks, from notes and images; it is a kind of personal encyclopedia made in drawings, and these drawings go in 100 bottles that are thrown into the sea in different places in the world. The method of the project has to do with chance. When you throw a bottle in the sea, it will find, or connect with, someone you do not know, and at a time and place you also do not know. It is completely outside of space and time, and therefore a new form of engaging with art. It does not go into a gallery or into a museum, but rather it goes to the sea to. . . .

Someone who will receive it. We began the interview with the idea of chance. . . .

Then a series of games with symbols and encounters begin that you cannot foresee. The bottle will be found by someone, and for that person the image of the drawing will mean something. It is a series of events I cannot control, and this fascinates me.

I imagine you keep copies of all this.

There is photographic documentation. I document the process with movies and photographs of the places where I throw the bottles, but the drawings in the bottles are originals with a note that briefly explains the project and gives details about how to contact me for further information. The installation is periodically exhibited, and each time there are less drawings and more documentation and photos in the video. There is also a map where I draw the trajectory, and I document photographically what is happening. This means that one day the piece will be only documentation, and there will be no drawings.

And perhaps many of the pieces will be lost.

Yes, and perhaps some will surface 100 years from now, who knows, transcending not only territory, but also time. The bottles are navigating, and no one knows when they will be picked up.

The project is incredibly original, and suggestive. And from now on, whenever I go to the shore, I will be looking hard for bottles! Thank you very much, it has been a great pleasure, Carlos.

Appendix 2

Carlos Estévez's Biographical Chronology

1969 Born in Havana, Cuba

EDUCATION

1992 Instituto Superior de Arte, Havana, Cuba
1991 Taller de Cine, Escuela Internacional de Cine y Televisión, Havana,
      Cuba
      Taller de Conservación y Restauración, Centro Nacional de
      Conservación, Restauración y Museología, Havana, Cuba
      Taller de Talla en Madera, Instituto Superior de Arte, Havana,
      Cuba
1989 Taller de Fotografía Manipulada, Fototeca de Cuba, Havana, Cuba
1987 Escuela Provincial de Artes Plásticas San Alejandro, Havana, Cuba
1983 Escuela Elemental de Artes Plásticas 20 de Octubre, Havana,
      Cuba

RESIDENCES

2005 Master Prints Series, Massachusetts College of Arts, Massachusetts,
      USA
      Montclair State University, New Jersey, USA
2003–
2004 Cité Internationale des Arts, Paris, France
2003 Sacatar Foundation, Isla Itaparica, Salvador de Bahía, Brazil
2002 Massachusetts College of Art, Boston, MA, USA
2001 TALLIX FOUNDRY, Beacon, NY, USA
2000 Nordic Artists' Centre, Dale, Norway
1998 Fundación Art-OMI, New York, NY, USA
      UNESCO-ASCHBERG, Nordic Artists' Centre, Dale, Norway

1997   Gasworks Studios, London, England
       Academia de San Carlos, Universidad Nacional Autónoma de
          México, Mexico City, Mexico

SOLO EXHIBITIONS

2008   Secret Keepers, Couturier Gallery, Los Angeles, CA, USA
       Hermetic Garden, Panamerican Art Projects, Miami, FL, USA
2007   New Wave from Cuba, Promo-Arte Gallery, Tokio, Japan
       Mirage Habitable, JM'ART Galerie, Paris, France
       Anamorfosis, Havana Galerie, Zurich, Switzerland
       Inner Voices, Sandra and Philip Gordon Gallery, Boston Art
          Academy, Boston, MA, USA
       Speak (Again) Memories, Contemporary Art Center New Orleans,
          Lupin Foundation Gallery, New Orleans, LA, USA
       Labyrinthus, Panamerican Art Projects, Dallas, TX, USA
       Two of a Kind, Alva Gallery, New London, CT, USA
2006   Observatorium, Alonso Art, Miami, FL, USA
       Le voyage inmmobile, Gómez Fine Art, San Juan, Puerto Rico
2005   Irreversible processes, Couturier Gallery, Los Angeles, CA, USA
       Existir en el tiempo, Olga M. & Carlos Saladrigas Gallery,
          Ignatian Center for Arts of Belén Jesuit, Miami, FL, USA
2004   Existential Gravitation, Diana Lowenstein Fine Arts, Miami, FL,
          USA
       Théories et explications, Selam Gallery, Paris, France
       Horror Vacui, Salle Edouard Marcel Sandoz et Michel David-
          Weill, Cité Internationale des Arts, Paris, France
       Sueños y desvelos, Alva Gallery, New London, CT, USA
2003   Botellas al mar, Casa del Lago, Mexico City, Mexico
       Ciudad Secreta, Exposición Colateral a la 8va. Bienal de La
          Habana, Casa Benito Juárez, Havana, Cuba
       La vida y sus implicaciones, Galería Sacramento, Aveiro, Portugal
       Human Transparency, Galería Couturier, Los Angeles, CA, USA
       Viridarium, Cuban Art Space, New York, NY, USA
       No Man's Land, Galeria 106, Austin, TX, USA
       La eternidad cotidiana, Havana Galerie, Zürich, Switzerland
2002   Circo Metafísico, Diana Lowenstein Fine Art, Miami, FL, USA
       El alma es un lugar, Centro de Arte Contemporáneo Wilfredo
          Lam, Havana, Cuba
       Circo cotidiano, Galería Pequeño Espacio, Consejo Nacional de las
          Artes Plásticas, Havana, Cuba

The Dark Theater, ALVA Gallery, New London, CT, USA
Dreamcomber, Bakalar Gallery, Massachusetts College of Art,
    Boston, MA, USA
2001 The Theater of the Soul, Chidlaw Gallery, Cincinnati, OH, USA
The Theater of Life, Galería Couturier, Los Angeles, CA, USA
Stains of Life (with Claudia Bernardi), Movimiento de Arte y
    Cultura Latinoamericana (MACLA), San José, CA, USA
Drawings and Sculpture, Space of the Center for Cuban Studies,
    New York, NY, USA
2000 Stains of Life (con Claudia Bernardi), Galería Habana, Havana,
    Cuba
1999 Bestiarium, Galería Couturier, Los Angeles, CA, USA
1998 Lieux Inconnus, Château de la Napoule, France
Mundo viviente (proyecto dentro de la exhibición colectiva Arte
    contemporáneo de Cuba; Ironía y sobrevivencia en la Isla
    utópica), Arizona State University Art Museum, Tempe, AZ,
    USA
Teatro invisible, Nordic Artists' Centre, Dale, Norway
1997 Visionario II, Galería Nina Menocal, Mexico City, Mexico
The Heart Is a Bridge, Gasworks Gallery, London, England
Visionario, Academia de San Carlos, Mexico City, Mexico
1996 Tratado ontológico, Galería Espacio Abierto, Revista Revolución y
    Cultura, Havana, Cuba
1995 El destino es tuyo (con Santiago Rodríguez Olazábal), Galería
    Latinoamericana, Casa de las Américas, Havana, Cuba
Revelaciones gnómicas, Museo Nacional Palacio de Bellas Artes,
    Havana, Cuba
1993 No sé por qué voy a los extremos (con Luis Gómez), Galería
    Habana, Havana, Cuba
1992 A través del universo, Centro de Desarrollo de las Artes Visuales,
    Havana, Cuba
1987 La cantidad hechizada, Casa del Joven Creador, Havana, Cuba
1984 Pinturas y dibujos, Galería Leopoldo Romañach, Havana, Cuba

GROUP EXHIBITIONS

2008 CIRCA Puerto Rico, Puerto Rico Convention Center, San Juan,
    PR
Feria Internazionale d'Arte Moderna e Contemporanea, Milan, Italy
Merrill Lynch Arte Americas, Miami Beach Convention Center,
    Miami, FL, USA

Spirits of LA, Los Angeles Municipal Art Gallery, Los Angeles, CA, USA

13th Annual Los Angeles Art Show, Los Angeles, CA, USA

2007 Colectiva de Navidad 2007, Allegro Galería, Panama City, Panama

Present ART XIV, Couturier Gallery, Los Angeles, CA, USA

Historias, Beatrice M. Haggerty Gallery, University of Dallas, Irving, TX, USA

RED DOT, Miami Beach, FL, USA

Art Miami, Winwood Distric, Miami, FL, USA

Shanghai Art Fair, Shanghai, China

Legacies 2007: Ceremonies and Celebrations, Alva Gallery, New London, CT, USA

A través del espejo, Arte Cubano Hoy, Allegro Galería, Panama City, Panama

Cuba Avant-Garde: Contemporary Cuban Art from The Farber Collection, Harn Museum of Art, Gainesville, FL, USA; John and Mable Ringling Museum of Art, Sarasota, FL, USA

Bale Latina, Basilea Kulurhaus Westquai 39 Dreilandereck, Basel, Switzerland

Los nuestros, Contemporánea Fine Arts, Miami, FL, USA

Merrill Lynch Arte Americas. Miami Beach Convention Center, Miami, FL, USA

Art-Miami, Gómez Fine Art Gallery, Miami, FL, USA

Laudible Latins, The Ormond Memorial Art Museum & Gardens, Ormond Beach, FL, USA

Layers: Collecting Cuban-American Art, Iris and B. Gerald Cantor Art Gallery, Worcester, MA, USA

New Millennium: Cuban Contemporary Artists, Galería Alovera. Guadalajara, Spain

2006 Cuban Art & Culture, Museum of Latin American Art, Long Beach, CA, USA

In Transition, Latinis Foundation, Limassol, Cyprus

Radicales Libres, Galería GE, Monterrey, Mexico

El Triunfo de la Locura (XI Aniversario), Galería Lyle O'Reitzel, Santo Domingo, Republica Dominicana

Do Outro Lado do Atlântico, Sete Artistas Cubanos na Universidade de Aveiro, Portugal

Siete artistas cubanos, Del otro lado del Atlántico, Galería Sacramento, Aveiro, Portugal

Diversidades del Caribe al Sur, Gómez Fine Art Galería, San Juan, Puerto Rico

Merrill Lynch Arte Americas, Coconut Grove Convention Center, Miami, FL, USA

Arte de Cuba, Centro Cultural Banco do Brasil, São Paulo, Rio de
    Janeiro and Brasilia, Brazil
Habana 1990's, Alonso Art, Miami, FL, USA
ART Miami, Miami Beach Conventional Center, USA
Blow out, The Cuban Art Space of the Center for Cuban Studies,
    New York, NY, USA
2005 Draw, Son Espace Gallery, Palafrugell, Girona, Spain
ArtLA, Los Angeles, CA, USA
AAF Contemporary Art Fair New York City, NY, USA
Being Good: Women's Moral Values in the New Millennium,
    ALVA Gallery, New London, CN, USA
Present Art XII, A Large Show of Small Works, Couturier
    Gallery, Los Angeles, CA, USA
Art Off The Main: The Show of Contemporary African,
    Caribbean & Latin American Art, New York, NY, USA
Arte América, The Latin American Art Fair, Coconut Grove, FL,
    USA
En Homenaje a María Zambrano, Museo de América, Madrid,
    Spain
The Dictionary Project, Brickbottom Gallery, Somerville, MA,
    USA
Palm Beach, America's International Art Fair, FL, USA
2004 Present Art XI, Couturier Gallery, Los Angeles, CA, USA
Cuba From The Inside Looking Out, Elaine L. DeRoy
    Auditorium, Wayne State University, Detroit, MI, USA
7 Artistas Cubanos, Galeria Sacramento, Aveiro, Portugal
« 50 × 70 » Obra sobre papel, Habana Galerie, Zurich, Switzerland
Exposición de grupo de primavera, Cité Internationale des Arts,
    Paris, France
2do Salón de Pequeño Formato, Espacio de Arte de ACEA'S,
    Barcelona, Spain
6th Art International Zurich, Switzerland
2003 XXV Colectiva de Dezembro, Galeria Sacramento, Aveiro,
    Portugal
31 Artistas Cubanos Contemporáneos en Chile, Galería BordeRío,
    Vitacura, Santiago, Chile
Contemporary Cuban Art and the Art of Survival, Natalie and
    James Thompson Gallery, San Jose State University, CA, USA
Inside/outside, Contemporary Cuban Art, Charlotte and Philip
    Hanes Art Gallery, Wake Forest University, Winston-Salem,
    NC, USA
Arte Cubano Contemporáneo, Subasta humanitaria, Casa de las
    Américas, Havana, Cuba.

Shuttered Cuba, Alva Gallery, New London, USA

Paranoia, Cyprus Art, Sant Feliu de Boada, Girona, Spain

Invadiendo territorios, Arte Cubano Contemporáneo, Museo Bellas Artes Gravinia, Palacio Conde Lumiares, Alicante, Spain

Cuban Art from the Permanent Collection, Arizona State University Art Museum, Tempe, AR, USA

2002 Arte de Cuba, Colección Ludwig, Russian State Musuem, Saint Petersburg, Russia.

XXIV Colectiva de dezembro, Galería Sacramento, Aveiro, Portugal

Diversities: Six Artists from Cuba, El Camino College Art Gallery, Torrance, CA, USA

Present Art IX: A Large Show of Small Works, Galería Couturier, Los Angeles, CA, USA

Boston Art Fair, Cyclorama, Boston, MA, USA

El arte por la vida, Salón Blanco del Convento de San Francisco de Asís, Havana, Cuba.

Subasta Habana.com Expo ON-LINE, Fundación Habana Club, Havana, Cuba

Intercidade, Juiz de Fora, Galeria Arlindo Daibert do Centro Cultural Bernardo Mascareñas, Minas Gerais, Brazil

Las Antillas/West Indies, Galería Haydee Santamaría, Casa de las Américas, Havana, Cuba

En torno al entorno, Centro de Desarrollo de las Artes Visuales, Havana, Cuba.

From a Black Hole, Cuba, Son Space, Molí de Pals, Girona, Spain

16 Artistas Cubanos en Beirut, Palacio de la UNESCO de Beirut, Lebanon

Cuba Fusión, Arts Council, Greenwich, CN, USA

Feria de Arte de Chicago, Navy Pier, Chicago, IL, USA

Arte cubano contemporáneo, Muestra colateral a la Bienal de São Paulo, Galería Marta Traba, Memorial América Latina, São Paulo, Brazil

2001 Contexto: Arte reciente de Cuba en la Colección Permanente, Museo del Bronx, New York, NY, USA

Tercer Salón de Arte Contemporáneo, Centro de Desarrollo de las Artes Visuales, Havana, Cuba

Up Up & Away, The Viewing Room, New York, NY, USA

Cuba: Five Odysseys, Gallery of the State University of California at Northridge, CA, USA

Cuba, Isla infinita, Arte contemporáneo, Museo de Arte Costarricense, San José, Costa Rica

Arte cubano: entre el lienzo y el papel, Sala Miró, Sede de la UNESCO, Paris, France.

Viva Cuba, Alva Gallery, New London, CN, USA

Feria de ARCO 2001, Madrid, Spain

2000   Arte Contemporáneo, Salon de Exposiciones de la Prefectura de
       Santo André, Santo André, São Paulo, Brazil

       Arte Contemporáneo cubano, Subasta Humanitaria, Casa de las
       Américas, Havana, Cuba

       7ma. Bienal de La Habana, Uno más cerca del otro, Fortaleza de
       la Cabaña, Havana, Cuba

       La gente en casa, 7ma Bienal de La Habana, Museo Nacional de
       Bellas Artes, Havana, Cuba

       Two Nations, Works on paper, White Water Gallery, North Bay,
       ON, Canada

       Contemporary Art from Cuba, The Art Institute of Boston at
       Lesley University, Boston, MA, USA

       De Valigia in Cuba, Centro Provincial de Artes Plásticas y Diseño,
       Havana, Cuba

       Una mano y las dos, Centro de Desarrollo de las Artes Visuales,
       Havana, Cuba

       Salón de invierno, Centro de Desarrollo de las Artes Visuales,
       Havana, Cuba

       Transforma, Casa de la Cultura Carmen Montilla, Havana, Cuba

       Bienal de Estandartes, IV Salón, Centro Cultural de Tijuana,
       Tijuana, Mexico

       International Young Art 2000, Sotheby's Tel Aviv, Israel; Sotheby's
       Chicago, USA; Sotheby's Vienna, Austria

1999   Con un poco de amor, Centro Provincial de Artes y Diseño,
       Havana, Cuba

       Arte Cubano, más allá del papel, Centro Cultural del Conde
       Duque, Madrid, Spain

       Sobre papel, Galería Nina Menocal, Mexico City, Mexico

       Sobre papel, Galería Couturier, Los Angeles, CA, USA

       Ajiaco, Galería La Acacia, Havana, Cuba

       Cuatro Artistas Cubanos, Geunkes & De Vil Gallery, Knokke,
       Belgium

       Imaginaciones Cubanas, Centro Cultural La Mercé, Girona, Spain

1998   II Salón de Arte Cubano Contemporáneo, Centro de Desarrollo de
       las Artes Visuales, Havana, Cuba

       La isla futura, Arte joven cubano, Centro de Cultura Antiguo
       Instituto, Gijón, Spain

       Arte Cubano de fin de siglo, Festival Iberoamericano de Cádiz,
       Baluarte de la Candelaria, Cádiz, Spain

       VI Bienal Internacional de Pintura, América: Vidas, Cuerpos e
       Historias, Cuenca, Ecuador

Un Siglo de Arte Joven, Arte Cubano en los 90s, VI Congreso de
UNEAC, Palacio de las Convenciones, Havana, Cuba

Seducciones, Centro de Arte Contemporáneo Wilfredo Lam,
Havana, Cuba.

Cuba, Drammen Museum, Drammen, Norway

Cubanías (de la Isla Caribeña 52 años después), Museo de Bellas
Artes, Buenos Aires, Argentina

Contemporary Art from Cuba: Irony and Survival on the Utopian
Island, Arizona State University Art Museum, Tempe, AR,
USA; Yerba Buena Center for the Arts at the DeYoung
Museum, San Francisco, CA; Cranbrook Art Museum,
Bloomfield Hills, MI, USA; Austin Museum of Art, Austin,
TX, USA; Grand Rapids Art Museum, Grand Rapids, MI,
USA; Museum of Latin American Art, Long Beach, CA, USA;
University Art Museum, University of California, Santa Barbara,
CA, USA; Spencer Museum of Art, University of Kansas,
Lawrence, KA, USA; Contemporary Art Museum, University of
South Florida, Tampa Bay, FL, USA

Maferefun Cuba, African Religious Symbols in Cuban Art, The
Metropolitan Pavilion Gallery, New York, NY, USA

Cent ans de peinture cubaine, Chaire Goya, Centre Universitaire
Méditerranée, Nice, France

International Art Weekend, Art-OMI, New York, NY, USA

New Art from Cuba, Trask Gallery, National Arts Club, New
York, NY, USA

Fragmentos a su imán, Galería Latinoamericana, Casa de las
Américas, Havana, Cuba

Agada Umbo Omode (la fuerza viene de todos), Centro de
Desarrollo de las Artes Visuales, Havana, Cuba

Comment peut-on être cubain? Maison de l'Amérique Latin, Paris,
France

La imagen y el laberinto, Arte Cubano Actual, Casa de las Artes,
Vigo, Iglesia de la Universidad, Santiago de Compostela, Spain

Feria de ARCO, Madrid, Spain

1997   El arte que no cesa, Centro de Arte Contemporáneo Wilfredo
Lam, Havana, Cuba.

Arte cubano actual, Centro de Arte Antiguo Instituto de
Jovellanos, Gijón, Spain

V Salón de Dibujo, Museo de Arte Moderno, Santo Domingo,
Dominican Republic

Salón Nacional de Grabado 97, Centro Provincial de Artes
Plásticas y Diseño, Havana, Cuba

Imaginaciones de otra Isla, Proyecto de Isla a Isla, Fundación Arismendi, Casa de la Cultura de Asunción, Isla Margarita, Venezuela

VI Bienal de La Habana, Recintos Interiores, Fortaleza San Carlos de la Cabaña, Havana, Cuba

El ocultamiento de las almas, Centro de Desarrollo de las Artes Visuales, Havana, Cuba Arte Contemporáneo del Caribe y Suecia, Galería Latinoamericana, Casa de las Américas, Havana, Cuba; Galería Mar Blanco, Stockolm, Sweeden

Presencias, Arte Cubano de fin de siglo, Sala de Exposiciones de la Cámara de Comercio, Santander, Pabellón de Exposiciones de la Ciudadela de Pamplona; Sociedad Económica de amigos del País, Málaga; Casa de las Artes, Vigo, Spain

First Public Exhibition of The Cuban Art, Space of the Center for Cuban Studies, Metropolitan Book Center, New York, NY, USA

1996   Plástica Cubana Actual, Embajada de la República de Cuba en Beijing, China Fotocentro, Gallery of the Journalist's Union, Moscow, Russia

A mitad del sueño, Casa de Cultura de Celaya, Mexico City, Mexico

Ni fresa ni chocolate, Convento de Santa Clara (CENCREM), Havana, Cuba

Mundo soñado, Casa de América, Palacio de Linares, Madrid, Spain

1995   Relaciones inconexas, Taller de serigrafía René Portocarrero, Havana, Cuba

Segunda Bienal Barro de América, Centro de Arte Lía Bermúdez, Maracaibo, Venezuela

Primer Salón de Arte Cubano Contemporáneo, Museo Nacional Castillo de la Real Fuerza, Havana, Cuba

Con Cuba de igual a igual, Edificio Cultural La Bolsa, Bilbao, Sala de Exposiciones del Ayuntamiento, Barakaldo, Biskay, Spain

Plástica Cubana Contemporánea, Centro Cultural de Belén, Lisbon, Portugal

Libro objeto, Centro Wilfredo Lam, Havana, Cuba

Imágenes de Martí, Casa del Lago, Mexico City, Mexico; Teatro Nacional Rubén Darío, Managua, Nicaragua; Museo de Arte Contemporáneo, Panama City, Panama; Fundación Guayasamín, Quito, Ecuador

Salón de Pintura Cubana Contemporánea Juan Francisco Elso, Museo Nacional Palacio de Bellas Artes, Havana, Cuba

Iluminación, Centro de Desarrollo de las Artes Visuales, Havana, Cuba

1994 La Jeune Peinture Cubaine, Centre Marquiniquais d'Action Culturelle, Fort de France, Martinique

1994 Utopía, Galería Espada, Centro de Desarrollo de las Artes Visuales, La Habana, Cuba

Minutos antes, Galería Paralelo 23, São Paulo, Brazil

Avances, Centro Provincial de Artes Plásticas, Guantánamo, Cuba

V Bienal de La Habana, Dados de Medianoche, Galería La Espuela de Plata, Centro de Desarrollo de las Artes Visuales, Havana, Cuba

Salón de la Ciudad 1994, Centro Nacional de Artes Plásticas y Diseño, Havana, Cuba

Cómprame y cuélgame, Centro de Desarrollo de las Artes Visuales, Havana, Cuba

1993 Dibujo no te olvido, Centro de Desarrollo de las Artes Visuales, Havana, Cuba

1992 Nacido en Cuba, Itinerant exposition in several cities in Mexico, Puerto Rico, and Venezuela

1989 III Bienal de la Habana, Muestra colateral del Instituto Superior de Arte, Havana, Cuba

Festival de la creación, Instituto Superior de Arte, Havana, Cuba

1984–
1986 Exposición de estudiantes en el marco de las Jornadas Científicas, Galería Leopoldo Romañach, Havana, Cuba

PRIZES

1998 Mención de Estímulo, VI Bienal Internacional de Pintura de Cuenca, Cuenca, Ecuador

1995 Gran Premio Primer Salón de Arte Cubano Contemporáneo, Havana, Cuba

Premio de la Revista Revolución y Cultura al Primer Salón de Arte Cubano Contemporáneo, Havana, Cuba

1994 Gran Premio Salón de la Ciudad, Havana, Cuba

Premio del Consejo Nacional de las Artes Plásticas al Salón de la Ciudad, Havana, Cuba

PUBLIC COLLECTIONS

Fundación Arte Viva, Rio de Janeiro, Brazil

Museo del Bronx, New York, USA

Bacardi Art Foundation, Miami, FL, USA
Fort Lauderdale Museum of Art, Fort Lauderlade, FL, USA
Association d'Art de La Napoule, France Drammens Museum for
    Kunst og Kulturhistorie, Drammens, Norway
Acerbo Histórico de la Academia de San Carlos, Mexico City,
    Mexico
Museo Nacional Palacio de Bellas Artes, Havana, Cuba
Kunst Forum Ludwig, Aachen, Germany
Colección Casa de las Américas, Havana, Cuba
Center for Cuban Studies, New York, NY, USA
Arizona State University Art Museum, Tempe, AZ, USA
OMI Foundation Collection, New York, NY, USA
MOLAA, Museum of Latin American Art, Long Beach, CA,
    USA
Private collections in Argentina, Brazil, Canada, England, France,
    Haiti, Holland, Mexico, Norway, Peru, Portugal, Spain, Sweden,
    Switzerland, the United States, and Venezuela

Appendix 3

Carlos Estévez's Images of Thought

Curated by Jorge J. E. Gracia
November 5, 2009–February 6, 2010

ACKNOWLEDGMENTS BY SANDRA H. OLSEN,
DIRECTOR OF UB ART GALLERIES

As early as 1907 the term "interpretation" in museums became synonymous with education while it simultaneously identified the unique characteristic of museum education as learning through the use of objects. Proclaiming to be centers of education and enlightenment, museums strived to avoid criticism that they appealed only to the educated few and collected objects valued by wealthy leaders by supporting programs and "interpretive" materials that could communicate certain truths, reveal meanings, and impart understanding of cultural heritage and scientific knowledge to the general public.

As museums and galleries became increasingly dependent upon government support, members of the public began to critically examine the educational value of museums and their role as interpreters of their cultural heritage. During the social upheaval of the 1960's various members of the public challenged the rights of museums to serve as cultural gatekeepers and questioned their authority and purpose. *How* and *when* were the objects acquired and *from whom*? *Who* interprets the objects and articulates their identity and with *what authority*? During the next two decades, while museums struggled to broaden the diversity of their exhibitions and programs and provide interpretive materials that offered multiple perspectives, numerous communities took control of their cultural identity and its interpretation by boldly founding cultural-specific museums around the nation.

Issues of cultural identity have been increasingly heightened by globalization and the *angst* it generates for the future world economy and environment. UB Art Gallery is extremely fortunate, therefore to be working a second time with SUNY Distinguished Professor and Samuel P. Capen Chair Jorge J. E. Gracia who has dedicated much of his research to questions of cultural identity with artworks as the instruments for discourse. This exhibition is the perfect sequel to the 2006 exhibition of Cuban American art he brought to

231

the gallery in conjunction with a National Endowment for the Humanities Seminar, "Negotiating Identities in Art, Literature and Philosophy: Cuban Americans and American Culture." Although the current project was initiated by Gracia's customary process of introducing a newly discovered artist, Carlos Estévez, to his ongoing website project, "Cuban Art Outside Cuba: Identity, Philosophy, and Art," his conversations with the artist led to a meticulous examination of the paintings and an extensive dialogue about the interpretation of art. For this publication and the exhibition, *Carlos Estévez's Images of Thought,* Jorge Gracia simultaneously assumes the challenges of art historians, curators and philosophers by tackling both a conceptual analysis and philosophical interpretation of the rich and complex paintings of Carlos Estévez. Typical of Professor Gracia's generosity, he not only invites us to join in the discussion but provides an intelligible framework for us to participate.

We are most grateful to Jorge Gracia for entrusting us with presenting the exhibition that accompanies his most recent publication. It is a privilege and always a pleasure to work with him. At the University at Buffalo, I wish to thank President John B. Simpson; Provost and Vice President for Academic Affairs Satish K. Tripathi; and Bruce Mccombe, Distinguished Professor and Dean of the College of Arts and Sciences. On the UB Art Gallery staff I thank Sandra Firmin, curator; Jennifer Markee, financial and general operations manager; Kitty Marmion, administrative assistant; and the external affairs officer and the preparator.

UB Art Gallery is funded by the UB College of Arts and Sciences, the visual Arts Building Fund, the Seymour H. Knox Foundation Fine Arts Fund, and the Fine Arts Center Endowment.

EXHIBITION CHECKLIST

Asterisks indicate that the work is featured or mentioned in this book. Hight precedes width precedes depth; dimensions are in inches.

1. *A través del universo* (Through the Universe), 1992, Wood, fabric, candle, glass eyes, 79 × 157 × 12, Collection of Mr. and Mrs. Howard Farber
2. *Homo absconditus* (Hidden Man), 1994, Wood, hair, candles, 79 × 79 × 12, Collection of Ms. Amarilys García
3. *El espacio es una condición mental* (Space is a Mental Condition), 1998, Watercolor on paper, 27.5 × 39, Collection of the artist
4. *Horadar* (Drill), 1998, Watercolor and watercolor pencil on paper, 27.5 × 39, Collection of Ms. Amarilys García
5. *Mecánica natural* (Natural Mechanics), 1998, Watercolor and watercolor pencil on paper, 27.5 × 39, Collection of Mr. Carlos Estévez Jr

6. *El secreto de la vida* (Life's Secret), 1998, Wood and branches sculpture, ca. 96 × 96 × 12, Collection of the artist

7. **Botellas al mar* (Bottles to Sea), 2000, Installation consisting of 83 drawings on paper and 83 bottles, each drawing ca. 36 × 5-10, Collection of the artist

8 **Oscilaciones de la fe* (Waverings of Faith), 2003, Oil and pencil on canvas, 37 × 64, Collection of Ms. Amarilys García

9. *Sueños paralelos* (Parallel Dreams), 2003, Oil on canvas, 40 × 80, Collection of Mr. Carlos Estévez Jr

10. *Gravitación existencial* (Existential Gravitation), 2004, Oil on canvas, 56 × 25, Collection of the artist

11. **Horror vacui* (Fear of Empty Spaces), 2004, Oil and pencil on canvas, 55 × 39.5, Collection of the artist

12. **El ser indeterminado* (Undetermined Being), 2004, Oil and pencil on canvas, 38 × 64, Collection of Mr. José A. Pérez-Gurri

13. **Procesos irreversibles* (Irreversible Processes), 2004, Oil and pencil on canvas, 51 × 77, Collection of the artist

14. *Ejercicios de conciencia* (Exercises of Conscience), 2005, Collage on paper, 19.5 × 12, Collection of Mr. Carlos Estévez Jr

15. **Pensamientos numerales* (Numerical Thoughts), 2005, Mixed media on paper, 20 × 30, Collection of Prof. and Mrs. Jorge Gracia

16. *Camera Man*, 2006, Wood, photographic lenses, ready-made glass, eyes, metal, 64 × ca. 48 × ca 48, Collection of the artist

17. *Cruzadas personales* (Personal Crusades), 2006, Collage on paper, 12 × 79, Collection of the artist

18. *Noah II*, 2006, Wood and paper, 47 × 95 × 21.5, Collection of the artist

19. **Self-fishing*, 2006, Collage on paper, 39 × 27.5, Collection of Prof. and Mrs. Jorge Gracia

20. *Teatro de sombras* (Theater of Shadows), 2006, Collage on paper, 39.5 × 14, Collection of Ms. Amarilys García

21. *Universo portátil* (Portable Universe), 2006, Collage on paper, 39.5 × 13, Collection of Mr. Carlos Estévez Jr

22. **Amores difíciles* (Difficult Loves), 2007, Pencil and gouache on Nepal paper, 30 × 20, Collection of Prof. and Mrs. Jorge Gracia

23. **Forging People*, 2007, Pencil and gouache on Nepal paper, 30 × 20, Collection of Prof. and Mrs. Jorge Gracia

24. **Vasos comunicantes* (Communicating Vessels), 2007, Ink on paper, 11 × 8, Collection of Prof. and Mrs. Jorge Gracia

25. *El juego de la eternidad ilusoria* (The Game of Illusory Eternity), 2008, Mixed media, 40 × 64 × 3, Collection of Mr. and Mrs. Howard Farber

26. *Theatrum mundi* (World Theater), 2008, Mixed media, 56 × 96 × 3, Pan American Collection
27. *El jardín de los senderos que se birfurcan* (The Garden of Forking Paths), 2009, Pencil and gouache on Nepal paper, 30 × 20, Collection of Prof. and Mrs. Jorge Gracia

Notes

PREFACE

1. Perhaps I should say "perceptual art" because my claims apply to all art to which we have access through the senses. However, since the examples I use and the works of Estévez I discuss in this book are visual, I will continue to speak of visual art. For the tactile aspect of pictures, see Dominic McIver Lopes, "Vision, Touch, and the Value of Pictures," *British Journal of Aesthetics* 42: 2 (2002): 191–201.

CHAPTER 1

1. See, for example, Lopes, *Understanding Pictures* (Oxford: Clarendon Press, 1996) and "Directive Pictures," *Journal of Aesthetics and Art Criticism* 62: 2 (2004): 189–96, James Elkins, *The Object That Stares Back* (San Diego, CA: Harcourt Brace & Co., 1996), and Gilles Deleuze, *Francis Bacon: The Logic of Sensation,* trans. Daniel Smith (New York: Continuum, 2005).

2. See Jean-Paul Sartre's "The Paintings of Giacometti," in *Situations,* trans. Benita Eisler (New York: Fawcett, 1965), 124–35; Jacques Derrida's *The Truth in Painting,* trans. Geoff Bennington and Ian McLeod (Chicago: University of Chicago Press, 1987); Deleuze's *Francis Bacon;* and Michel Foucault's *The Order of Things: An Archeology of the Human Sciences* (New York: Pantheon, 1970), ch. 1.

3. See Walter Benjamin, *The Arcades Project,* ed. Rolf Tiedemann, trans. Howard Eiland, illus. Kevin McLaughlin (Cambridge, MA: Harvard University Press, 2002); Martin Heidegger, *Ontology: The Hermeneutics of Facticity,* trans. John van Buren, 26–27 (Indianapolis: Indiana University Press, 1988); Foucault, *This Is Not a Pipe,* trans. J. Harkness (Berkeley: University of California Press, 1983); and Julian Young's discussion of Heidegger's "The Origin of the Work of Art," in the first chapter of *Heidegger's Philosophy of Art* (Cambridge: Cambridge University Press, 2001).

4. For example, Arthur C. Danto, *After the End of Art: Contemporary Art and the Pale of History* (Princeton, NJ: Princeton University Press, 1997).

5. Cited by Daniel W. Smith in "Translator's Introduction," in Deleuze, *Francis Bacon,* xx.

6. See, for example, Gracia, Carolyn Korsmeyer, and Rodolphe Gasché, eds., *Literary Philosophers: Borges, Calvino, Eco* (New York: Routledge, 2002).

7. Sigmund Freud himself has an interpretation of Leonardo da Vinci's *Madonna and Child with St. Anne,* in *Leonardo da Vinci: A Memory of His Childhood,* ed. James Strachey and Anna Freud (London: Art Paperbacks, 1987).

8. Plato, *The Republic,* book V, in *The Collected Dialogues of Plato, including the Letters,* ed. Edith Hamilton and Huntington Cairns, 688–720 (New York: Pantheon Books, 1961). For a view that emphasizes the cognitive value in art, see Nelson Goodman, *Languages of Art: An Approach to a Theory of Symbols* (Indianapolis, IN: Hackett, 1976), 248, 262–65.

9. See Jerrold Levinson, "Emotion in Response to Art: A Survey of the Terrain," in *Emotion and the Arts,* ed. Mette Hjort and Sue Laver, 20–34 (New York: Oxford University Press, 1997).

10. Elkins, *What Painting Is: How to Think about Oil Painting, Using the Language of Alchemy* (New York: Routledge, 1999), 93; see also 2, 5.

11. Danto has argued that there is something similar in the logic of words and art, in that both words and art contrast with "real things," but this is not to say "that art is a language." See *The Transfiguration of the Commonplace: A Philosophy of Art* (Cambridge, MA: Harvard University Press, 1981), 82–83.

12. Danto, *The Transfiguration of the Commonplace,* 88.

13. Foucault, *The Order of Things,* 48.

14. I have explored the identity of literary works in Gracia, "Borges's 'Pierre Menard': Philosophy or Literature?" in *Literary Philosophers,* 85–108. For the use of words in art, see also Foucault's understanding of one of Magritte's works as a calligram, in *This Is Not a Pipe,* particularly ch. 2.

15. Theodor W. Adorno claims that artworks are indeed logical and even syllogistic, but what he understands by this is quite different from what is usually meant by, say, Aristoteleans and Fregeans. The syllogisms in question lack both concepts and judgments, having more to do with what Adorno calls experience and empirical thought. See *Aesthetic Theory,* trans. Robert Hullot-Kentor (Minneapolis: University of Minnesota Press, 1997), 136. And Stanley Cavell has claimed that the logic of aesthetic claims and ordinary language philosophy is not different. See "Music Discomposed," in *Must We Mean What We Say?* (Cambridge: Cambridge University Press, 1976), 189. See also J. M. Bernstein's criticism of this claim in *Against Voluptuous Bodies: Late Modernism and the Meaning of Painting* (Stanford, CA: Stanford University Press, 2006), 78 ff.

16. One of the chapters in Foucault's *This Is Not a Pipe* is entitled "To Paint Is Not to Affirm," 53.

17. Adorno, *Aesthetic Theory,* 136, 137. And some artists, such as Magritte, agree. See Suzi Galik, *Magritte* (New York: Thames and Hudson, 1985), 12.

18. Adorno, *Aesthetic Theory,* 130.

19. For examples of the ways artists talk about their art, see the interviews in Gracia, Lynette M. F. Bosch, and Isabel Alvarez Borland, eds., *Identity, Memory, and Diaspora: Voices of Cuban-American Artists, Writers, and Philosophers* (Albany: State University of New York Press, 2007), and Gracia's Web site, *Cuban Art Outside Cuba: Identity, Philosophy, and Art,* http://www.philosophy.buffalo.edu/capenchair/CAOC/index.html.

20. Peter Lamarque and Stein Haugom Olsen seem to extend this point to literature, in *Truth, Fiction, and Literature: A Philosophical Perspective* (Oxford: Clarendon Press, 1994), 365.

21. Adorno, *Aesthetic Theory*, 130–33.

22. Bernstein, *Against Voluptuous Bodies*, 8. For Bernstein, this is not a problem of art and philosophy per se but rather a reflection of a deeper problem having to do with what he calls "the abstraction of modernity" (122).

23. Danto, *The Transfiguration of the Commonplace*, vii.

24. Bernstein, *Against Voluptuous Bodies*, 230 ff.

25. Danto seems to be moving in this direction in *After the End of Art*, 37.

CHAPTER 2

1. The bibliography at the end of this book has a section on Cuban art, where pertinent sources are listed, but see in particular Juan A. Martínez, *Cuban Art and National Identity: The Vanguardia Painters 1927–1950* (Gainesville: University Press of Florida, 1994), and Bosch, *Cuban-American Art in Miami: Exile, Identity, and the Neo-Baroque* (London: Lund Humphreys Press, 2004).

2. See Gracia, "Cuban-American Identity and Art," in *Cuban-American Literature and Art: Negotiating Identities*, ed. Alvarez Borland and Bosch (Albany: State University of New York Press, 2009), pp. 175–89.

3. See the interview with him on Gracia's Web page, *Cuban Art Outside Cuba: Identity, Philosophy, and Art*.

4. For revealing interviews about the work of some Cuban artists, see Gracia, Bosch, and Alvarez Borland, eds., *Identity, Memory, and Diaspora*, and Gracia's Web pages, *Cuban Art Outside Cuba* and *Negotiating Identities in Art, Literature, and Philosophy: Cuban Americans and American Culture*, a 2006 NEH Summer Seminar, http://www.philosophy.buffalo.edu/contrib/events/neh06.html.

5. Taken and edited from http://www.carlosestevez.net/.

CHAPTER 20

1. I discuss interpretation in more detail in Gracia, *A Theory of Textuality: The Logic and Epistemology* (Albany: State University of New York Press, 1995), 147–79, and *How Can We Know What God Means? The Interpretation of Revelation* (New York: Palgrave, 2001). For other conceptions and discussions of interpretation, see Paul Ricoeur, "Creativity in Language: Word, Polysemy, Metaphor," in *The Philosophy of Paul Ricoeur: An Anthology of His Work*, ed. Charles E. Reagan and David Stewart, 128 (Boston, MA: Beacon Press, 1978); J. W. Meiland, "Interpretation as a Cognitive Discipline," *Philosophy and Literature* 2 (1978): 25; Morris Weitz, *Hamlet and the Philosophy of Literary Criticism* (Chicago: University of Chicago Press, 1964), ch. 15; C. L. Stevenson, "On the Reasons That Can Be Given for the Interpretation

of a Poem," in *Philosophy Looks at the Arts*, ed. Joseph Margolis, 127 (New York: Scribner, 1962); Margolis and Tom Rockmore, eds., *The Philosophy of Interpretation* (Oxford: Blackwell, 2000); Stephen Davies, *Philosophical Perspectives on Art* (Oxford: Oxford University Press, 2007); and Robert Stecker, *Interpretation and Construction: Art, Speech, and the Law* (Malden, MA: Blackwell, 2003). I refer to specific views and the corresponding literature later.

2. See Danto, *The Transfiguration of the Commonplace*, 119, and Lopes, *Understanding Pictures*, 162–63, 158.

3. Lamarque and Olsen, *Truth, Fiction, and Literature*, 257.

4. Davies, *The Philosophy of Art* (Malden, MA: Blackwell, 2006), 111. See also Kendall L. Walton's discussion of "objects of representation," in his *Mimesis as Make-Believe: On the Foundations of the Representational Arts* (Cambridge, MA: Harvard University Press, 1990), 106–37, and Richard Wollheim, *Art and Its Objects*, 2nd. edition (Cambridge: Cambridge University Press, 1980).

5. Stecker emphasizes the need to recognize the multiple aims people have when interpreting artworks in his *Interpretation and Construction*, 52–55.

6. For a brief excursus into meaning in art, see Danto, *After the End of Art*, 195. See also "Art and Meaning," in *Theories of Art Today*, ed. Noël Carroll, 130–40 (Madison: University of Wisconsin Press, 2000). Among those who recognize the role of understanding in interpretation is Stecker, in *Interpretation and Construction*, 21. However, he unnecessarily narrows down this role to the understanding of the work under interpretation (72). A broader object seems more appropriate, as I argue below.

7. Foucault, *This Is Not a Pipe*, 32, 44.

8. I discuss meaning in Gracia, "Meaning," in *Dictionary for the Theological Interpretation of the Bible*, ed. Kevin J. Vanhoozer, 492–99 (Grand Rapids, MI: Baker Bookhouse, 2005). Some philosophers have questioned the viability of the concept of meaning. See, for example, W. V. O. Quine, "On What There Is," reprinted in *From a Logical Point of View* (Cambridge, MA: Harvard University Press, 1953).

9. See E. D. Hirsch Jr., *Validity in Interpretation* (New Haven, CT: Yale University Press, 1967).

10. Saul A. Kripke, *Naming and Necessity* (Cambridge, MA: Harvard University Press, 1987). I discuss this theory in chapter 6 of Gracia, *Individuality: An Essay on the Foundations of Metaphysics* (Albany: State University of New York Press, 1988).

11. A. J. Ayer, *Language, Truth, and Logic* (New York: Dover, 1936).

12. G. Frege, *Collected Papers* (Oxford: Oxford University Press, 1984).

13. See Goodman, *Languages of Art*, 58.

14. Deleuze, *Francis Bacon*, 6, 82.

15. Foucault, *This Is Not a Pipe*, chs. 3, 5. See also James Harkness, "Translator's Introduction," in Foucault, *This Is Not a Pipe*, 9.

16. Cited by Harkness in "Translator's Introduction," in Foucault, *This Is Not a Pipe*, 12.

17. H. P. Grice, "Meaning," *Philosophical Review* 66 (1957): 377–88.

18. For non-mental forms, see Plato, *The Republic*, book V; for abstract objects, see Frege, *Collected Papers*; for mental concepts or images, see John Locke, *An Essay Concerning Human Understanding* (New York: Dover, 1959); and for the

result of mental or neurological states, see J. Fodor, *Psychosemantics* (Boston, MA: MIT Press, 1987).

19. Quine, *Word and Object* (Cambridge, MA: Harvard University Press, 1960).

20. Gracia, "Borges's 'Pierre Menard.'"

21. L. Wittgenstein, *Philosophical Investigations* (Oxford: Oxford University Press, 1953).

22. M. Dummett, *Truth and Other Enigmas* (London: Duckworth, 1978).

23. See J. L. Austin, *How to Do Things with Words*, ed. J. Urmsum (Cambridge, MA: Harvard University Press, 1962).

24. John Searle, *Expression and Meaning* (Cambridge: Cambridge University Press, 1975).

25. See Davies, *The Philosophy of Art*, 114–22.

26. The classic statement of intentionalism has been given by Hirsch, in *Validity in Interpretation* (see, for example, p. 25). See also S. Knapp and W. B. Michaels, "Against Theory," *Critical Inquiry* 8 (1982): 723–42, "Against Theory 2," *Critical Inquiry* 14 (1988): 49–68; and Nicholas Wolterstorff, "Toward an Ontology of Works of Art," *Nous* 9 (1975): 136. For more recent discussions, see William Irwin, *Intentionalist Interpretations: A Philosophical Explanation and Defense* (Westport, CT: Greenwood Press, 1999); Paisley Livingstone, *Art and Intention: A Philosophical Study* (Oxford: Clarendon Press, 2005); and Lopes, who argues in particular against an intentionalist view of interpretation in art, in *Understanding Pictures*, ch. 8. Danto seems to come on the side of intentionalists in *The Transfiguration of the Commonplace*, 129–30.

27. For discussions of these issues, see Irwin, ed., *The Death and Resurrection of the Author* (Westport, CT: Greenwood Press, 2002), and Gracia, *Texts: Ontological Status, Identity, Author, Audience* (Albany: State University of New York Press, 1996).

28. In the specific case of pictorial art, Lopes has distinguished between artist meaning and pictorial meaning—which correspond roughly to the first and third categories I list. See Lopes, *Understanding Pictures*, ch. 8. And Davies has tried to strike a middle ground between intentionalism (where the intention of the author is paramount) and anti-intentionalism (where the intention of the author is irrelevant), with what he calls "a value-maximizing theory." He aims to go beyond the intention of an author while maintaining the integrity of the work. See *Philosophical Perspectives on Art*, 16.

29. I have discussed this issue in Gracia, *A Theory of Textuality*, 111ff.

30. Davies, *The Philosophy of Art*, 126.

31. Ibid., 113.

32. See for example, Foucault, "What Is an Author?," in *Language, Counter-Memory, Practice: Selected Essays and Interviews*, ed. Donald F. Bouchard, 113–38, trans. Donald F. Bouchard and Sherry Simon (Ithaca, NY: Cornell University Press, 1977).

33. For more on this, see Gracia, *How Can We Know What God Means?*

34. A good example of how the various factors about which I have been speaking function is a film interpretation of a literary work. One particularly instructive example concerns film interpretations of Bram Stoker's *Dracula*, whose main character has inspired more films than any other literary character in the history of literature.

See Gracia, "From Horror to Hero: Film Interpretations of Stoker's *Dracula*," in *Philosophy and the Interpretation of Pop Culture*, ed. Irwin and Gracia, 187–214 (Lanham, MD: Rowman & Littlefield, 2007).

35. Danto, *The Transfiguration of the Commonplace*, 208.

36. I discuss this issue in detail in the context of philosophical texts in Gracia, *Philosophy and Its History: Issues in Philosophical Historiography* (Albany: State University of New York Press, 1991), ch. 5. Much of what I say there can be applied, *mutatis mutandis*, to art. Stecker has explored and emphasized the importance of the aims of interpretation in art in *Interpretation and Construction*, 5–7, 34–37.

37. Foucault, "What Is an Author?"

38. Davies appears to defend a nonauthorial, but nonetheless unitary, interpretation in *The Philosophy of Art*, 130–31.

39. The conference took place at the University at Buffalo on October 26 and 27, 2007. For the program and further details, see http://www.philosophy.buffalo.edu/events/conferences/forging/.

CHAPTER 21

1. See Carroll, "Introduction," in *Theories of Art Today*, 3–24, and Davies, *Definitions of Art* (Ithaca, NY: Cornell University Press, 1991), *The Philosophy of Art*, 26–51, and *Philosophical Perspectives on Art*.

2. One of the main leaders of this effort was Weitz. See "The Role of Theory in Aesthetics," *Journal of Aesthetics and Art Criticism* 15 (1956): 27–35.

3. Gracia, *A Theory of Textuality*, 52–59.

4. Ibid.; see also Korsmeyer, "On Distinguishing 'Aesthetic' from 'Artistic,'" *Journal of Aesthetic Education* 11: 4 (1977): 45–57; George Dickie, *Art and the Aesthetic: An Institutional Analysis* (Ithaca, NY: Cornell University Press, 1974), 182–200; Monroe C. Beardsley, "Aesthetic Experience Regained," *Journal of Aesthetics and Art Criticism* 28 (1969): 3–11; and Davies, *The Philosophy of Art*, 52–58.

5. From Gracia, *A Theory of Textuality*, 48. Dickie has defended the artifactuality of "artworks" in *Aesthetics: An Introduction* (Indianapolis, IN: Bobbs-Merrill, 1971), ch. 11, and also in *Art and the Aesthetic*, 25, 34, 38. John Dewey has done so in *Art as Experience: An Introduction* (New York: G. P. Putnam's Sons, 1980), 48–49. Artifactuality is widely accepted as a requirement of art, and some authors appear to make it a sufficient condition of it. For attacks on artifactuality, see Jack Glickman, "Creativity in the Arts," in *Culture in Art*, ed. Lars Aagaard-Morgensen, 143–44 (Atlantic Highlands, NJ: Humanities Press, 1976); Weitz, "The Role of Theory in Aesthetics"; and R. J. Sclafani, "'Art' and Artifactuality," *Southwestern Journal of Philosophy* 1: 3 (1970): 103 ff. For a response to some of the arguments against the artifactuality of art, see Margolis, "The Ontological Peculiarity of Works of Art," *Journal of Aesthetics and Art Criticism* 35 (1976): 37–46.

6. Because of the difficulties in the determination of what constitutes artistic and aesthetic experiences, many aestheticians have abandoned the attempt to use these notions for the understanding of art and instead have turned to other criteria.

Dickie, for example, defines an *artwork* as an artifact that has certain relationships to a social institution. See *Aesthetics*, 98–108. But not everyone agrees. Davies, for example, unpacks the notion of aesthetic in term of properties that are "objective features perceived in the object of appreciation when it is approached for its own sake." And he contrasts this to artistic properties that bring in the context. See Davies, *The Philosophy of Art*, 52–58.

7. Gracia, *A Theory of Textuality*, 48.

8. Erwin Panofsky recognizes the connection between art objects, artifactuality, and aesthetic experience but comes up with a view very different from mine when he defines "a work of art as a man-made object demanding to be experienced aesthetically." See Panofsky, "The History of Art as a Humanistic Discipline," in *Meaning in the Visual Arts: Papers in and on Art History* (Garden City, NY: Doubleday, 1955), 1–25.

9. Walton has argued that the category of aesthetic is given too much emphasis when it comes to art, because not all art is meant to be observed and thus to be aesthetically experienced. Art is more a matter of action and performance than of reception and observation. See "Style and the Products and Processes of Art," in *The Concept of Style*, ed. Berel Lang, 72–103 (Ithaca, NY: Cornell University Press, 1987).

10. I have not raised the question of forgeries because it is largely irrelevant here. Let it suffice to say that I do not regard the notions of artistic value and aesthetic value as equivalent, and that I consider artistic value to be socially conditioned and historically determined. See Gracia, "Falsificación y valor artístico," *Revista de Ideas Estéticas* 116 (1971): 327–33. For a different approach, see Arthur Koestler, "The Aesthetics of Snobbery," *Horizon* 7 (1965): 80–83.

11. Panofsky, "The History of Art as a Humanistic Discipline," 11.

12. For some, the aesthetic has to do with the "delectable," but for others it does not. Poussin seems to have been the first to have proposed "delectation" as the end of art, although the medievals had held long before that *delectatio* was the mark of the beautiful. See A. Blunt, "Poussin's Notes on Painting," *Journal of the Warburg Institute* 1 (1937): 344–51. The notion of aesthetic experience and its use to characterize art is frequently contested. For example, D. Dutton raises important questions about it in the context of forgeries, in "Artistic Crimes," in *The Forger's Art: Forgery and the Philosophy of Art*, ed. D. Dutton, 172–87 (Berkeley: University of California Press, 1983); see also the article by Walton, cited earlier.

13. Note that the artifactuality condition makes possible, contrary to Dickie, for one to be mistaken in conferring the status of art object ("work" for Dickie). This view avoids some of the objections raised against Dickie's theory. For Dickie, see *Art and the Aesthetic*, 50.

14. Gracia, *A Theory of Textuality*, 4.

15. One could argue that the production of a theory involves an aesthetic dimension, and to that extent perhaps Kant may have had an aesthetic experience from producing the theory proposed in *Critique of Pure Reason*. If this is so, then perhaps one also could argue that the readers of the book can have a vicarious aesthetic experience. However, the aesthetic experience in this case is not produced by the text as such but by the theory, which is the meaning of the text—the aesthetic

object is not the text, but what I call elsewhere *the work*. See *A Theory of Textuality*, ch. 3, where I conceive a work as the meaning of certain texts or objects for which society has developed rules to fulfill a specific cultural function.

CHAPTER 22

1. There seem to be as many understandings of philosophy as there are philosophers, so it would be futile to try to provide here an outline of these different positions. I instead offer a broad understanding that I have defended elsewhere. See Gracia, *Metaphysics and its Task: The Categorial Foundation of Knowledge* (Albany: State University of New York Press, 1999).

2. For other objections, see H. P. Grice, D. F. Pears, and P. F. Strawson, "Metaphysics," in *The Nature of Metaphysics*, ed. D. F. Pears, 4–7 (London: Macmillan, 1957).

3. Lopes, "Pictures and the Representational Mind," *Monist* 86: 4 (2003): 633.

4. Elkins, *The Object That Stares Back*, 11.

5. For an in-depth exploration of the way various kinds of factors (e.g., cognitive, aesthetic, artistic, etc.) interact in the evaluation of paintings, see Lopes, *Sight and Sensibility: Evaluating Pictures* (New York: Oxford University Press, 2005), chs. 1, 3.

6. I have provided a view of these in Gracia, *A Theory of Textuality*, 168–76.

7. These expressions were made famous by Danto in "Philosophy as/and/of Literature," in *Literature and the Question of Philosophy*, ed. Anthony Cascardi, 1–23 (Baltimore, MD: The Johns Hopkins University Press, 1989).

APPENDIX 1

1. Filmed by Norma Gracia, transcribed by Patricia Díaz, translated by Ernesto Rosen Velásquez, and edited by Jorge J. E. Gracia. The Spanish version of this interview is available in Gracia, *Cuban Art Outside Cuba: Identity, Philosophy, and Art:* http://www.philosophy.buffalo.edu/capenchair/CAOC/index.html.

Bibliography

ON CARLOS ESTÉVEZ

Albertini, Rosanna. "Carlos Estévez: The Theater of Life." In *Carlos Estévez: The Theater of Life*. Exhibition Catalogue. Los Angeles: Couturier Gallery, 2001.

Block, Holly, ed. *Art Cuba: The New Generation*. New York: Abrams, 2001, 68, 69, 70, 152.

Bondil, Nathalie. *Cuba: Art and History from 1868 to Today*. Exhibition Catalogue. Montreal: The Montreal Museum of Fine Arts, 2008, 348 and 398.

García Gutiérrez, Enrique. "Le voyage inmobile." In *Carlos Estévez*. Exhibition Catalogue. San Juan, PR: Gómez Fine Art Galería, 2006.

Gracia, Jorge J. E. *Cuban Art Outside Cuba: Identity, Philosophy, and Art*. http://www.philosophy.buffalo.edu/capenchair/CAOC/index.html, 2006–.

Grant, Annette. "Cubans Making Lot Out of Little." In *New York Times*, June 11, 2000.

Keough, Jeffrey, and Lisa Tung. "Foreword." In *Carlos Estévez: Dreamcomber*. Exhibition Catalogue. Boston, MA: Huntington Gallery, Massachusetts College of Art, 2002.

Luis, Carlos M. "The Transparent Being." In *Carlos Estévez: The Transparent Being*. Exhibition Catalogue. Los Angeles: Couturier Gallery, 2003.

Mena Chicuri, Abelardo G., et al. *Cuba AvantGarde: Contemporary Cuban Art from the Farber Collection/Arte contemporáneo cubano de la colección Farber*. Gainesville, FL: Samuel P. Harn Museum of Art, 2007, 97–101.

Museo Nacional de Bellas Artes. Havana: Colección de Arte Cubano, 2001, 269.

Petrova, Yevgenia. *Art from Cuba: The Ludwig Collection*. Ludwig Forum for International Art. Peter and Irene Ludwig Foundation. St. Petersburgh: Palace Editions, 2005, 76–79, 163, 179–180.

Pinos-Santos, Carina. "Viaje al centro del hombre, una travesía de Carlos Estévez." *Revolución y Cultura* 5 (1995): 33–34.

Schneider Enríques, Mary. "Behind the Malecón: The Unexpected Visions of Carlos Estévez." In *Carlos Estévez: Dreamcomber*. Exhibition Catalogue. Boston, MA: Huntington Gallery, Massachusetts College of Art, 2002.

Sullivan, Edward J. "The *Bestiarium* of Carlos Estévez." In *Carlos Estévez: Bestiarium*. Exhibition Catalogue. Los Angeles: Couturier Gallery, 1999.

Veigas, José, et al. *Memoria. Cuban Art of the 20th Century*. Los Angeles: California/International Arts Foundation, 2003, 151.

Weinstein, Joel. "Knowingness." In *Existir en el tiempo/Existing in Time*. Exhibition Catalogue. Miami, FL: The Olga M. & Carlos Saladrigas Gallery, The Ignatian Center for the Arts, 2005.

ON CUBAN ART

II Salón de Arte Cubano Contemporáneo. Exhibition Catalogue. Havana: Consejo Nacional de Artes Plásticas, et al., 1998.

Alvarez, Pedro. *How Havana Stole from New York the Idea of Cuban Art*. Santa Monica, CA: Smart Art Press, 2000.

The American Experience: Contemporary Immigrant Artists. Exhibition Catalogue. Philadelphia and New York: The Balch Institute of Ethnic Studies, 1985.

Blanc, Giulio. *Cuban Artists of the Twentieth Century*. Fort Lauderdale, FL: Fort Lauderdale Museum of Art, 1993.

———. *The Post-Miami Generation*. Exhibition Catalogue. Miami, FL: Cuban Museum of Arts and Culture, 1990.

———. *The Miami Generation*. Exhibition Catalogue. Miami, FL: Cuban Museum of Arts and Culture, 1984.

Blanc, Giulio, et al. *Cuba/U.S.A.: The First Generation*. Exhibition Catalogue. Washington, DC: El Fondo del Sol, 1991.

Block, Holly, ed. *Art Cuba: The New Generation*. New York: Abrams, 2001.

Bosch, Lynette M. F. "Layers: Collecting Cuban-American Art." In *Layers: Collecting Cuban-American Art*, ed. Jorge J. E. Gracia, 8–20. Exhibition Catalogue. Buffalo, NY: University at Buffalo Art Galleries, 2006.

———. *Cuban-American Art in Miami: Exile, Identity, and the Neo-Baroque*. London: Lund Humphreys Press, 2004.

———. *Past Cuba: Identity and Identification in Cuban-American Art*. Exhibition Catalogue. Fairfield, CT: Fairfield University and St. Lawrence University, 1997.

———. *Islands in the Stream: Seven Cuban-American Artists*. Exhibition Catalogue. Cortland: State University of New York at Cortland, 1993.

Boswell, Thomas D., and James R. Curtis. *The Cuban-American Experience: Culture, Images, and Perspectives*. Totowa, NJ: Rowman & Allanheld, 1984.

Brown, David H. *Santería Enthroned: Art, Ritual, and Innovation in Afro-Cuban Religion*. Chicago: University of Chicago Press, 2003.

Camnitzer, Luis. *New Art of Cuba*. Austin: University of Texas Press, 2003. First published in 1994.

Caribe insular: Exclusión, fragmentación y paraíso. Exhibition Catalogue. Madrid: Casa de América, 1998.

Cobas, Roberto, ed. *Museo Nacional de Bellas Artes: Colección de Arte Cubano*. Collection Catalogue. Barcelona: "Sa Nostra" Caja de Baleares, Ambit, 2001.

Cockcroft, James D., and Jane Canning. *Latino Visions: Contemporary Chicano, Puerto Rican, and Cuban-American Artists*. Danbury, CT: Franklin Watts Press, 2000.

Cuba: La isla posible. Exhibition Catalogue. Barcelona: Ediciones Destino, 1995.

Cuba Siglo XX: Modernidad y sincretismo. Exhibition Catalogue. Islas Canarias: Centro Atlántico de Arte Moderno, 1996.

Díaz Burgos, Juan Manuel, ed. *Cuba: 100 años de fotografía, 1898–1998.* Murcia: Mestizo A.C., 1998.

Fernández, Antonio Eligio (Tonel). "Cuban Art: The Key to the Gulf and How to Use It" and "Cuban Art: The Path of Humor." In *Memoria: Cuban Art in the 20ᵗʰ Century,* ed. José Veigas, et al., 31–33, 43–44. Los Angeles: California International Arts Foundation, 2001.

———. "Tree of Many Beaches: Cuban Art in Motion (1980–1990)." In *Contemporary Art from Cuba: Irony and Survival on the Utopian Island,* ed. Marilyn Zeitlin, 39–66. New York: Delano Greenidge Editions, 1998.

———. "Alternative Humour and Comic Strips: Notes on the Cuban Case." In *The Unknown Face of Cuban Art,* ed. Laurie Short. Sunderland: Northern Center for Contemporary Art, 1992.

Fuentes-Pérez, Ileana, et al. *Outside Cuba: Contemporary Cuban Visual Arts/Fuera de Cuba: Artistas cubanos contemporáneos.* Exhibition Catalogue. New Brunswick: Rutgers University Press, 1987.

García, Manuel. *Historia de un viaje: Artistas cubanos en Europa.* Exhibition Catalogue. Valencia: Generalitat Valenciana, 1997.

Gómez-Sicre, José. *Art of Cuba in Exile.* Miami, FL: Editorial Munder, 1987.

González Mandri, Flora María. *Guarding Cultural Memory: Afro-Cuban Women in Literature and the Arts.* Charlottesville: University of Virginia Press, 2006.

Gracia, Jorge J. E. "Cuban-American Identity and Art." In *Cuban-American Literature and Art: Negotiating Identities,* ed. Isabel Alvarez Borland and Lynette M. F. Bosch, pp. 175–89. Albany: State University of New York Press, 2009.

———. *Cuban Art Outside Cuba: Identity, Philosophy, and Art.* http://www.philosophy. buffalo.edu/capenchair/CAOC/index.html, 2006–.

———, ed. *Layers: Collecting Cuban-American Art.* Buffalo: University at Buffalo Art Galleries, State University of New York, 2006.

Gracia, Jorge J. E., Lynette M. F. Bosch, and Isabel Alvarez Borland, eds. *Identity, Memory, and Diaspora: Voices of Cuban-American Artists, Writers, and Philosophers.* Albany: State University of New York Press, 2007.

Gracia, Jorge J. E., Lynette M. F. Bosch, and Isabel Alvarez Borland. *Negotiating Identities in Philosophy, Art, and Literature: Cuban Americans and American Culture.* Buffalo, NY: National Endowment for the Humanities Seminar, 2006. http://www.philosophy.buffalo.edu/contrib/events/neh06.html.

Herrera, Andrea O'Reilly. " 'Defying Liminality': The Journeys of Cuban Artists in the Diaspora." In *Cuba: Idea of a Nation Displaced,* ed. Andrea O'Reilly Herrera, 301–11. Albany: State University of New York Press, 2007.

Howe, Linda S. *Cuban Writers and Artists after the Revolution: Transgression and Conformity.* Madison: University of Wisconsin Press, 2003.

Jaffee McCabe, Cynthia, and Daniel J. Boorstin. *The Golden Door: Artist-Immigrants of America, 1876–1976.* Exhibition Catalogue. Washington, DC: Smithsonian Institution Press, 1976.

Joselitt, David. *Loin de Cuba*. Exhibition Catalogue. Aix-en-Provence: Musèe des Tapisseries, 1999.

Juan, Adelaida de. "La mujer pintada en Cuba." *Temas* 5 (1996): 38–46.

Kuba O.K.: Aktuelle kunst aus Kuba = arte actual de Cuba. Exhibition Catalogue. Düsseldorf: Städtische Kunsthalle, 1990.

Kuebler, Joanne. *Art of the Fantastic: Latin America, 1920–1987*. Indianapolis, IN: Indianapolis Museum of Art, 1987.

Kunst aus Kuba: Sammlung Ludwig/Art of Cuba: The Ludwig Collection. Bad Breisig: Palace Editions, 2002.

La dirección de la mirada: Neue Kunst aus Kuba, Art actuel de Cuba, Arte cubano contemporáneo. Exhibition Catalogue. Vienna and New York: Springer, 1999.

La gente en casa: Colección Contemporánea Museo Nacional. Exhibition Brochure. Havana: Museo Nacional de Bellas Artes, 2000.

Libby, Gary R. *Cuba: A History in Art*. Daytona Beach, FL: The Museum of Arts and Sciences, 1997.

Loomis, John A. *Revolution of Forms: Cuba's Forgotten Art Schools*. Princeton, NJ: Princeton Architectural Press, 1999.

Made in Havana. Exhibition Catalogue. Sydney: Art Gallery of New South Wales, 1989.

Martínez, Juan A. "*Lo blanco-criollo* as *lo cubano* in the Symbolization of a Cuban National Identity in Modernist Painting of the 1940s." In *Cuba, The Elusive Nation: Interpretations of National Identity*, ed. Damian J. Fernández and Madeline Cámara. Gainesville: University Press of Florida, 2000.

———. *Cuban Art and National Identity: The Vanguardia Painters 1927–1950*. Gainesville: University Press of Florida, 1994.

Mena Chicuri, Abelardo G., et al. *Cuba AvantGarde: Contemporary Cuban Art from the Farber Collection/Arte contempóraneo cubano de la colección Farber*. Gainesville, FL: Samuel P. Harn Museum of Art, 2007.

Montes de Oca, Dannys. *El oficio del arte*. Exhibition Catalogue. Havana: Centro de Desarrollo de las Artes Visuales, 1995.

Monzón, Lissette, and Darys J. Vázques. "El mercado del arte en los márgenes de la ideología y la realidad." *ArteCubano* 3 (2001): 8–15.

Mosquera, Gerardo. "Persistencia del uso." In Catalogue, *Museo Nacional de Bellas Artes*. Havana: Museo Nacional de Bellas Artes, 2003.

———. *Contemporary Art from Cuba*. New York: Arizona State University Art Museum: Delano Greenridge Editions, 1999.

———. "The Infinite Island: Introduction to New Cuban Art." In *Contemporary Art from Cuba: Irony and Survival in the Utopian Island*, ed. Marilyn A. Zeitlin, 23. Tempe: Arizona State University Art Museum, 1997.

New Art from Cuba. Exhibition Catalogue. London: Whitechapel Publications, 1995.

Noceda Fernández, José Manuel, et al. *Kcho: La jungla*. Exhibition Catalogue. Turin: Hopeful Monsters, 2002.

Santana, Andrés Isaac. *Imágenes de desvío: La voz homoerótica en arte cubano contemporáneo*. Santiago de Chile: J. C. Saez, 2004.

Santis, Jorge, and Carol Damian. *Breaking Barriers: Selections from the Museum of Art's Permanent Contemporary Cuban Collection.* Exhibition Catalogue. Fort Lauderdale, FL: Fort Lauderdale Museum of Art, 1997.

Seppälä, Marketta, ed. *No Man Is an Island: Young Cuban Art.* Pori: Pori Art Museum, 1990.

Short, Laurie, ed. *The Unknown Face of Cuban Art.* Sunderland: Northern Center for Contemporary Art, 1992.

Utopian Territories: New Art from Cuba. Exhibition Catalogue. Vancouver: University of British Columbia, 1997.

Veigas, José, et al. *Memoria: Cuban Art of the 20th Century.* Los Angeles: California International Arts Foundation, 2003.

Viera, Ricardo. *Latin American Artist Photographers from the Lehigh University Art Galleries Collection.* Exhibition Catalogue. Bethlehem, PA: Lehigh University Art Galleries/Museum Operation, 2001.

Weiss, Rachel. "Performing Revolution." In *Collectivism after Modernism: The Art of Social Imagination after 1945,* ed. Blake Stimson and Gregory Sholette, 115–62. Minneapolis: University of Minnesota Press, 2007.

While Cuba Waits: Art from the Nineties. Santa Monica, CA: Smart Art Press, 1999.

Zeitlin, Marilyn A., ed. *Contemporary Art from Cuba: Irony and Survival in the Utopian Island.* Tempe: Arizona State University Art Museum, 1997.

SOURCES USED

Adorno, Theodor W. *Aesthetic Theory.* Minneapolis: University of Minnesota Press, 1997.

Alcoff, Linda M. *Visible Identities.* Oxford: Oxford University Press, 2006.

Anaximenes. *Fragments.* In *An Introduction to Early Greek Philosophy; The Chief Fragments and Ancient Testimony, with Connecting Commentary,* ed. John Mansley Robinson, 41–56. New York: Houghton Mifflin, 1968.

Anderson, Benedict. *Imagined Communities: Reflections on the Origins and Spread of Nationalism.* London: Verso Editions, 1990. Originally published in 1983.

Anselm. *Monologion and Proslogion.* Translated by Jasper Hopkins. Minneapolis, MN: A. J. Banning Press, 1986.

Aristophanes. *The Clouds.* In *Two Classical Comedies,* comp. Peter D. Arnott. New York: Appleton-Century-Crofts, 1967.

Aristotle. *Metaphysics.* In *The Complete Works of Aristotle,* ed. Jonathan Barnes, vol. 2, 1552–1728. Princeton, NJ: Princeton University Press, 1984.

———. *On the Soul.* In *The Complete Works of Aristotle,* ed. Jonathan Barnes, vol. 1, 641–92. Princeton, NJ: Princeton University Press, 1984.

———. *Physics.* In *The Complete Works of Aristotle,* ed. Jonathan Barnes, vol. 1, 315–446. Princeton, NJ: Princeton University Press, 1984.

———. *Posterior Analytics.* In *The Complete Works of Aristotle,* ed. Jonathan Barnes, vol. 1, 39–113. Princeton, NJ: Princeton University Press, 1984.

Augustine. *The City of God.* 2 vols. Indianapolis, IN: St Maur Theological Center, 1979.

———. *Retractations.* In *Saint Augustine: The Problem of Free Choice,* trans. Dom M. Pontifex. London: Longmans, 1955.

———. *On Free Will.* In *Augustine: Earlier Writings,* trans. J. H. S. Burleigh, vol. 6. London: SCM Press, 1953.

———. *On the Teacher.* In *Augustine: Earlier Writings,* trans. J. H. S. Burleigh, vol. 1. London: SCM Press, 1953.

Austin, J. L. *How to Do Things with Words.* Edited by J. Urmsum. Cambridge, MA: Harvard University Press, 1962.

Ayer, A. J. *Language, Truth, and Logic.* New York: Dover, 1936.

Bambrough, Renford. "Literature and Philosophy." In *Wisdom: Twelve Essays,* ed. Renford Bambrough, 274–92. Oxford: Blackwell, 1974.

Banton, Michael. *Racial Theories.* Cambridge: Cambridge University Press, 1987.

Beardsley, Monroe C. "Aesthetic Experience Regained." *Journal of Aesthetics and Art Criticism* 28 (1969): 3–11.

Benjamin, Walter. *The Arcades Project.* Edited by Rolf Tiedemann, translated by Howard Eiland, and illustrated by Kevin McLaughlin. Cambridge, MA: Harvard University Press, 2002.

Bergson, Henri. *Creative Evolution.* Translated by Arthur Mitchel. New York: The Modern Library, 1944.

Bernstein, J. M. *Against Voluptuous Bodies: Late Modernism and the Meaning of Painting.* Stanford, CA: Stanford University Press, 2006.

Blunt, A. "Poussin's Notes on Painting." *Journal of the Warburg Institute* 1 (1937): 344–51.

Bonaventure. *Sermons on the Six Days.* In *Philosophy in the Middle Ages,* ed. Arthur Hyman and James J. Walsh, 456–61. Indianapolis, IN: Hackett, 1973.

Burger, John. *Ways of Seeing.* New York: Viking Press, 1973.

Butler, Judith. *Gender Trouble: Feminism and the Subversion of Identity.* New York: Routledge, 1999.

Carroll, Noël, ed. *Theories of Art Today.* Madison: University of Wisconsin Press, 2000.

Cavalli-Sforza, Luka L., et al. *The History and Geography of Human Genes.* Princeton, NJ: Princeton University Press, 1994.

Cavell, Stanley. "Music Discomposed." In Stanley Cavell, *Must We Mean What We Say?* Cambridge: Cambridge University Press, 1976.

Code, Lorraine. "Voice as Voicelessness: A Modest Proposal?" In *Philosophy in a Feminist Voice,* ed. Janet Kourany, 204–30. Princeton, NJ: Princeton University Press, 1998.

Comte, Auguste. *The Positive Philosophy.* New York: AMS Press, 1974.

Conley, Tom. "A Trace of Style." In *Displacement: Derrida and After,* ed. Mark Krupnick, 74–93. Bloomington, IN: Indiana University Press, 1983.

Corlett, J. Angelo. *Race, Racism, and Reparations.* Ithaca, NY: Cornell University Press, 2003.

Danto, Arthur. *After the End of Art: Contemporary Art and the Pale of History.* Princeton, NJ: Princeton University Press, 1997.

———. "Philosophy as/and/of Literature." In *Literature and the Question of Philosophy*, ed. Anthony Cascardi, 1–23. Baltimore, MD: Johns Hopkins University Press, 1987.

———. *The Transfiguration of the Commonplace: A Philosophy of Art*. Cambridge, MA: Harvard University Press, 1981.

Darwin, Charles. *On the Origin of Species*. New York: New York University Press, 1988.

Davies, Stephen. *Philosophical Perspectives on Art*. Oxford: Oxford University Press, 2007.

———. *The Philosophy of Art*. Oxford: Blackwell, 2006.

———. *Definitions of Art*. Ithaca, NY: Cornell University Press, 1991.

De Beauvoir, Simone. *The Second Sex*. Translated and edited by H. M. Parshley. New York: Alfred A. Knopf, 1993.

Deleuze, Gilles. *Francis Bacon: The Logic of Sensation*. Translated by Daniel Smith. New York: Continuum, 2005.

Derrida, Jacques. *The Truth in Painting*. Translated by Geoff Bennington and Ian McLeod. Chicago: University of Chicago Press, 1987.

Descartes, René. *Discourse on Method*. In *A Discourse on Method and Selected Writings*. Translated by John Veitch, 1–68. New York: Dutton and Co., 1951.

Dewey, John. *Art as Experience: An Introduction*. New York: G. P. Putnam's Sons, 1980.

Dickie, George. *Art and the Aesthetic: An Institutional Analysis*. Ithaca, NY: Cornell University Press, 1974.

———. *Aesthetics: An Introduction*. Indianapolis, IN: Bobbs-Merill, 1971.

Du Bois, W. E. B. "The Conservation of Races." In *W. E. B. Du Bois Speaks: Speeches and Addresses 1890–1919*, ed. Philip F. Foner, 73–85. New York: Pathfinders, 1970.

Dummett, M. *Truth and Other Enigmas*. London: Duckworth, 1978.

Dutton, D. "Artistic Crimes." In *The Forger's Art: Forgery and the Philosophy of Art*, ed. D. Dutton, 172–87. Berkeley: University of California Press, 1983.

Eliot, T. S. "Tradition and the Individual Talent." In *Selected Essays 1917–1932*. London: Faber and Faber, 1932.

Elkins, James. *What Painting Is: How to Think about Oil Painting, Using the Language of Alchemy*. New York: Routledge, 1999.

———. *The Object That Stares Back*. San Diego, CA: Harcourt Brace, 1996.

Empedocles. *On the Nature of Things*. In *An Introduction to Early Greek Philosophy: The Chief Fragments and Ancient Testimony, with Connecting Commentary*, ed. John Mansley Robinson, 151–73. New York: Houghton Mifflin, 1968.

Epictetus. *Discourses*. In *Discourses and Enchiridion*. Roslyn, NY: Published for the Classics Club by W. J. Black, c1944.

Fodor, J. *Psychosemantics*. Boston, MA: MIT Press, 1987.

Foucault, Michel. *Power*. Edited by James D. Faubion and translated by Robert Hurley, et al. New York: New Press, 2000.

———. *This Is Not a Pipe*. Berkeley: University of California Press, 1983.

———. "What Is an Author?" Translated by Donald F. Bouchard and Sherry Simon. In *Language, Counter-Memory, Practice: Selected Essays and Interviews*, ed. Donald F. Bouchard, 113–38. Ithaca, NY: Cornell University Press, 1977.

———. *The Order of Things: An Archeology of the Human Sciences.* New York: Pantheon, 1970.

Frege, G. *Collected Papers.* Oxford: Oxford University Press, 1984.

Freud, Sigmund. *Leonardo da Vinci: A Memory of His Childhood.* London: Art Paperbacks, 1987.

Gablik, Suzi. *Magritte.* New York: Thames and Hudson, 1992.

Gadamer, Hans-Georg. "Goethe and Philosophy." In *Literature and Philosophy in Dialogue: Essays in German Literary Theory,* ed. Robert H. Paslick, 1–19. Albany: State University of New York Press, 1994.

———. "On the Circle of Understanding." In *Hermeneutics versus Science? Three German Views,* ed. John M. Connolly and Thomas Keutner, 68–78. Notre Dame, IN: University of Notre Dame Press, 1988.

———. "Plato and the Poets." In *Dialogue and Dialectic: Eight Hermeneutical Studies in Plato.* Translated by P. Christopher Smith, 39–72. New Haven, CT: Yale University Press, 1980.

Glickman, Jack. "Creativity in the Arts." In *Culture in Art,* ed. Lars Aagaard-Morgensen, 130–46. Atlantic Highlands, NJ: Humanities Press, 1976.

Goodman, Nelson. *Languages of Art: An Approach to a Theory of Symbols.* Indianapolis, IN: Hackett, 1976.

Gracia, Jorge J. E. *Latinos in America: Philosophy and Social Identity.* Oxford: Blackwell, 2008.

———. "From Horror to Hero: Film Interpretations of Stoker's *Dracula.*" In *Philosophy and the Interpretation of Pop Culture,* ed. William Irwin and Jorge J. E. Gracia, 187–214. Lanham, MD: Rowman & Littlefield, 2007.

———. *Surviving Race, Ethnicity, and Nationality: A Challenge for the Twenty-First Century.* Lanham, MD: Rowman & Littlefield, 2005.

———. "Meaning." In *Dictionary for the Theological Interpretation of the Bible,* ed. Kevin J. Vanhoozer, 492–99. Grand Rapids, MI: Baker Bookhouse Co., 2005.

———. *Old Wine in New Skins: The Role of Tradition in Communication, Knowledge, and Group Identity.* Marquette University 67th Aquinas Lecture. Milwaukee, WI: Marquette University Press, 2003.

———. "Borges's 'Pierre Menard': Philosophy or Literature?" In *Literary Philosophers: Borges, Calvino, Eco,* ed. Jorge J. E. Gracia, Carolyn Korsmeyer, and Rodolphe Gasché, 85–108. New York: Routledge, 2002.

———. *How Can We Know What God Means? The Interpretation of Revelation.* New York: Palgrave, 2001.

———. *Hispanic/Latino Identity: A Philosophical Perspective.* Oxford: Blackwell, 2000.

———. *Metaphysics and its Task: The Search for the Categorial Foundation of Knowledge.* Albany: State University of New York Press, 1999.

———. *Texts: Ontological Status, Identity, Author, Audience.* Albany, NY: State University of New York Press, 1996.

———. *A Theory of Textuality: The Logic and Epistemology.* Albany: State University of New York Press, 1995.

———. *Philosophy and Its History: Issues in Philosophical Historiography.* Albany: State University of New York Press, 1991.

———. "Notes on Ortega's Aesthetic Works in English." *Journal of Aesthetic Education* 11 (1977): 117–25.

———. "Falsificación y valor artístico." *Revista de Ideas Estéticas* 116 (1971): 327–33.

Grice, H. P. "Meaning." *Philosophical Review* 66 (1957): 377–88.

Grice, H. P., D. F. Pears, and P. F. Strawson. "Metaphysics." In *The Nature of Metaphysics*, ed. D. F. Pears, 1–22. London: Macmillan, 1957.

Grosz, Elizabeth. *Volatile Bodies: Toward a Corporeal Feminism.* Bloomington: Indiana University Press, 1994.

Gunther, York. "Emotion and Force." In *Essays on Nonconceptual Content.* Boston, MA: MIT Press, 2003.

Hare, Peter, ed. *Doing Philosophy Historically.* Buffalo, NY: Prometheus Books, 1988.

Harkness, James. "Translator's Introduction." In Michael Foucault, *This Is Not a Pipe*, 1–12. Berkeley: University of California Press, 1983.

Hegel, G. W. H. *Phenomenology of Spirit.* Translated by Howard P. Kainz. University Park: Pennsylvania State University Press, 1994.

Heidegger, Martin. *Ontology: The Hermeneutics of Facticity.* Translated by John van Buren. Indianapolis: Indiana University Press, 1988.

———. *Being and Time.* Translated by John MacQuarrie and Edward Robinson. London: SCM Press, 1962.

Heraclitus. *Fragments.* In *An Introduction to Early Greek Philosophy: The Chief Fragments and Ancient Testimony, with Connecting Commentary*, ed. John Mansley Robinson, 87–105. New York: Houghton Mifflin, 1968.

Hirsch, Jr, E. D. *Validity in Interpretation.* New Haven, CT: Yale University Press, 1967.

———. "Objective Interpretation." *PMLA* 75 (1960), 463–79.

Hume, David. *An Inquiry Concerning Human Understanding.* La Salle, IL: Open Court Press, 1963.

Irwin, William, ed. *The Death and Resurrection of the Author.* Westport, CT: Greenwood Press, 2002.

———. *Intentionalist Interpretations: A Philosophical Explanation and Defense.* Westport, CT: Greenwood Press, 1999.

Judovitz, Dalia. "Philosophy and Poetry: The Difference between Them in Plato and Descartes." In *Literature and the Question of Philosophy*, ed. Anthony J. Cascardi, 24–51. Baltimore, MD: Johns Hopkins University Press, 1987.

Kant, Immanuel. *Critique of Pure Reason.* Translated by Norman Kemp Smith. Rev. 2nd ed. New York: Palgrave Macmillan, 2003.

Kierkegaard, Søren. *Either/Or.* Edited by Robert L. Perkins. Macon, GA: Mercer University Press, 1995.

———. *Fear and Trembling.* Translated by Walter Lowrie. Princeton, NJ: Princeton University Press, 1941.

Knapp, S., and W. B. Michaels. "Against Theory 2." *Critical Inquiry* 14 (1988): 49–68.

———. "Against Theory." *Critical Inquiry* 8 (1982): 723–42.

Koestler, Arthur. "The Aesthetics of Snobbery." *Horizon* 7 (1965): 80–83.

Korsmeyer, Carolyn. "On Distinguishing 'Aesthetic' from 'Artistic.'" *Journal of Aesthetic Education* 11: 4 (1977): 45–57.

Kripke, Saul A. *Naming and Necessity.* Cambridge, MA: Harvard University Press, 1987.

Kusch, Martin, ed. *The Sociology of Philosophical Knowledge.* Dordrecht: Kluwer Academic Publishers, 2000.

Lamarque, Peter, and Stein Haugom Olsen. *Truth, Fiction, and Literature: A Philosophical Perspective.* Oxford: Clarendon Press, 1994.

Levinson, Jerrold. "Emotion in Response to Art: A Survey of the Terrain." In *Emotion and the Arts,* ed. Mette Hjort and Sue Laver, 20–34. New York: Oxford University Press, 1997.

Lewontin, R. C. "Race." In *Encyclopedia Americana,* vol. 23, 116–22. Danbury, CT: Grolier, 1998.

Livingstone, Paisley. *Art and Intention: A Philosophical Study.* Oxford: Clarendon Press, 2005.

Locke, John. *An Essay Concerning Human Understanding.* New York: Dover, 1959.

Lopes, Dominic McIver. *Sight and Sensibility: Evaluating Pictures.* Oxford: Oxford University Press, 2007.

———. "Directive Pictures." *Journal of Aesthetics and Art Criticism* 62: 2 (2004): 189–96.

———. "Pictures and the Representational Mind." *Monist* 86: 4 (2003): 632–52.

———. "Vision, Touch, and the Value of Pictures." *British Journal of Aesthetics* 42: 2 (2002): 191–201.

———. *Understanding Pictures.* Oxford: Clarendon Press, 1996.

Lovejoy, Arthur. *The Great Chain of Being: A Study of the History of an Idea.* Cambridge, MA: Harvard University Press, 1936.

Marcus Aurelius. *Meditations.* Translated by John Long. Mineola, NY: Dover, c1997.

Margolis, Joseph. "The Ontologial Peculiarity of Works of Art." *Journal of Aesthetics and Art Criticism* 35 (1976): 37–46.

Margolis, Joseph, and Tom Rockmore, eds. *The Philosophy of Interpretation.* Oxford: Blackwell, 2000.

Marx, Karl. *Economic and Philosophical Manuscripts of 1844.* Edited by Dirk Struik and translated by Martin Milligan. New York: International Publishers, 1964.

Meiland, J. W. "Interpretation as a Cognitive Discipline." *Philosophy and Literature* 2 (1978): 23–45.

Nietzsche, Friedrich. *The Will to Power.* Translated by Walter Kaufmann and R. J. Hollingdale. London: Weidenfeld & Nicolson, 1968.

———. *Beyond Good and Evil.* Translated by Marianne Cowan. South Bend, IN: Gateway Editions, 1955.

Ortega y Gasset, José. *Man and People.* New York: Norton, 1957.

Panofsky, Erwin. *Meaning in the Visual Arts: Papers in and on Art History.* Garden City, NY: Doubleday, 1955.

Parmenides. *On Nature.* In *An Introduction to Early Greek Philosophy: The Chief Fragments and Ancient Testimony, with Connecting Commentary,* ed. John Mansley Robinson, 107–26. New York: Houghton Mifflin, 1968.

Pelagius. *Letters of Pelagius and His Followers.* Translated and edited by B. R. Rees. Rochester, NY: Boydell Press, 1991.

Peter Abelard. *The Story of Abelard's Adversities.* Translated by J. T. Muckle. Toronto: Pontifical Institute of Mediaeval Studies, 1954.

Plato. *Meno.* In *The Collected Dialogues of Plato,* ed. Edith Hamilton and Huntington Cairns, 353–84. New York: Pantheon Books, 1961.

———. *Phaedrus.* In *The Collected Dialogues of Plato,* ed. Edith Hamilton and Huntington Cairns, 475–525. New York: Pantheon Books, 1961.

———. *The Republic.* In *The Collected Dialogues of Plato,* ed. Edith Hamilton and Huntington Cairns, 575–844. New York: Pantheon Books, 1961.

Pythagoras. *Fragments.* In *An Introduction to Early Greek Philosophy: The Chief Fragments and Ancient Testimony, with Connecting Commentary,* ed. John Mansley Robinson, 57–84. New York: Houghton Mifflin, 1968.

Quine, W. V. O. *Word and Object.* Cambridge, MA: Harvard University Press, 1960.

———. "On What There Is." In W. V. O. Quine, *From a Logical Point of View.* Cambridge, MA: Harvard University Press, 1953.

Ricoeur, Paul. "Creativity in Language: Word, Polysemy, Metaphor." In *The Philosophy of Paul Ricoeur: An Anthology of His Work,* ed. Charles E. Reagan and David Stewart, 109–33. Boston, MA: Beacon Press, 1978.

Sartre, Jean-Paul. *Being and Nothingness.* New York: Routledge, 2003.

———. *No Exit and Three Other Plays.* New York: Vintage International, 1989.

———. "The Paintings of Giacometti." In Jean-Paul Sartre, *Situations.* Translated by Benita Eisler. New York: Fawcett, 1965.

Sclafani, R. J. " 'Art' and Artifactuality." *Southwestern Journal of Philosophy* 1: 3 (1970): 103–10.

Searle, John. *Expression and Meaning.* Cambridge: Cambridge University Press, 1975.

Stecker, Robert. *Interpretation and Construction: Art, Speech, and the Law.* Malden, MA: Blackwell, 2003.

Stevenson, C. L. "On the Reasons That Can Be Given for the Interpretation of a Poem." In *Philosophy Looks at the Arts,* ed. Joseph Margolis, 121–39. New York: Scribner, 1962.

Tertullian. *On the Prescription of Heretics.* In *On the Testimony of the Soul and On the "Prescription" of Heretics,* trans. T. Herbert Bindley. London: Society for the Promotion of Christian Knowledge, 1914.

Thomas Aquinas. *Summa theologiae.* Edited by Thomas Gilby. Garden City, NY: Image Books, 1969–.

Thomasson, Amie L. *Fiction and Metaphysics.* Cambridge: Cambridge University Press, 1999.

van den Berghe, Pierre L. "Does Race Matter?" In *Race and Racism,* ed. Bernard Boxill, 101–13. Oxford: Oxford University Press, 2001.

Voltaire. *Candide.* New York: Bantam Classics, 1984.

Von Vacano, Diego A. *The Art of Power: Machiavelli, Nietzsche, and the Making of Aesthetic Political Theory.* Lanham, MD: Lexington Books, 2007.

Walton, Kendall L. *Mimesis as Make-Believe: On the Foundations of the Representational Arts.* Cambridge, MA: Harvard University Press, 1990.

———. "Style and the Products and Processes of Art." In *The Concept of Style,* ed. Berel Lang, 72–103. Ithaca, NY: Cornell University Press, 1987.

Weber, Max. "What Is an Ethnic Group?" In *The Ethnicity Reader: Nationalism, Multiculturalism, and Migration*, ed. M. Guibernau and J. Rex, 15–26. Cambridge: Polity. 1997.

Weitz, Morris. *Hamlet and the Philosophy of Literary Criticism*. Chicago: University of Chicago Press, 1964.

———. "The Role of Theory in Aesthetics." *Journal of Aesthetics and Art Criticism* 15 (1956): 27–35.

Whitehead, Alfred North. *Process and Reality: An Essay in Cosmology*. New York: Free Press, 1978.

William of Ockham. *Philosophical Writings: A Selection*. Translated by Philotheus Boehner. Indianapolis, IN: Bobbs-Merrill, 1964.

Wittgenstein, L. *Philosophical Investigations*. Oxford: Oxford University Press, 1953.

Wollheim, Richard. *Art and Its Objects*, 2nd edition. Cambridge: Cambridge University Press, 1980.

———. *On Art and the Mind*. Cambridge, MA: Harvard University Press, 1974.

Wolterstorff, Nicholas. "Toward an Ontology of Works of Art." *Nous* 9 (1975): 115–42.

Young, Julian. *Heidegger's Philosophy of Art*. Cambridge: Cambridge University Press, 2001.

Index